Suffering and Salvation in Ciudad Juárez

Nancy Pineda-Madrid

D1113993

Fortress Press
Minneapolis

SUFFERING AND SALVATION IN CUIDAD JUÁREZ

Cover image: Antonio Zazueta Olmos
Cover design: Lindsey Brunsman, faceoutstudio
Book design: PerfecType, Nashville, TN

Library of Congress Cataloging-in-Publication Data
Pineda-Madrid, Nancy.
Suffering and salvation in Ciudad Juárez / Nancy Pineda-Madrid.
p. cm.
Includes bibliographical references.
ISBN 978-0-8006-9847-8 (alk. paper)
1. Suffering—Religious aspects—Christianity. 2. Salvation—Christianity.
3. Women—Crimes against—Mexico—Ciudad Juárez. 4. Ciudad Juárez
(Mexico) —Social conditions. I. Title.
BT732.7.P45 2011
261.8'328082097216—dc22   2011009401

Manufactured in the U.S.A.

15 14 13 12 11 1 2 3 4 5 6 7 8 9 10

To Larry, the one in whom my soul delights

To Raquel Madrid and Gustavo Salaiz Pineda, my parents,
To Idaila García and Trinidad Torres Madrid, my maternal
grandparents,
To Isidora Salaiz and Pablo Nava Pineda, my paternal grandparents,
for giving me wings to fly

To the memory of the girls and women killed in Ciudad Juárez

Contents

Foreword

The themes of suffering and salvation have, of course, been central to Christian theology from the beginning. A central question for theology has been whether we can hope for salvation from sin and its consequences, so often experienced with seemingly unbearable cruelty. How can (or rather, how *dare*) one speak of a loving God in the face of suffering, especially the suffering of the innocent victims? This is the question so many theodicies have attempted to answer. In one way or another, however, these have all failed, for theologies will always fail to make sense of what, at bottom, can never make sense. As the Jewish theologian Irving Greenberg has averred concerning the Holocaust: "To talk of love and of a God who cares in the presence of the burning children is obscene and incredible."[1] In the presence of the burning children, theology is reduced to silence. Greenberg suggests, however, that we still are not paralyzed: "to leap in and pull a child out of a pit, to clean its face and heal its body, is to make the most powerful statement—the only statement that counts." The only credible response is *practical*.

It is an irony of history that "modern atheism," so often born of the inability to reconcile a loving God with the intractable reality of innocent suffering, has its origins not among the victims of that suffering but among those of us who look on from a distance, not among the burning children (so many of whom continue to struggle and hope even in the midst of horror) but among those of us standing at the edge of the pit and wondering what to make of it all. If there is to be a credible "theodicy," then it will be found in the very midst of those victims of history who continue to cry out, to struggle every day for survival in a world that obsessively seeks their elimination.

That is where Nancy Pineda-Madrid dares to locate her theology, in order to ask whether Christian claims of salvation can be credible in the face of the brutal extermination of the women and girls of Ciudad Juárez, Mexico. Pineda-Madrid calls for a re-imagining of the themes of salvation and suffering as social, communal realities. For too long, she argues, Christians have interpreted both salvation and suffering in individualistic terms. This impedes the ability of Christians to respond adequately to evil, which so often presents itself not only in our hearts but also in our social structures. Evil becomes prematurely "spiritualized" and perceived as a fundamentally theoretical or theological issue—the challenge that meaninglessness represents for the believer—rather than the fundamentally practical issue that it is—the challenge that injustice represents for faith.

Pineda-Madrid's masterful work in practical theology looks to the quite particular case of Ciudad Juárez to discern how that community's practices of resistance are themselves religious "texts" that reveal the abiding presence and ongoing salvific work of a God who, despite all the available evidence, is indeed a God of love. As in the Gospels themselves, where the first evangelizers were the women at the tomb, so will the women of Ciudad Juárez be for us the unlikely witnesses to the Good News.

Roberto S. Goizueta
Margaret O'Brien Flatley Professor of Catholic Theology
Boston College

Acknowledgments

This book has various points of origin. Indeed, Ciudad Juárez (Chihuahua, Mexico) has been significant to me virtually all my life and, arguably, even before my life began. It is the city that my paternal grandfather, Pablo Nava Pineda, spent time in as a teenager before he crossed into El Paso, Texas, in 1914 in search of a better life in the United States. During my own childhood and youth, almost every Sunday evening my parents would take my siblings and me out for a family dinner in Juárez, made even more enjoyable by the ever-present Mariachis. As a high school student at El Paso's Loretto Academy, many fellow students and good friends were young women from Ciudad Juárez, where we, together with our families, celebrated our high school graduation. I am deeply blessed by this history.

In 2006, while teaching at Boston College, I had the privilege of sitting in on a seminar offered by M. Shawn Copeland entitled "Social Suffering." The idea of social suffering haunted me for weeks and months and eventually led me to understand more deeply the evil transpiring in Juárez. In so many ways Shawn pushed me and supported me through my journey with this project. At roughly the same time, María Pilar Aquino also kept encouraging me to write about the feminicide in Juárez. Without her clear sense of my ability to bring this book into being, it would not have come about. Finally, my mother, Raquel M. Pineda, who has worked for years to end illiteracy among women in Juárez, kept me up to date with her firsthand accounts and regular newspaper clippings. She and other women have worked for many years to keep Centro Santa Catalina viable. This center, located in Juárez, helps women there learn to read, write, and earn a living through the crafts they make. Without this trinity of women, Shawn, María Pilar, and Raquel, I would not have written this book. Gracias.

I am truly grateful to Fortress Press, particularly J. Michael West and Susan Johnson, who encouraged this project and supported it in ways too numerous to mention. I appreciate immensely the Louisville Institute and its visionary director, Jim Lewis. This institute provided me funding so that I could take a year to develop an initial draft of each chapter of this book. Moreover, during the summer of 2010 I took part in a human rights delegation to study feminicide in Guatemala. The Guatemalan Human Rights Commission/USA and its insightful, caring director, Amanda Martin, did much to open my eyes to the severity and evil of feminicide in Guatemala and thereby help me to appreciate further the significance of this transnational tragedy. Gracias.

Colleagues from Boston College and other universities have assisted me greatly by generously offering their advice and counsel throughout this process. I am in debt to Colleen Griffith, Rosemary Carbine, Lisa Sowle Cahill, Elisabeth Schüssler Fiorenza, Rosemary Radford Ruether, Jen Bader, Dominic Doyle, Robert Lasalle-Klein, and Gary Macy for their sage insights. Monica Maher and Rafael Luevano, both of whom have published on feminicide, were valuable conversation partners always generously willing to share their perspective on this tragedy. Alejandro García-Rivera, my former mentor who recently passed away, also played a vital role in this book. He introduced me to the work of Josiah Royce and helped me to imagine ways that theology can address itself to evil. Frank Oppenheim S.J. patiently and faithfully pushed me to greater precision in my understanding of Royce's contribution. Many other Boston College colleagues and staff have extended their kindness and concern during this process: Hosffman Ospino, Neto Valiente, Jim Keenan, Mary Ann Hinsdale, Jane Regan, John Shea, Theresa O'Keefe, Jim Weiss, John McDargh, Maura Colleary, and Mary Magennis. Gracias.

Several journalists have risked much, including their lives, to bring Juárez's feminicide to our attention. My work draws significantly on the contributions of Diana Washington Valdez (*El Paso Times*) and Alfredo Corchado (*Dallas Morning News*). Gracias.

Many friends and family members extended personal encouragement and support for my project throughout its evolution. We shared good food, good wine, and good conversation: Ana María Pineda, Eddie Fernandez, Kirk Wegter-McNally, Jennifer Wegter-McNally, Greg Zuschlag, Mark McVann, Ricardo González Sanchez, Kathleen Fischer, Annette Andrews, Patty Repikoff, Michele Pineda Fernandez, Angela Fernandez Velasquez, Esther Pineda, Liz Kowalczyk, Michael Feloney, and of course my father, Gustavo S. Pineda. Their support kept my spirits going in the midst of New England's bleak winters. Gracias.

I must give thanks to many Boston College graduate students who worked as research assistants and were thoughtful critics of my work. I offer my thanks to Elena Mireles, Erika Meyer, Becky Camacho, Ladivel Diaz, and Teri Elliot-Hart. I am particularly indebted to Bobby Rivera, who tracked down many sources early on in the development of this book. Gracias.

Without the unwavering support of both Tom Groome and Roberto Goizueta for my work at Boston College and for this book project in particular, this book would not be. I am privileged to count them both as my good friends. They have bent over backward and moved mountains to help me. This book will see the light of day because of their faith in me. Gracias.

Francine Cardman and Mike Raschko both have been faithful friends and caring supporters. But more than this, or better said as an expression of it, they each read the entire manuscript and shared with me their ideas and critiques. Francine's keen insights quite literally transformed the quality of this book. Years ago Mike introduced me to theology, and I am theologian today because of what he modeled for me. Even now all these years later his questions and judgment remain my guide. I am a better thinker and theologian because of the contribution of these good friends. Gracias.

Most importantly, however, I thank Larry Gordon, my life partner whose patience, love, and compassion have lifted me up throughout this long process. Larry has read this manuscript and has pushed me always to be my best. Gracias!

Introduction

Salvation addresses God's saving presence among human beings, which was inaugurated at creation, given ultimate expression through the person of Jesus the Christ, and continues in the dynamic action of the Holy Spirit in history. In the second half of the twentieth century, widely influential theologians such as Karl Rahner, Edward Schillebeeckx, Rosemary Radford Ruether, and Gustavo Gutiérrez[1] argued that the human quest for salvation entails not a flight from the world but an engagement with the world.

This book builds on their contributions and suggests a reimagining of salvation. This book is therefore also a theodicy with a practical emphasis, one that begins with and continually returns to the standpoint of those who suffer. Suffering brought on by collective evil, and our corresponding drive for release from such suffering, reveals that *community* is a necessary condition for the possibility of salvation. *Suffering and Salvation in Ciudad Juárez* takes up the task of a Latina feminist constructive proposal of salvation guided by an examination of the feminicide in Ciudad Juárez, ongoing since 1993, and the practices of resistance that have been developed in response to this atrocity.

Feminicide, a term widely used by feminist social scientists, refers to the killing of girls and women by men in an exceptionally brutal

1

manner, on a massive scale, and with impunity for the perpetrators. Use of this term indicates that we must analyze critically the power dynamics involved. Horrific violence is growing along the U.S.-Mexico border, and in Juárez specifically. Both men and women are targets of violence. In fact, every year more men are brutally murdered than women. In 2010 more than three thousand people were murdered in Juárez. And as this book goes to press, over one hundred people have already been killed since January 1, 2011, in little over a month. Obviously, this outpouring of violence is an atrocity that needs to be addressed.

However, the focus of this book is the horrific killing of girls and women, because this feminicide warrants particular attention. Females are being targeted because they are female. In April of 1994, the Rwandan government called upon the Hutu majority to kill the Tutsi minority. Tutsis were killed simply because they were Tutsi.[2] Somewhat similarly, in Ciudad Juárez females are being killed because they are female. This is a difficult phenomenon to comprehend. It seems too incredible to be real, but in fact this phenomenon is transpiring in various countries in the Americas (for example, Guatemala, Honduras, and Canada, among others).[3] And while men are being murdered at an alarming rate, these killings are not hate crimes based on gender coupled with a desire to assert power.

This book is deeply rooted in the particular, and its import is its reflection on the insights this particularity provides for a reimagining of salvation. The particularity is the experience of Latinas in Ciudad Juárez who have suffered feminicide. In this book their experience does not function as a theological norm for universal truth claims. Rather, "context" serves as a theological norm. Claims to truth, meaning, and significance invariably emerge out of a particular context. The Ciudad Juárez feminicide (just as any given context) provides an angle on truth yet does not represent truth in an ultimate way.

What serves as a theological norm in this book is the contextual rootedness of all knowing. This is not to say that all claims to theological knowing are relative. Indeed, they are not. Some theological claims are much more adequate than others, making the issue one of criteria and judgment. I stand with feminist thinkers who attempt to "unearth the politics of epistemology,"[4] in my case as they come to light in the Christian doctrine of salvation. My commitment here does not reduce theological knowledge to politics but rather recognizes the complexity inherent in making any and all theological claims.

Recognizing this complexity is crucial because the politics of theological discourse matters and matters greatly. As Latin American liberation theologian Ignacio Ellacuría warns, "There is an ahistorical conceptual universality and there is an historical, or historicized, conceptual universality. The former may seem more theoretical and more universal; that is not so much because it conceals a historicity that by its concealment operates perversely, as because it ignores the universal dimension of historical reality. If theology does not reflect critically on what specific historical praxis the conceptualizations come from and what praxis they lead to, it places itself at the service of a history that the concept may be trying to negate."[5] In short, I believe that the universal is mediated by the particular, and the political impact of our theological constructs matters.

Consonant with these ideas of particularity, history, and context, Mary McClintock Fulkerson once described theology as a "response to a wound." Like a wound, the work of constructing theology begins with an experience so compelling that it demands a response. "Wounds like the idolatries of the German church compelled Karl Barth to articulate a theology of the Word; falsely universal white theologies in a context of deeply entrenched racism compelled James Cone to write black theology."[6] The wound of feminicide in Juárez, too, compels a response. This book is a response. In Juárez, we find a rapidly accelerating destruction of society under the weight of feminicide and an extended culture of violence. The violence against women signals a sociocide, a complete collapse and deterioration of the bonds of society. The aim of this book is to argue that if salvation is to be meaningful today, then it must speak to the overwhelming evil of feminicide. A social, communal response is now required.

While Christian salvation must be interpreted as both individual and social, in the here-and-now of feminicide a social interpretation takes on greater urgency. This book begins with a "reading" of the suffering of the victims of this atrocity, described and analyzed in terms of both its social, political, as well as cultural and symbolic dimensions. This "reading" shows the multilayered need for release from suffering, or alternatively, the longing for salvation.

The prevailing understanding of salvation, namely satisfaction atonement theologies focused primarily on Jesus' death, fall far short of an adequate response to the suffering of feminicide. In contrast, the religious practices designed by those who have suffered feminicide hold a clue to a more adequate understanding of salvation. Those who have lost loved ones have created religious practices of resistance that are richly suggestive of how salvation emerges in history and of its *social* character. These practices indicate that *community* is necessary for the realization of salvation.

In chapter 1, I briefly clarify the meaning of "feminicide" and then proceed with a thick description of this particularly heinous evil. It concerns the overwhelming, brutal, ritualized murdering of young, poor Latinas in large numbers with impunity for the perpetrators. This trauma began in 1993 in Ciudad Juárez, Estado de Chihuahua, just over the U.S.-Mexico border from El Paso, Texas (the region of my childhood, adolescence, and young adult years). In this chapter I consider the political, social, and economic conditions that create an ideal climate for these killings to begin and continue. I consider also the ways these conditions have been manipulated to prevent any accountability. A "prepolitical" society has been established with no agreed-upon norms for behavior and no civil context for developing norms.

And so I ask: How are we to regard this suffering? What are we to make of it? How are we to understand it? I draw on the work of Paul Farmer and Arthur Kleinman to answer these questions, but I also extend their work to create what I term a "social-suffering hermeneutic," a way of regarding the suffering of others. Through this lens, I consider the significance embedded first in how we identify the suffering; second, the various interests competing to promote how they would like others to view this suffering; and finally, the interplay of, on the one hand, the destructive political and economic interests that lead to the suffering of vulnerable populations in society and, on the other hand, the consequential personal accounts of suffering. By attending to the interplay of powerful interests and personal accounts, this hermeneutical approach not only addresses itself to the social origins of feminicide but also compels us to see what is at stake in our response.

This chapter then establishes that the feminicide destroys not only female human lives but also indicates the destruction of society, sociocide. Accordingly, on the surface it might appear that this book is concerned with the absence of meaningful government to investigate these brutal killings and to get to the bottom of whatever hidden conspiracy or strategy sustains this brutality. That, however, is not the focus of this book. Rather, a more serious problem is suggested, namely the underlying, deep-rooted presence of evil and the tragic consequences that result. Widely divergent theories have been developed to explain the feminicide, but taken together these conflicting theories suggest that the insidiousness of evil emerges from a much deeper level, thereby raising not only political but theological questions.

Chapter 2 further develops a social-suffering hermeneutic by focusing on the cultural-symbolic dimensions of female suffering. I consider social imaginaries and how they function, which leads to an examination of certain conventional Latina cultural representations of suffering (for example, the dualism of Guadalupe-La Malinche, La Llorona, and Coyolxauhqui). These "cultural representations" of suffering command our attention because they come packaged in an alluring narrative that presents how women (and men) should relate to their experience of suffering, and they come wrapped in a mantle of desirability. Powerful interests have manipulated and commodified these representations to serve their own end and have done so for generations. This commodification of suffering fosters a worldview that women either unconsciously absorb or consciously resist. Either way, the horrific suffering brought on by feminicide drives a relentless urge for release, for justice, and for healing. The chapter concludes by reframing the human quest for salvation through a series of theological questions. What is the relationship between salvation and ethics? What is the relationship between salvation and female humanity? What is the relationship between salvation and history? What is the relationship between salvation and the image of God?

Having explored some of the soteriological questions that emerge out of the feminicide at the end of chapter 2, the next chapter turns to the Christian tradition to consider one of the most influential theological constructs in soteriology. Anselm's *Cur Deus Homo* (CDH) and the satisfaction atonement theologies that it spawned deserve significant attention. In many ways, they occupy space in the Christian religious imagination of our own day. Today, Anselm and his progeny are in many respects still setting the terms of the salvation debate. This chapter, before it delineates the argument set forth in CDH, places Anselm in his context, trying to understand the world that spawned CDH. Next, I examine the Gadamerian notion of "effective history" in relation to Anselm's legacy. Finally, I offer an analysis and critique of Anselm's model, thereby demonstrating its inadequacy to illuminate the experience of Latinas as outlined in chapters 1 and 2. Essentially, contemporary satisfaction atonement theologies have led to the separation of salvation from ethics to disastrous effect. This analysis concludes with attention to the ways this model leads to the exclusion of particular insights pertinent to the experience of Latinas. This chapter thus establishes the need to rethink salvation in light of Latinas' experience.

David Tracy tells us that when it comes to the question of evil, the religious sensibilities of those who know oppression and suffering—their songs, protests, prayers, and laments—often bear particularly insightful theological wisdom.[7] Chapter 4 returns to the experience of feminicide but this time to discover the practices of resistance that courageous (mostly) women have developed as their response to their suffering. It is my contention that their practices of resistance reveal much about how Latinas experience salvation (articulated in chapter 4), which stands in contrast to satisfaction atonement theologies. Latinas' practices of resistance to feminicide suggest much about how we might understand the meaning of salvation today (which will be developed in chapter 5).

Chapter 4 continues by examining how, through these practices, Latinas connect Christian religious symbols (for example, the cross and exodus) to symbols that affirm female humanity (for example, days honoring women and their courage, the color pink). This connection manifests itself in public actions that not only validate female humanity but also subvert the destructive political interests and damaging cultural-symbolic representations that idealize female suffering. These practices foreground the universal community of humanity and creation; they point toward a social conception of salvation. Not only do the practices of resistance inherently stand against all that undermines the humanity of women—they likewise stand against all that renders religion banal and domesticated. They stand in solidarity with the women who have suffered feminicide, both those directly affected and all female humanity, which has come under threat. Through these practices, practitioners have thwarted efforts to domesticate the faith and have ensured that the radical message of the Christian gospel remains vital. I call attention to the subversive character of the religious practices of resistance, an angle on popular religious practices not significantly developed in U.S. Latino/a theological discourse. This chapter tills the soil for the constructive theological work done in chapter 5.

Chapter 5 begins with the claim that embedded in our response to suffering lies the possibility of salvation. Through practices of resistance, which are ritualized responses, the members of the victims' families and other supporters have created community and affirmed that community is foundational to life. The practices not only create community but also forge the beginning of a salvific community. A salvific community makes the spiritual unity of the world more visible and demands that the crucified people (those who have suffered feminicide) be brought down from the cross. I delineate the marks of a salvific community, drawing connections to the practices of resistance. The central thesis of this chapter and the book is that through our response to suffering we learn that community is the condition for the possibility of salvation.

1

Suffering— A Social Reality

Suffering brought on by structural evil makes demands of us. It demands that we[1] recognize the ways in which our collective decisions can create an increased likelihood that the most vulnerable among us will suffer and suffer mightily. Yet it likewise asks us to consider how we *see* the suffering of others.[2] How we perceive the suffering of others can make an enormous difference in whether we see, or not, its origins in social structures of human making.

When suffering is situated within a social, political ambit, as is done by liberation and political theologians (for example, M. Shawn Copeland, Gustavo Gutiérrez, Ivone Gebara, Johann Baptist Metz, and Jürgen Moltmann), then the public relevance of theology takes on flesh. Liberation and political theologies concern themselves not only with the hopes, pains, and fears of humanity, not only with the intellectual import of age old beliefs, but also with the current state of society and the world, the injustices present therein, and the suffering that results. In these articulations, theology continuously strives to be more self-aware and self-critical about the nature of its larger impact. Needless to say, this impact is understood not merely in terms of personal decisions but, just as importantly, in terms of the infrastructures we create—social, political, and economic—that give shape to our world. Consequently, these theologies judge themselves based on their contribution to the furtherance of the reign of God in our social and political life, in this world as well as the next.

What is more, our souls weigh in the balance in our response to suffering. This statement reflects not only a personal truth, to be sure, but a social truth as well. How our communities respond to suffering matters. Through our collective choices, we can become more or less humane, more or less responsive to God's grace.

This book asserts that salvation is realized in the world, albeit partially, only when we act in a manner that makes the essential unity of the whole human community more visible. Said another way, community makes possible the realization of salvation. However, the Christian tradition has always affirmed the personal nature of salvation, a claim this book does not attempt to supplant. Nonetheless, an exclusively individual understanding of salvation distorts the meaning of the doctrine of salvation and is, in the end, inadequate. We must affirm both individual and social salvation. Liberation theologians, like Gustavo Gutiérrez and Jon Sobrino, have extended our understanding of sin to include social sin. If sin is both individual and social, then so must be salvation.

This first chapter argues that if we "read" the suffering of the feminicide in a way that invites our critical awareness of how we appropriate unjust suffering, then we "see" more transparently the horrific evil of this collective and personal tragedy. In turn, the urgency of the question of salvation comes to the fore, a topic that I will begin to address in chapter 2.

In order to develop this claim, this chapter begins with a particularly horrific example of suffering, the feminicide in Ciudad Juárez, precipitated by a wide array of social circumstances of complex origin. This first section attempts to understand what this phenomenon is, some of the reasons it came about, and what is at stake in our response. The feminicide must be considered among the most physically violent assaults on the humanity of girls and women and consequently a frontal attack on God's salvific intention for all human beings, women and men alike. The next section attends to how this kind of suffering might be "read" so as to make clear the ways in which far too often the suffering of the most vulnerable—in this case poor, dark-skinned females—is presented as unavoidable and less affecting. It is too often depicted as an unfortunate, capricious happening, one far removed from social structures that we have a hand in sustaining if not creating. Third, this chapter engages in a "reading" of the suffering brought on by the feminicide, a reading that encourages a more critical awareness of its larger significance. Finally, this chapter concludes with an acknowledgment of the ways in which this reading of the feminicide needs to go further. It must take our social imaginal world into account.

Feminicide in Ciudad Juárez

Gender-based violence against women has a long, tragic history. Social conflict, war, and societal change have been and continue to be waged on many fronts, particularly through violent acts against women's bodies. Such violence has taken the form of sexual torture, rape, disappearances, and murder, to name but a few. Indeed, twentieth-century examples can be found in the conflicts in Bosnia-Herzegovina, Rwanda, Vietnam, Argentina, Yugoslavia, El Salvador, Peru, Haiti, Guatemala, Honduras, Congo, and Mexico, among other countries. Gender-based violence has come under greater scrutiny in recent years due, in part, to the work of the Women's Caucus for Gender Justice, which successfully argued before the "newly constituted International Criminal court (ICC) at the Hague"[3] that "Gender crimes are incidents of violence targeting or affecting women exclusively or disproportionately, not because the victims of such crimes are of a particular religion or race, but *because* they are women."[4] As Rosa-Linda Fregoso and Cynthia Bejarano have pointed out, the last decade of the twentieth century has seen a rise in such crimes.

Among feminist scholars of the law, the social sciences, and theology, as well as among feminist human rights activists, the terms *femicide* and *feminicide* have been used to refer to the murder of females because they are female. Frequently, scholars use these two terms interchangeably. Even so, as the discourse has evolved (and continues to evolve) distinctions between the two have emerged. Anthropologist and sociologist Marcela Lagarde has pointed out that *femicide* and *homicide* are synonyms, *femicide* specifying the murder of women. But the term *femicide* is insufficient to speak of the tragedy in Ciudad Juárez because, like homicide, it does not refer to systematic violence based on gendered power inequalities. Further, as Fregoso and Bejarano explicated, *femicide* is a term that has been developed by feminist scholars in the United States, especially by feminist sociologist Diana Russell.[5] Thus, discursively it reflects the movement of a concept from "its usage in the English-language (North) to a

Spanish-speaking (South) context."[6] The term *feminicide* is taken from the Spanish *feminicidio*, a concept first documented in the Dominican Republic in the 1980s by feminist activists who used it in their campaign to bring violence against women to an end. Lagarde introduced this term into scholarly discourse in 1987. *Feminicidio*, and thus feminicide, linguistically reflects the way that the Spanish language creates a compound out of two terms with Latin roots, that is, *femina*, meaning "female," and *caedo, caesum,* meaning "to kill," with an *i* used to link them.[7]

My choice of the term *feminicide* reflects not only this history laid out by Fregoso and Bejarano but also their definition, which follows:

> Building on the generic definition of *femicide* as "the murder of women and girls *because* they are female" [the definition advanced by Diana Russell], we define *feminicide* as the murders of women and girls founded on a gender power structure. Second, feminicide is gender-based violence that is both public and private, implicating both the state (directly or indirectly) and individual perpetrators (private or state actors); it thus encompasses systematic, widespread, and everyday interpersonal violence. Third, feminicide is systemic violence rooted in social, political, economic, and cultural inequalities. In this sense, the focus of our analysis is not just on gender but also on the intersection of gender dynamics with the cruelties of racism and economic injustices in local as well as global contexts. Finally, our framing of the concept follows Lagarde's critical human rights formulation of feminicide as a "crime against humanity."[8]

According to this definition, feminicide builds on femicide but now includes the phenomenon of impunity for the perpetrators because the state is implicated, either explicitly or implicitly, and makes clear that this crime transpires on a large scale, that is, it is widespread and rooted in the structural inequalities that render some women and girls acutely vulnerable. To this I would add one further descriptor, namely, that the killings are exceptionally brutal and vicious, a point exemplified in the case of Ciudad Juárez and several of the other cases listed above.[9]

Most journalists and other investigators agree that the Ciudad Juárez feminicides began in 1993, with one of the first victims being identified as Alma Chavarría Fávila, who was brutally raped, anally and vaginally. Some journalists state that she was a five-year-old girl, while others claim she was a young woman. Her body revealed that she was severely beaten and eventually murdered through strangulation.[10] In April of 2009, the *El Paso Times* reported that since 1993 more than six hundred girls and women have been tortured, raped, and murdered, most between the ages of ten and thirty. Many more are missing.[11] "Nearly all of the victims [have been] poor, young, and slender, with dark flowing hair and warm, reddish brown complexions."[12]

Juárez, a city of over two million inhabitants, sits directly on the U.S.-Mexican border alongside El Paso, Texas. Only a fairly insignificant Rio Grande river separates the two cities. During the past sixteen years, repeated investigations (local, state, national, and international) into these murders by "the authorities" have ended in failure. One early telling example is found in the experience of forensics chief and criminologist Oscar Maynez Grijalva. He began his investigation of these crimes in 1994 only to have his reports consistently ignored by his superiors in the Chihuahua state attorney general's office (Procuraduría General de Justica del Estado de Chihuahua). In time, his superiors instructed him to plant evidence to incriminate innocent men. When he refused, he began receiving threats and eventually was forced to resign.[13] Journalists, scholars, critics, and public officials have all offered a wide range of explanations for the feminicide, which collectively indicate conflicting possibilities.[14] Rosa Linda Fregoso has posed a list of questions illustrating the spectrum of theories:

> Are they committed by a single or multiple sex serial killers? By the police- and state-sponsored paramilitary groups? By the "Juniors" (sons of the elite)? By traffickers of illegal human organs? By an underground economy of pornography and snuff-films? By a satanic cult? By narcotraffickers? By unemployed men envious of women workers? By men expressing rage against poverty? By men threatened by changing sex roles? By abusive spouses or boyfriends?[15]

Fregoso has further noted that these widely divergent explanations have served to fuel the sense of terror and trauma that currently grip Juárez, making the people's capacity to resist this evil far more difficult.

⚭　　⚭　　⚭

The following story of seventeen-year-old María Sagrario González Flores helps develop in some detail one example. Sagrario's story is fairly typical of the victims. In 1996 the González family moved from the interior state of Durango to the Juárez area in search of a better life. By 1998 Sagrario, along with her father, Jesús, and sister Guillermina, were employed at a maquiladora.[16] Managers at this plant had Sagrario change her shift to early morning from the overnight shift, which she, her father, and older sister had all shared. This meant that Sagrario would have to travel alone and leave home at 4:00 a.m. to make it to work on time. The poverty of the Gonzálezes forced them to live in an outer lying area of Juárez in a one-room home thrown together with tar paper and wood, a home without running water.

On April 16, 1998, Sagrario's shift ended at 3:00 p.m., yet at 10:00 p.m. she had not returned home. Frantic, Jesús took his oldest daughter, Guillermina, and the two went looking for Sagrario. They quickly figured out that she was not with her boyfriend, who at 10:00 p.m. was at the same maquiladora plant working his own shift. They went to the local jail in downtown Juárez seeking help from the Juárez police, asking that they commence a search for Sagrario. Jesús' request was met with a patronizing response and the suggestion that Sagrario had run off with her boyfriend. The police made it clear that they would do nothing in the effort to find Sagrario, even though over the previous five years Juárez had a rapidly growing list of missing young women who turned up tortured, raped, and dead.[17]

Having had no luck with the Juárez municipal police, Jesús González then sought help from the district attorney's office and the state police. These offices were charged with handling the investigations of the string of murdered young women in Juárez. But this office, too, rebuffed Jesús, claiming that he had to wait twenty-four hours before he could file a missing persons report. He argued that he was looking for his daughter alive, not dead, but to no avail. After checking the local area hospitals, Jesús and his son Juan began their own search for Sagrario along the path she typically traveled. Fairly quickly the family sought the help of neighbors, who organized themselves and began a search in the desert where other victims had been found.

After the family had been searching for two weeks, they learned that a body had been found in the desert area called Loma Blanca. Sagrario's mother, Paula, took her son Juan and went to the police station on May 1 to find that the young woman's body was clothed with a company smock with the name Sagrario embroidered on it. The murdered girl was indeed

Sagrario. She had been stabbed five times and strangled. Police thought that Sagrario had also likely been raped, but her body was too decomposed for them to make a definitive judgment.

To add further torment to the González family's anguish, the police claimed that Sagrario was murdered while living a *doble vida* ("double life"), earning a second salary selling herself as a prostitute to Juárez men, a preposterous accusation.[18] The family found it unbelievable that investigators would make such a statement. Many Juárez residents had a growing suspicion that the police, both municipal and state, were either directly involved in the murders or, at the very least, orchestrating a cover-up for the guilty parties. The family buried Sagrario's remains in a simple desert cemetery. They could not afford a casket or the 150 dollars required for a proper burial. They decorated the dirt mound of Sagrario's resting place with plastic flowers.[19]

✖   ✖   ✖

This feminicide raises many searing issues and haunting questions. Scholars have just begun exploring and debating the various ways to interpret the "social identities of the victims and the meaning of their deaths"[20] as well as how to construct a meaningful cultural narrative of these brutal murders.

For the purpose of this chapter, I want to focus on how these killings represent an overt attack on female human beings, brown-skinned and economically poor. Not only were these girls and young women brutally murdered, but also, several of their bodies revealed a severed right breast and a left nipple bitten off. Other bodies were dismembered. Still others revealed a triangle carved into their backs with a knife or other sharp object or had a gang symbol carved on their backs. In at least one case, a woman's vagina was penetrated with a knife and then cut up into pieces; her mouth was cut up as well, both carved to resemble a "flower." Bodies of victims were left in public places as if to make an intentional and politically embarrassing statement.[21]

The killers could continue their brutality with ongoing impunity because a sufficient number of officials at every level of government had been corrupted. This has made the state complicit in these ongoing murders and guilty of crimes against humanity. Interrogations have revealed that some perpetrators kill girls and women as a sport, a competition to see who could rape and kill the most girls and women, or as a way for drug cartels to mark their territory, or to "celebrate" successful drug runs across the border.[22] What this rather brief account makes evident is that we are not dealing strictly with the murdering of girls and women, an evil tragedy to be sure, but rather with a more heinous *ritualized* killing of girls and women.

This ritualized killing of girls and women undoubtedly reflects misogynistic and entrenched pathological proclivities on the part of the perpetrators. But it also represents something more: the logic of a patriarchal sociopolitical system; the attempt to construct and inscribe power hierarchies; a denial of the political existence of girls and women; and the use of girls' and women's bodies for asserting control.

First, it represents the most heinous logic of a patriarchal,[23] or better, kyriarchal[24] sociopolitical system. When, as in this case, the genitalia and breasts of the girls and women victims, the most overt corporeal symbols of female humanity, become the focal targets of the assault on these girls and women, and when these brutal killings are allowed to continue with impunity for over eighteen years, then this tragedy carries with it a much larger social significance. At the very least, we must acknowledge the presence of a social order that has given rise to practices that "result in the death and the devaluation of female lives."[25] We must ask ourselves: What is the social condition that allows for the possibility of the proliferation of sexual violence? What are the roots of this condition? What keeps it vital and thriving? No doubt, the state and other major social institutions play a major role as they politically structure this social world.

Second, we need to recognize that the ritualized killing of girls and women is an extreme attempt to construct and inscribe power hierarchies. The perpetrators, through the act of killing, strive "to promote the authority of forces deemed to derive from beyond the immediate situation."[26] These ritualized killings are a product of a social mindset that sees girls and women as subjects in need of kyriarchal control, in a world in which a kyriarchal mindset is uncritically assumed as "God-given," as the way things are and are meant to be. This has led rather easily to females becoming the targets of economic exploitation in the maquiladoras of Juárez, which in turn serves to make the extermination of girls and women appear explicable and, tragically, less horrific. This layered subordination of girls and women rooted in a kyriarchal culture creates a devaluation of female lives.

The devaluation of female lives expresses itself in a number of ways. To be sure, it is evident in the brutal nature of the killings. However, it is perhaps more striking in the state-sanctioned terrorism of poor women that has taken hold in Mexico.[27] In fact, Mexico's legal system has served to promote violence against women within the private sphere. "Under current Mexican law, if injuries inflicted during interfamilial violence heal within fifteen days, the woman cannot file charges against her domestic partner; if the injuries heal after fifteen days but are not permanent, the aggressor is merely fined."[28]

Third, the state has created a system of investigation designed to remove the identity of the victims for the purpose of denying their political existence. Multiple investigations at every possible level of government (local, state, national, and international) have been intentionally compromised or botched. Evidence has been consistently mishandled, lost, or destroyed. In many cases, when a body is eventually found, it has been so decomposed that it is no longer possible to determine the details related to the murder. State agents, attorneys, journalists, activists, and others who have attempted to expose the truth of these killings have been threatened, assassinated, or have had a family member killed.[29] Thus, even in the wake of the deaths of the victims, the surviving family members have been denied the right to seek justice on behalf of their murdered daughter, sister, mother, or friend. The government itself is culpable of denying political standing to victims and their surviving family members.

Finally, the killers use girls and women's bodies for the purpose of asserting their unmitigated control of Juárez and beyond.

> In fact, the various feminicides in Mexico make evident the exercise of power across the social spectrum: the power of the state over civil society; the rich over the poor; the white elite over racialized people; the old over the young; men over women. The feminicides constitute a novel kind of "dirty war," one waged by multiple forces against disposable female bodies. The women targeted in these unprecedented border feminicides represent the "stigmatized bodies," those "marked for death in drug wars and urban violence." . . . Feminicide in Juárez exposes the reality of overlapping power relations on gendered and racialized bodies as much as it clarifies the degree to which violence against women has been naturalized as a method of social control.[30]

Women's bodies are used to mark territory and demonstrate power. These killings are "politically motivated sexual violence" that is based on a kyriarchal culture and its attendant infrastructure.[31] As Diana Washington Valdez has noted: "There is no one in Mexico who can protect anyone who seeks to investigate this."[32] All of which points to the killers' use of fear, trauma, and ultimately social terror so as to control the territory and overpower any threat to the ongoing work of evil here.

This experience of evil has cut short the lives of victims and forever changed the lives of the remaining family members and friends. This experience of evil confronts us with an ongoing horror, an evil that is many evils. The list of evils includes not only the unjust murders but also their brutality; the erasure and denial of the political standing of victims and their families; the betrayal of a government that terrorizes rather than protects its people; a lingering social imagination that appears to accept that poor, young women are disposable; the seeming pedestrian view that female humanity matters much, much less. These are but some of the evils.[33]

⊠   ⊠   ⊠

How we regard suffering matters theologically. If the suffering of the feminicide's victims and their families is seen as an aberration, as the tragic lot of an unfortunate handful of victims and their families, then the desire for release from this evil, that is, for healing from God, can be described as the journey of the directly affected individuals. Moreover, if the victims are somehow to blame for the onslaught of their suffering and murder, then their suffering can be reduced to the effect of their own personal sin. Indeed, religious and civil authorities have made just such an argument.[34] If, however, this horrific suffering is regarded as the by-product of social structures—economic, political, religious, cultural—then the drive for God's salvific grace needs to be seen as one we pursue socially, collectively.

The Juárez feminicide provokes the question: How best to delineate this experience of suffering? On the one hand, we can no doubt analyze its social, political, and economic dimensions and develop an understanding of a wide range of factors that put the feminicide's victims at high risk for great suffering. Indeed, we desperately need an analysis of our national and international infrastructures that leaves in plain sight the human collateral damage brought on by these structures. Even so, as

Rebecca Chopp warns, "Knowledge of suffering cannot be conveyed in pure facts and figures, reportings that objectify the suffering of countless persons. The horror of suffering is not only its immensity but the faces of anonymous victims who have little voice, let alone rights, in history."[35] Analysis alone does not go far enough. On its own, analysis can offer a short-sighted picture, one that leaves us aware but not engaged.

On the other hand, the personal stories of pain, like that of María Sagrario González Flores, would likely leave us engaged but not responsible. We are genuinely moved by the account of her brutal death. We insist that it stop. Her tragic story carries the power to move us. Yet the interrelated social-political systems that create a middle-class lifestyle for some and structural violence for many are not transparent for us. We find it difficult to see, much less accept, the ways in which our middle-class "must-have" products lead to a world that is ultimately destructive for the most vulnerable among us, like Sagrario. "The dynamics and distribution of suffering are still poorly understood."[36] So, as Robert McAfee Brown tells us, "The world that is satisfying to us is the same world that is utterly devastating to them,"[37] yet we still do not understand this connection well.

This leaves us with a dilemma. How do we "read" suffering, particularly that of the most vulnerable in our world? Why does our response to this question matter? What is at stake in our response to this question?

A Social-Suffering Hermeneutic

There are assumptions implicit in the ways we typically, perhaps unreflectively, regard the pain of others. Far too often, suffering has been dichotomized in a way that separates the analysis of individual experience from that of the social experience of suffering. Conventional dichotomies keep separate "individual from social levels of analysis, health from social problems, representation from experience, suffering from intervention."[38] When these common and accepted dichotomies frame the discussion of suffering, as is often so in "anthropology, social history, literary criticism, religious studies, and social medicine," then we no longer can grasp with clarity either the ways in which human suffering is at once both collective and individual or that the ways of "experiencing pain and trauma can be both local and global."[39] We need an approach to suffering that subverts these typical dichotomies.

Prior to the advent of liberation theologies in the late 1960s, theological discourse considered the question of suffering from the perspective of individual experience. Undoubtedly, one of the great contributions of liberation theologies has been to call our attention to unjust collective suffering in its many forms. However, the feminicide today demands that we once again examine how we understand the interlocking nature of individual and collective suffering and why attention to this relationship is crucial.

To begin, we need to appreciate that our perception of widespread human suffering has been powerfully shaped by the media and the commercial interests behind it. The media presents human suffering to us after it has been spun, digested, and "packaged." What results is human suffering as a commodity. "Packaged" images of suffering are presented so that they "appeal emotionally and morally." They often spell trouble because human suffering comes to us "remade, thinned out, and distorted," basically prepackaged in an essentialized, naturalized, or sentimentalized form, typically so that it serves some commercial purpose.[40] In the process, viewers become desensitized to and overwhelmed by serious suffering, yet grateful that it is not readily visible in their own neighborhoods, that it remains at a safe distance, physically and emotionally.

Today's packaged images of suffering "produce moral fatigue, exhaustion of empathy, and political despair"[41] and are distributed globally. We the "consumers" of suffering are left feeling that there is far too much suffering; it is too complex to be readily understood and too complicated to alleviate. This undermines any attempt at creating more just structures. We can find ourselves unable to respond except, perhaps, by writing a check. It is as if we are in a catatonic state. My point is that powerful interests put forward seductive depictions of suffering that are anything but transparent. We need to recognize this and to discern these depictions for what they are. We need to become more critically aware of the commercial and political interests that drive the most ubiquitous depictions of suffering. They shape how we appropriate suffering, in other words, how we make sense of the suffering of others, the reason for their suffering, and our relationship to their suffering. Often this occurs subconsciously. And it matters because how we appropriate another's suffering will, to a large degree, dictate our response. Packaged images of suffering, while skewed, do serve a constructive purpose. Without media depictions of others' suffering, we would be far less able to identify human needs and to develop compassionate responses to them. But this is insufficient.

We need to address ourselves to the angle taken in these depictions and how this angle has shaped our appropriation. Valid appropriations of human suffering are themselves complex to achieve. As the Kleinmans rightly observe, "To develop valid appropriations, we must first make sure that the biases of commercial emphasis on profit-making, the partisan agendas of political ideologies, and the narrow technical interests that serve primarily professional groups are understood and their influence controlled."[42] For theologians, our commitment to distinguish valid appropriations of suffering matters greatly. The search for more valid appropriations is not an attempt to reduce suffering to a "common" experience but rather is an attempt to recognize the complexity of the distinctive ways suffering is understood.

Cognizant of this dilemma, some theorists and theologians (Paul Farmer, M. Shawn Copeland, Rebecca Chopp, and others) have sought means of delineating suffering in a fashion that links social, political analysis with personal stories of suffering. Their focus directs attention to the ways that "structural violence" leads to insidious, extreme, and tragically avoidable human suffering. This interpretation of suffering, namely, linking personal accounts of extreme suffering *to* the social matrix that precipitates them, has been termed by some theorists "social suffering."

Building on this work, I propose a *social-suffering hermeneutic* that foregrounds the ways in which wider social forces coalesce to mar individual human lives. Thus, individual experience is read from within the larger social matrix that defines the parameters of that individual experience.

To develop a social-suffering hermeneutic, we need to understand what distinguishes this approach. We may identify four primary distinguishing factors in a social-suffering hermeneutic: (1) it foregrounds the praxiological nature of the experience of suffering; (2) it recognizes the presence of our interests in the naming of suffering; (3) it attends to the interplay between societal problems and personal suffering; and (4) it discerns the ways in which "core symbol systems and cultural discourses" are used to mediate suffering as a social experience.

First, a social-suffering hermeneutic foregrounds the praxiological nature of the experience of suffering. By "praxiological" I mean that the human experience of suffering (and all human experience) always already reflects praxis. By "praxis" I refer to the integral relation that exists between human thought and action (or practice). Theory shapes experience and experience shapes theory in a never-ending cycle. This means that there can be neither a project of "pure theory" that is ahistorical, that claims a view from nowhere, nor can there be an understanding of action as strictly instrumental, cut off from discernment and insight. How the experience of suffering is depicted and named shapes that experience and creates a framework that gets triggered by future experiences of suffering. Conversely, experiences of suffering inform and transform what suffering means. Until suffering is "named" through words and other forms of expression, that experience remains inchoate and devoid of its power to shape lives for good or for ill.

In the process of naming the experience of suffering, one may understand that experience more transparently. One may identify what the experience of suffering means, namely, what is important about the experience. Accordingly, one may become less of a passive receptacle in the face of that experience. Through the process of naming, we can take greater possession of our lives. To understand that suffering is necessarily and unavoidably praxiological means that we do not unreflectively assume that the experience of suffering is merely a given. While we may claim that the experience of suffering—physical, emotional, and the like—is simply there, the minute we in any way acknowledge it we are, in fact, interpreting suffering. Suffering, like all forms of human experience, is interpreted. With interpretation comes some active purpose or interest.[43]

Second, a social-suffering hermeneutic recognizes the presence of interests in our naming of suffering. Interests, be they economic, political, social, or ecclesiastical, strongly influence how we understand suffering and how we respond to the diverse forms of suffering in our world. Varied interests compete for our attention as they put forward processes that attempt to guide our response to suffering along a certain line of thought and a certain mode of behavior. "These processes involve both authorized and contested appropriations of collective suffering."[44] A given appropriation would be "authorized" if it reflects the viewpoint of the dominant economic interests of a society. Conversely, it would be "contested" if it challenged those interests.

Examples of social suffering like the Ciudad Juárez feminicide serve as the terrain for the construction and contestation of the social order and of theological order as well. When a narrative is put forward to describe the feminicide, it serves as a kind of "map" of the "legitimate" parameters of our personal and collective worldview and reflects a particular point of view, one that serves the interests of some to the detriment of others. A given narrative may offer some explanation for why this horror has befallen the women and city of Ciudad Juárez, and, given the scale of this atrocity, the explanation may contain assumptions about the relationship of human beings to evil and human beings to God. Kleinman, Das, and Lock offer a compelling example of how interests drive the naming of suffering and in so doing reflect a worldview that appears inevitable but is not. They write:

> The devastating conflicts in Bosnia, Rwanda, Zaire, Somalia, and Afghanistan are made over from national and regional disasters into trans-national tragedies that are "seen" and "felt" as part of the stream of everyday experience in the intimacy of homes thousands of miles away, at a safe distance. Social suffering is a feature of cultural representation both as spectacle and as the presentation of the real. But cultural technologies now exist to fashion the "real" in accord with the interests of power to a degree hardly imagined in the past. What W. J. T. Mitchell calls the gap between representation and responsibility is a master moral dilemma. How we "picture" social suffering becomes that experience, for the observers and even for the sufferers/perpetrators. What we represent and how we represent it prefigure what we will, or will not, do to intervene. What is not pictured is not real. Much of routinized misery is invisible; much that is made visible is not ordinary or routine. The very act of picturing distorts social experience in the popular media and in the professions under the impress of ideology and political economy.[45]

When the interests of political and economic power collude to determine the appropriation and commodification of suffering, and when this is packaged for mass consumption, this process of packaging creates and bends the experience of social and personal suffering so as to further the interests of power. These interests forge the "gap" between representation and responsibility and seek to maintain it. We cannot recognize valid appropriations of human suffering if we do not understand this gap.

Third, a social-suffering hermeneutic attends to the interplay between societal problems and personal suffering. This interplay is evident in public suffering that is widespread (genocide in Rwanda, for example) or in economic exchange that leads to the ongoing destruction of human lives (such as sex tourism) or in the varied clustering of major social problems. When major problems coalesce, they create an intensive, compounded experience. Sufferers may experience substance abuse, domestic violence, depression, poverty, despair, and tuberculosis concurrently as part and parcel of living in a disintegrating community. To identify such a cluster of problems as solely individual, meaning peculiar to this single individual, is a severe distortion. The "blame-the-victim" strategy is a common example of such distortion. What such a cluster of human problems indicates is the "often close linkage of personal problems with societal problems. It reveals too the interpersonal grounds of suffering: in other words, that suffering is a social experience."[46] As M. Shawn Copeland tells us, "Torture, genocide, extermination, 'ethnic cleansing,' 'disappearance,' enslavement, cultural decimation, protracted systemic racism,"[47] to name a few, all exemplify this interplay of the personal and social.

Finally, a social-suffering hermeneutic discerns the ways in which "core symbol systems and cultural discourses" are used to mediate suffering as a social experience. These core symbol systems may be in the form of classical images, folktales, stories, or metaphors, and they involve mythic stories of group origins. Regardless, they map the terrain of suffering and thereby offer the raw material by which suffering is depicted and authorized, whether in popular culture or by powerful social institutions. Every depiction furthers a particular point of view. These cultural representations, because they are living symbols, can be manipulated to give continuous birth to a worldview that clarifies the boundaries within which we find what is "legitimate" and beyond which we are not suppose to venture. Hans-Georg Gadamer refers to the ongoing interpretation of these symbols through the course of history as their "effective history."[48] The effective history of these cultural representations and symbols mediates the construction of social and self-identity.[49]

This historical process, needless to say, is an inherently political one. The dominant political power will invariably put forward in compelling fashion the "legitimate," "authorized," or "conventional" view of who we are in the world. As living symbols, cultural representations serve as one nerve center of society well situated to cast forth their appeal to a wide range of audiences. Accordingly, the clever manipulation of symbols and cultural representations becomes a powerful tool in the endeavor to shape hearts and minds. This can alter social experience in ways that shift the tide of our historical understanding of suffering.

Social suffering affects not only the desperately poor of the two-thirds-world countries but also the most poor and powerless within the so-called first world. Disintegration affects the poor of the first and two-thirds worlds alike, and the concurrent phenomenon of suffering is not merely coincidental but causal. It reveals the global impact of a political economy that feeds on a permanent substructure of powerless people whose presence is seemingly a "necessary" by-product in the production of an ongoing comfortable lifestyle for the upper classes.[50] As Kleinman, Das, and Lock observe:

> Social suffering results from what political, economic, and institutional power does to people and, reciprocally, from how these forms of power themselves influence responses to social problems. Included under the category of social suffering are conditions that are usually divided among separate fields, conditions that simultaneously involve health, welfare, legal, moral, and religious issues. They destabilize established categories. For example, the trauma, pain, and disorders to which atrocity gives rise are health conditions; yet they are also political and cultural matters. Similarly, poverty is the major risk factor for ill health and death; yet this is only another way of saying that health is a social indicator and indeed a social process.[51]

In sum, a social-suffering hermeneutic develops a critical awareness of the appropriation of suffering (that is, praxiological, interests, interplay of social and personal, cultural representations). This self-conscious hermeneutic fosters an awareness of how conventional social experience can appear to be "natural" and "normal." Yet this "appearance" of normality, while ubiquitous, often conceals the workings of power that inflict suffering on the vulnerable and innocent among us.[52]

If we employ a social-suffering hermeneutic, then we will ask questions of the feminicide such as: Which population is most at risk of great suffering? How might we identify those who are most at risk to sustain debilitating suffering? chronic suffering? Who will likely experience the enduring assault of racism? sexism? classism? rape? torture? Are certain forms of institutionalized violence "demonstrably more noxious than others?"[53] Which population stands the greatest mortal risk? Whose economic, ecclesiastical, political, social, and commercial interests are served by keeping this experience of suffering invisible? What are the conventional ways that cultural representations have been presented in popular culture or promoted by powerful social institutions? Such questions serve as a point of departure for a social-suffering hermeneutic.[54]

"Reading" the Feminicide

A social-suffering hermeneutic casts the suffering brought about by the feminicide in a particular light, one that enables us to recognize that in the depiction and naming of this suffering lies great power to shape, even determine, that experience. Chapter 2 will lay out how this depiction further shapes the theological issues presented by the feminicide. Every victim of the feminicide confronted a cluster of social problems with origins well beyond their purview. These problems placed Latinas, like María Sagrario González Flores, and their families at extremely high risk for experiencing the most brutal human violence and dehumanizing institutional power. The proverbial odds were stacked against Sagrario. For us to recognize what is behind her horrific death would mean recognizing our own responsibility for the circumstances that led to her death, a recognition that is, in the words of Al Gore, "an inconvenient truth."

The Praxiological Nature of the Experience of Suffering

By foregrounding the praxiological nature of the experience of suffering, we call attention to how the killing of the girls and women of Juárez gets named and how we thus understand the suffering it produces. Along with many feminist theorists, I have chosen to identify it as *feminicide*. Others use either *femicide*, *homicide*, *murders*, or *killings*. Terms like *homicides*, *murders*, and *killings* remain commonplace, but in this circumstance they are vague and misleading. These terms obfuscate the significance of the tragedy of the Juárez feminicide. They suggest that what the victims have unfortunately suffered is random, haphazard, and arbitrary—the work of a small group of sociopaths and nothing more. Moreover, these terms ignore questions of race, class, and gender. While the racialization of Mexican Americans and Mexican nationals in the United States can be traced back to the politics, economics, and ideology (Manifest Destiny) surrounding the Treaty of Guadalupe-Hidalgo in 1848, these racial politics consistently come to the fore every time it is economically beneficial to U.S., white, corporate interests. The feminicide is one recent example of many.

The term *femicide* is marginally better. *Femicide* has been widely used to identify the Juárez murders because *femicide* explicitly introduces gender as central to these killings. It calls attention to the sex of the victim, and arguably, it directs us toward the way that gender identity is constructed within society. The term *femicide* signifies that the killing was motivated by the fact that the victim was female. As anyone who reads newspapers knows, violence in Juárez is rampant; bodies are mounting by the week. And as the documenting of the feminicide demonstrates, a large number of victims are victims because they are female. Still, the term *femicide* falls short. *Femicide*, along with the terms identified above, fails to suggest an underlying systemic evil as integral to this brutal taking of life. While these terms do suggest a horrific, tragic failing, they invariably indicate that the pertinent severe failure must be fairly limited and arbitrary. It "must be" a failure borne by one or a few individuals and certainly not a tragedy involving a widespread, tacit, banal participation in evil, a situation that demands that all of us consider our own complicity. These terms are all shortsighted ways of naming the Juárez tragedy.

Each renders invisible or distant the need for a systemic analysis. What has transpired and continues is not the murders of a few girls and women here and there, the possible work of a serial killer, but rather the ongoing ritualized killing of hundreds of poor, brown girls and women over more than fifteen years' time. The circumstances suggest that this is the work of many, not merely a few. The feminicide's duration and the arrests and forced confessions of a few innocent men[55] means that the perpetrators, whoever they are, enjoy unmitigated impunity. The state must be viewed as complicit if not directly responsible, as Rosa Linda Fregoso, Melissa Wright, and many other scholars have argued.[56] As we have already seen, the girls and women are not simply murdered. Their corpses reveal that they have been violently raped, that their breasts and genitalia have been savagely mutilated. Though hundreds of men are murdered in Juárez every year, unlike women victims the men's "bodies are rarely mutilated or raped."[57] Most often their deaths are linked to drug violence, or at least that is the intent of the perpetrators.

By naming this suffering *feminicide*, we make visible what otherwise remains invisible. *Feminicide* turns our attention toward the roots of this experience of suffering as virile "misogynist sexism, racist classism, and expansionist colonialism."[58] These roots suggest some of the deep-seated sensibilities that give rise to this horrific feminicide, killings marked by their brutality, by their sheer numbers, and by the impotence of civil authorities who have, for the most part, no desire to end them or, worse, a direct role in them. Naming them as *feminicide* begins to lay bear what is transpiring and to thwart all efforts to conceal the roots of this social trauma.[59]

A dramatic shift in gender roles likewise has influenced how this suffering is named. Some interpreters of the feminicide argue that Juárez's entrenched patriarchal culture coupled with the "farm-to-factory" transition of young women has fueled this atrocity. Many young women and their families came to Juárez from rural settings in which the women were necessarily dependent upon the men in the family to do much of the hard labor of farm work. However, as young women became the primary wage earners and thus the primary providers for their children, the relationships between these young women and the men in their lives shifted. These women were no longer dependent upon the financial support of the men. Employers sought out few men for jobs in the maquiladoras. Over time a growing number of young women began to realize that they did not need a husband, especially if he was abusive and did not have a job. This shift in gender roles, some claim, has contributed to a quasi-public acquiescence to the feminicide as a punishment for women who transgress seemingly "divinely ordained" gender roles.[60]

Some scholars suggest that the feminicide has been played off as a kind of billboard warning to women who want to assert themselves. A staff member of Casa Amiga, a crisis center for women confronting domestic violence in Juárez, reported that women are sharing accounts of the male partners threatening them with their lives if they do not "stay in line," claiming that women can be easily beaten or killed and the authorities will not investigate.[61] How we name the suffering of the feminicide is not just a question of acknowledging the enormous, multifaceted character of the suffering but instead requires a shift in how we perceive the structural, systemic roots from which it springs.

The Presence of Disparate "Interests"

When various groups lay claim in the name of various interests to how we perceive suffering, they create contested ground, in which competing narratives shape our understanding of the suffering of the feminicide's victims. Economic interests, the state's interests, and the interests of dominant institutions (including the church) all come into play by means of various, competing narratives, each of which attempts to commodify and package this suffering according to its own interpretation.

The first of these, economic interests, constitutes one of the most fiercely debated perceptual terrains. As the outrage in response to the feminicide escalated, so did a critique of the expansion of transnational capitalism and global neoliberalism. This rapid expansion grew out of, in part, the passage of the North American Free Trade Agreement, better known as NAFTA, in 1993, which facilitated much more porous borders in the interest of "free trade."[62] Proponents of this common critique argued that economic globalization led to the exploitation and in turn to the extermination of girls and women. As Fregoso recounts

> During the 1990s, Ciudad Juárez was the largest export-processing zone on the border, host to roughly 350 manufacturing plants own primarily by U.S. transnational corporations. These plants employed roughly 180,000 workers who were paid around $23 per week in take-home pay, a little less than $4 per day, or fifty cents per hour. . . . Antiglobalization perspectives provide valuable insight into how Juárez figures as the "local" embodiment of the way of global neoliberalism (market-based development) under the coordination and direction of the Group of Eight (G8), the IMF [International Monetary Fund], the WTO [World Trade Organization], and the World Bank; of the concentration of economic power in transnational corporations; of the internationalization of social divisions; and of the subordination of national economies to global forces. Without doubt, global and transnational dynamics implode into the geography of Ciudad Juárez.[63]

In response to this crucible, those critical of the expansion of global capitalism developed arguments that drew connections between the exploitation of female workers in the maquiladoras and the extermination of women in the feminicide. These often were interpreted as part of "a single process." Both were interpreted as "expressions of the exercise of power and gender hierarchies," and each served, in part, "to explain the other."[64] In fact, the female workers came to be known as *mujeres desechables* ("disposable women"). In spite of this reasoning, the feminicide was, by and large, erroneously connected to the maquiladora industry. While the overwhelming majority of all the victims were poor, dark-skinned women, overall, only a small number of them worked in Juárez's maquiladoras.[65] And yet, this connection remains popular in the minds of many interested in critiquing global capitalism.

It seems as if those critical of global capitalism would have us view the feminicide's victims and its survivors as passive victims, poor, brown women unfortunately caught up on the wrong side of inevitable, capitalist "change and progress." And in some representations of the killings of women, such as the documentary *Maquila: A Tale of Two Mexicos*, the feminicide's victims are depicted not only as "victims of globalization but as subjects in need of patriarchal regulation."[66] In others, such as *Performing the Border*, women are portrayed "not as being in need of regulation and surveillance, but rather as the very objects of regulation and surveillance."[67] Such examples contribute to the linking of the exploitation of women workers in the maquiladoras with women victims of the feminicide. For women to be "in need of patriarchal regulation" or to be "objects of regulation and surveillance" means that they are seen as victims or as objects of global capitalism. Perhaps more insidiously, these third-world women become fodder, serving as the objects of first-world feminist definitions, which miss seeing the ways these women resist their situation in spite of the enormous sacrifice and courage such resistance entails.[68]

In the second narrative of suffering, according to the state's interests, the state viewed its interests in this feminicide not in terms of protecting its female citizenry from extreme gender violence but in terms of deflecting attention from its horrific abdication of civil responsibility. When the state no longer could deny the growing number of these horrific killings, it began to deploy a blame-the-victim strategy. It defended this strategy by arguing that the victims were engaged in nonnormative sexual behavior, by which the state meant that these women were leading a *doble vida* ("double life") as prostitutes, were associating with lesbians, were influenced by women from the United States, and thus were becoming more independent and promiscuous.

According to this line of thinking, the victims brought the feminicide upon themselves because of their essentially "immoral" behavior. Thus they are to be held responsible for the violence directed against them. Concurrent with this line of thinking was a "patriarchal nostalgia for an earlier era of male authority in which women remain wedded to the private sphere of domesticity and motherhood."[69] Eventually, widespread pressure from hundreds of national, international, and transnational human-rights groups laid bare "state corruption and indifference,"[70] forcing the state to change its account of these killings but not to alter its failure to investigate.

In 2001 the state adopted a new narrative strategy of reporting that it was conducting an "investigation" into each case of the various "homicides" of women. With regularity the state argued that each case was independent and discrete and therefore unrelated to other cases. By so doing, it sought to undermine "the more general and systematic phenomenon of violence against women."[71] This new narrative strategy helped the state generate the perception of its authority and professionalism, which it used to combat allegations of its corruption. The strategy also allowed the state to claim that female "homicides" were a normal part of life in any major city and to discredit the accusations being put forward by women's-rights and human rights activists. The state accused these groups of "politicizing" the murders.[72]

The state has consistently focused on those arguing that the accelerated growth of transnational capitalism and global neoliberalism bear primary responsibility for the extermination of female bodies in Juárez. This narrative strategy has

> worked to absolve the state of its complicity and perhaps even direct involvement in the murders of poor and dark-skinned women in Ciudad Juárez. . . . As the master narrative for the Left, globalism generates a problem of interpretation that is unable to account for the consolidation of a new form of state-sanctioned terrorism in Mexico. The state, however, is in many ways directly implicated in the culture of feminicide in the region. In February 2002, for example, state agents ambushed and assassinated Mario Cesar Escobedo Anaya, a defense attorney for one of the suspects in the killings, who was leading charges against police for their use of torture in extracting confessions.[73]

The state's role and complicity must be foregrounded, because doing so provides greater clarity on the extreme degree of vulnerability marking the lives of young, poor, dark-skinned women in Ciudad Juárez. In the end, the feminicide is a crime of the state "which tolerates the murders of women and neither vigorously investigates the crimes nor holds the killers accountable."[74]

While the state must be held accountable, Alicia Schmidt Camacho makes clear the complexity of such an assertion. She calls for an examination of *subjetividad desnacionalizada* ("denationalized subjectivity").[75] To understand the suffering of the feminicide's victims and survivors, Schmidt Camacho claims, we need to situate the feminicide in the context of the borderlands, not merely in Ciudad Juárez or Mexico. The U.S. government's militarization of the borderlands has generated a new wave of criminal organizations who use the desert for clandestine commercial activity that traffics in human beings dubbed "illegal"[76] by the United States. This has contributed significantly to the borderlands functioning as essentially "denationalized space." Schmidt Camacho posits: "In light of this feminicide, we need to distinguish the idea of "crimes against humanity" from its legal definition as a project of a nation-state. [The feminicide], in turn, directs us to new forms of human rights violations that have arisen as a result of the erosion of the [nation-state] because of globalized capital."[77]

We need to develop an internationally binding understanding of world citizenship that applies to Mexican women and all the world's women. This would be one part of a viable strategy to resist the condition of denationalized subjectivity in the face of violence against women, irrespective of any particular nation-state's culpability.[78] Schmidt Camacho's contribution here matters immensely because it directs attention to the ways in which global capital has increasingly compromised the nation-state. The standard of living enjoyed by a majority in the United States and the industrialized West comes at a terrible price. Yet this argument must not be used to let the Mexican state or the United States off the hook.

As far as the state is concerned, the suffering of the feminicide's victims and survivors becomes a secondary concern in the face of the state's more pressing interest to save face through damage-control narrative strategies—a highly dubious endeavor but one the state tenaciously pursues. It is a dubious endeavor because the Juárez feminicide has transpired while the buying and selling of the law has escalated to a new level, not only in its breadth among the rank and file but also in its reach, extending up to the highest levels of authority in the city of Ciudad Juárez and in the state of Chihuahua as well.

The careful research of journalists like Diana Washington Valdez, Alfredo Corchado, and Teresa Rodríguez, among others, details the corruption within the local Juárez police, the Chihuahua state police, the local district attorney's office, and so on. Their research suggests that the governor's office in the state of Chihuahua is at least complicit in the feminicide, cooperating by launching ever new investigations but ensuring that they will ultimately be stymied. Scapegoats for the feminicide have been identified and tortured assiduously until confessions were elicited while the real criminals continue their killing spree unabated. The police, particularly the state police, have been directly implicated in the feminicide.[79] The suffering of the feminicide's victims and their families remains obscured because in this context the law and civil authority is a sham.

Attendant to these phenomena, the victims' plight has become much more obscure. NAFTA made the border porous so as to facilitate greater economic prosperity for U.S. corporations, but this in turn made Ciudad Juárez a highly attractive locale for competing drug cartels feeding the United States' escalating demand for cocaine, among other drugs. Because of NAFTA, it is now far easier to move drugs across the border. The drug cartel activity in Juárez has made corruption, violence, lawlessness, and impunity normative throughout the city, creating a climate of escalated risk for all city residents, particularly the most vulnerable—poor, dark-skinned, young women.

In 2004 authorities arrested several state policemen suspected of drug trafficking and murder. These arrests led to the confession of a man named Alejandro García, who claimed to have taken part in the murders of some of the women at the orders of both the state police and the Vicente Carrillo Fuentes drug cartel. This confession revealed a drug gang that counted corrupt municipal and state police among its members. One unidentified interviewee claimed that each time a major drug shipment crossed the border into the United States without being discovered, members of the drug gang would celebrate by killing women. Some gang members wanted to wear a "trophy of their success," so they would bite off the left nipple from the breast of their female victims and wear it on a chain around their neck. Yet in the following couple of years, even with the work of a federal special prosecutor and with evidence that implicated some 130 Chihuahua state officials, the feminicide continued. Many officials initially implicated were later exonerated.[80]

Adding to the obscurity of the suffering of the feminicide's victims is a largely invisible but organized network that has methodically worked to terrorize victims' family members, and all others, who start asking too many questions. The creation of a "reign of terror" is to ensure that the feminicide can continue with impunity, in part through the silencing of any public critique of the murders. Accordingly, any attempt to critique the corruption of the authorities or their immunity is met with a swift, brutal response. Journalists have recorded accounts of the police terrorizing women by brutally beating them, by gang raping them, by threatening to kill their spouses and children, or by showing them pictures of the dead bodies of women who had been raped and tortured. Faceless others have terrorized women by sending out anonymous death threats and by shooting and wounding their children.[81]

Moreover, those government officials who have made a sincere attempt to pursue the real criminals in this case have had their findings ignored, their efforts thwarted, been asked to falsify documents, and been coerced into stepping down from their positions. The source of this hideous pressure on them has remained for the most part hidden. One of the elements of the reign of terror is that its originating source is not transparent. Yet it exerts significant control over life and death. The dominant forces here strategize, on the one hand, to minimize if not mute any public critique of the feminicide and, on the other, to escalate the experience of terror in the private realm—all of which serves to shape how the extreme suffering of the feminicide is "understood," or better said, misunderstood and distorted. For example, Sagrario González's family members have been threatened and dismissed as they have repeatedly tried to keep the case of her murder in the public view. In response, authorities have systematically shunned and minimized the González family's experience and employed a blame-the-victim strategy to trivialize her murder.

Finally, the third narrative of suffering, that of social institutions like the church, also influences how the feminicide is perceived and how those who are suffering are to be regarded. While feminicide's survivors have turned to religious imagery in their grief and outrage (see chapter 4), it appears that Christian church authorities scandalously have remained silent concerning the feminicide or have also adopted a blame-the-victim strategy.[82] Roman Catholic Bishop Renato Ascencio León, Juárez's ordinary since 1994, was quoted in 2009 as stating that women need to change the way they dress and act, and he suggested that women's "immodesty" is responsible for provoking men's sexual aggression. Some have suggested that his comments, made at the Catholic Church's Sixth World Meeting of Families (Mexico City, January 2009), could lead one to believe that he blames the victims of the feminicide for bringing about their rape, murder, and sexual mutilation.[83]

Julia Monárrez Fragoso observed that Catholic Church officials also criticize the mothers who have protested their daughters' murders, claiming that these mothers have created divisions in society by means of their criticism of civil authorities. She rightly notes the hypocritical, not to mention unprincipled, nature of this position, particularly given the outrage church officials stirred up against civil authorities when a Mexican cardinal was assassinated. Basically, Monárrez Fragoso is correct when she argues that as late as 2003 churches in Juárez—Catholic and Protestant (mainline and evangelical)—had not publically taken a position in support of the murdered girls and women. However, there are some members of religious communities and other religious leaders who have spoken out and acted on behalf of these victims.[84]

The Episcopal Conference of Bishops in Mexico (CEM) has issued a major pastoral exhortation ("Que en Cristo Nuestra Paz México Tenga Vida Digna") as well as various public letters and statements calling attention to the violence that has erupted in several sectors of Mexico and urging the Mexican people to work at rebuilding the peace.[85] In addition, the six bishops of the state of Chihuahua have likewise issued a brief statement. Given the violence in the state, the Chihuahua bishops implore all who live within the state to turn to God and work toward an end to the violence.[86]

While some of the statements acknowledge in a general way that young women in Mexico are victims of discrimination and violence, none directly addresses the horror of the feminicide. The 115-page pastoral exhortation issued by CEM devotes only a few paragraphs to the violence against women. In one paragraph, the document offers an insubstantial critique of those who hold the female victims themselves responsible for the violence they experience. The critique is insubstantial because it reduces violence against women to cases of domestic violence and claims that those who criticize women fail to understand the social, economic, and cultural conditions that prevent women from leaving their violent domestic relationship.[87] And while several Mexican bishops have individually issued letters addressing the violence and calling for it to end, sadly and incredibly, as of this writing Bishop Renato Ascencio León of Juárez has not issued such a letter addressing violence in general, much less the violence against women. At the very least, the inattention to the Juárez feminicide by Mexico's Roman Catholic Episcopal leadership suggests that this suffering is not that significant in the minds of the episcopacy.

The Interplay between Societal Problems and Personal Suffering

The above analysis of the way interests shape how we regard the feminicide for the most part described the macro level. A social-suffering hermeneutic, however, attends to the interplay of societal problems and personal suffering. Attention to consequential personal suffering foregrounds the particular experience of victims like Sagrario González and thus keeps the macro level of analysis from becoming merely an abstraction. By staying in touch with personal accounts of the victim's experience, we realize that this feminicide urgently demands our response.

In the case of Sagrario González, a number of factors coalesced in her life suggesting that she and other women like her were extremely vulnerable and quite likely to suffer unjustly, severely. Tragically, too many of them have ended up brutally murdered. Sagrario was young (seventeen years of age), slender, poor, an employee of a maquiladora company, and, needless to say, female. She was in several respects the quintessential embodiment of the great majority of feminicide victims. Not only was Sagrario's family desperately poor, but they also lived in a city where the concerns of the poor were and are summarily disregarded by local authorities who are themselves part of the working poor and so are forced to accept bribes to provide for their own families.

The struggle to survive forced the González family to relocate to Juárez. Along with her family, Sagrario was a transplant from the state of Durango, having lived in Juárez about two years at the time of her murder. Many families, likely hers as well, had known a simple, rural life and then moved to the sprawling metropolis of Juárez, Chihuahua, a city of some two million people, among the largest in Mexico. The adjustment necessitated by such a move was enormous. All of these factors contributed to her vulnerability.

Sagrario, like most young women, was desperate for work, given the extreme poverty of her family. Maquiladora managers sought out young women for their labor force. Managers found that such women had fresh energy for work, had a great deal of manual dexterity, did not question authority, and did not complain about sudden changes in their work shifts or about demanding work quotas. In short, they were a corporate manager's dream. Sagrario's murderers abducted her within days of when her work hours changed. They took her while she was in transit from the maquiladora to her home. After her work hours changed, she traveled late at night by herself because her work shift no longer coincided with the work shifts of her sister or father.[88] The economic interests of U.S. corporations feed upon and profit greatly from the desperation and vulnerability of young female maquiladora workers like Sagrario.

Sagrario's horrific murder and the subsequent suffering of her family are exacerbated by a culture of entrenched, pervasive sexism that undermines "the adoption of public policies that would protect women."[89] In this particular kind of cultural milieu, authorities easily and mindlessly dismissed the concerns of Sagrario González's family. For example, the police authorities told Mr. González that his daughter probably either ran off with her boyfriend or that, unbeknownst to him, she was leading a double life as a prostitute. The clear message was that Sagrario, the victim, was to blame for supposedly being out alone late at night and/or for allegedly "dressing suggestively." Authorities had no supporting evidence for this assertion.[90]

The underlying message is that the lives of poor, young women are of a different and lesser human nature. Within a cultural context of pervasive interlocking systems of domination, the suffering of the feminicide victims is of a lesser order of significance. It is regarded as suffering that can be more easily overlooked without much ado. When Sagrario's body was eventually found and identified, it was so decomposed that they could only establish that she had been stabbed repeatedly and strangled. As with the stories of many victims, it was impossible to establish definitively whether or not Sagrario was victim to one of the drug cartel's celebrations. But she could have been. No doubt, the perpetrators want everyone in the community with a conscience to fear, to be too afraid to go public with the demand for justice.

Conclusion

Thus far, a social-suffering hermeneutic has offered us an angle of vision on the naming of suffering and its significance, and on the varied interests that seek to manipulate our understanding. In addition, we have seen how larger social forces coalesce in a fashion that generates many human casualties, captured in the suffering of Sagrario González and her family.

But our rational analysis of this suffering, while utterly crucial, is insufficient. The analysis thus far does not take into account society's tacit acquiescence to these atrocities. This tacit acquiescence emerges from a general sense, typically not expressed, that such suffering, while tragic to be sure, is nevertheless an enduring evil. No doubt, a widespread gender hierarchy operates. To put it plainly, if women in Juárez were killing poor men in large numbers, sexually mutilating their bodies, and making a public display of this, it would not be allowed to continue for well over eighteen years. What makes the reverse not just possible but a reality? What gives rise to this subconscious orientation? What feeds the tenacity of this orientation?

A social-suffering hermeneutic recommends a deeper level of reflection—namely, a consideration of the way core symbols and cultural discourses are interpreted so as to manipulate how Latinas themselves, and society at large, understand suffering. To understand what renders certain human lives inconsequential, and therefore disposable, recommends an analysis on a deeper level. Only at the conclusion of such analysis can we begin to understand what is at stake in asking the theological question of salvation.

2

Suffering, Social Imaginaries, and the Making of Evil

I f we are to understand the complexity of the appropriation of suffering within society, and if we are to grasp why social, political, and even some religious authorities deem the suffering of Latinas to be of a lesser significance than that of others, then we need to recognize the presence of a hegemonic imaginary worldview as it is generated and sustained by reigning stereotypes of Latinas. Too often these stereotypes have served to dehumanize Latinas by caricaturing them as "pawns" available to service the needs of others in the private and public realms but lacking any sense of agency. The worldview forged by these stereotypes encourages as well as condones, at least implicitly, many of the forms of institutionalized violence and structural evil suffered by Latinas. This same worldview operates to keep Latina suffering entrenched and seemingly legitimate while it additionally bears a connection to the U.S. demand for illegal drugs and many U.S. corporations' demands for excessive profit margins.

This chapter continues the development of what I term a *social-suffering hermeneutic*. The first chapter delineated how this "reading" of suffering clarifies the praxiological nature of suffering; the ways that particular interests strive to shape our reading; and the interplay of societal problems and personal suffering. This chapter takes up the fourth distinctive feature of a social-suffering hermeneutic by turning our attention to the cultural-symbolic dimensions of suffering. Building on the first chapter, it explores some of the roots of the evil that led to the eventuality of the feminicide. Some cultural-symbolic roots serve to "legitimize" unjust suffering, making it palatable, making it appear unavoidable.

Although the evil of the feminicide operates on a political and economic level, this chapter argues that a dominant, social imaginary worldview is created and sustained, to a significant degree, by limited and limiting stereotypes of Latina womanhood that dehumanize Latinas as well as keep Latina suffering entrenched and seemingly legitimate. This recontextualizes Christian salvation.

To speak of a "social imaginary worldview" carries a particular challenge because of its elusiveness. A social imaginary worldview tends to be much more implicit than explicit, operative at a subconscious level rather than on the plane of our awareness. It concerns our precognitive, prethematic grasp of the world and the ways this grasp orients how we perceive the world around us and our place in it. The first section thus focuses on the notion of a social imaginary worldview as it is developed in the writings of three theorists—Charles Taylor, Octavio Paz, and Emilie Townes—with an eye toward the underside of our imaginal, social existence. The next section extends the first by examining the ways in which particular paradigmatic, female, cultural-symbolic representations mediate our imaginal, social existence and are manipulated to create a seemingly integral and legitimate relation between Latinas and suffering. Here I argue that these representations contribute to a social climate predisposed to an evil like the feminicide. The final section of this chapter clarifies how this feminicide, in light of the foregoing social-suffering hermeneutical analysis, recontextualizes our interrogation of salvation and what it means today.

Social Imaginaries and the Making of Evil

A social-suffering hermeneutic necessarily includes attention to the ways in which core symbol systems or cultural representations portray suffering as a social experience. They depict, among other things, how a given society understands the place of suffering in societal life. Since these cultural representations powerfully shape our imaginal social existence, they are used to define what is deemed a "legitimate" view of our place and the place of suffering in the world. The inherently political nature of these cultural representations has meant, and continues to mean, that they are useful for either good or for ill. Powerful economic and political interests regularly manipulate these cultural representations, often to evil effect. No doubt the clever manipulation of these cultural representations has contributed to a climate that has made the tragedy of the feminicide possible and, to some degree, probable. Yet before this chapter turns to particular representations, I want to explore our imaginal social existence that these representations help to generate.

Three scholars theorize on imaginal social existence. Charles Taylor makes clear its ubiquitous character and the ways ordinary people imagine their social space in precognitive, prethematic fashion. Octavio Paz shows that this implicit organization of social space cannot be portrayed without explicit, sustained attention to gender and the relation between gender and violence. Emilie Townes cogently argues that particular narratives and stereotypes make possible "the cultural production of evil."[1]

Charles Taylor has described at length the character and nature of our imaginal social existence through what he describes as a common, widespread "implicit grasp of social space," in other words, our shared operative sense of how things in society do proceed. He identifies this felt sense as a "social imaginary." We operate with a social imaginary, Taylor claims, well before we ever think about it or attempt to consciously understand it. To clarify, this operative "social imaginary," or shared understanding of the moral order, is simply that: an understanding of moral order *as it is*; it is *not* an understanding of moral order *as it should be*. This social imaginary, that is, this given conception of moral order, assigns particular characteristics to the world and to divine action within it such that a given set of moral norms appears right, merits our pursuit, and is at least partially realizable.[2] Taylor insightfully elaborates and emphasizes the implicit character of this notion. He writes:

> By social imaginary, I mean something much broader and deeper than the intellectual schemes people may entertain when they think about social reality in a disengaged mode. I am thinking, rather, of the ways people imagine their social existence, how they fit together with others, how things go on between them and their fellows, the expectations that are normally met, and the deeper normative notions and images that underlie these expectations.

There are important differences between social imaginary and social theory. I adopt the term imaginary (i) because my focus is on the way ordinary people "imagine" their social surroundings, and this is often not expressed in theoretical terms, but is carried in images, stories, and legends. It is also the case that (ii) theory is often the possession of a small minority, whereas what is interesting in the social imaginary is that it is shared by large groups of people, if not the whole society. Which leads to a third difference: (iii) the social imaginary is that common understanding that makes possible common practices and a widely shared sense of legitimacy.[3]

Taylor's observation here may be extended to suggest that a society in which feminicide not only emerges but also endures has become subject to a manipulation of its "images, stories, and legends" so that they forge a "moral order" that implies that violence against women is just this side of "tolerable." Horrific, unimaginable, to be sure, but just within the realm of "toleration" in a world still riddled with injustices and still producing lives marked by desperation. Functionally, the Juárez feminicide reflects at least some minimum, marginal level of social acquiescence, or it would not continue. Bear in mind that Taylor's social imaginary is precognitive. Atrocious as this sounds, our inability to bring this feminicide to an end suggests a broad, tacit acquiescence to the notion that the lives of these sufferers matter less and therefore are "expendable."

Nonetheless, in developing his notion of social imaginaries, Taylor argues that, of course, social imaginaries can be false in that they can and do distort the realities of daily experience. Societies often claim to live by a value or principle that they imagine as realized in their experience (for example, the equality of all citizens within a democratic state) yet cover up and ignore the ways huge sectors of the society are systematically excluded from this principle. Indeed, various spheres of what Taylor calls "false consciousness" can and do mark a society's understanding of itself. If, for example, a society professes and believes that all citizens are equal yet disproportionately incarcerates particular sectors (for example, Blacks and Latinos/as), it develops a "false consciousness" in that some can be fairly confident of their just treatment before the law (for example, Whites), while others cannot. Those confident feel a sense of righteousness and the others anger or depression.

Even so, according to Taylor, social imaginaries cannot be reduced to mere ideology because some people do engage "in a form of democratic self-rule, even if not everyone, as our comfortable self-legitimations imagine. Like all forms of human imagination, the social imaginary can be full of self-serving fiction and suppression, but it also is an essential constituent of the real. It cannot be reduced to an insubstantial dream."[4] So for Taylor, the social imaginary, irrespective of its various elements of "self-serving fiction and suppression," is invariably part of the real. In other words, Taylor calls our attention to a dissonance between the social, moral society we imagine ourselves to be and the social world we have de facto created.

But this creates a problem within Taylor's thought. His considerations of "false consciousness" lack full development, most certainly from the perspective of the victims of "social suffering," and therefore end up attenuated. Consequently, for a consideration of how societies appropriate social suffering, Taylor's account, at least as he develops it in his *Modern Social Imaginaries*, provides a somewhat useful but nonetheless limited construct. While he does help us to recognize the significance of people imagining their social existence and the precognitive dynamic of social imaginaries, he does not help us, much beyond an initial discussion, to understand well and grapple effectively with the presence of false consciousness and of distortion. What we need is a more intellectually robust and searing consideration of what he refers to with his idea of false consciousness.[5]

Among the most widely read philosophers to address the idea of a social imaginary worldview in Latin America is the ever controversial 1990 Nobel Prize laureate Octavio Paz. Indeed, he recognizes its potent presence. In his words: "There is among Mexicans, men and women, a universe of buried images, desires, and impulses. I attempted a description (of course insufficient—a mere glimpse) of the world of repressions, inhibitions, memories, appetites, and dreams which Mexico has been and is."[6] However, and much more importantly, Paz foregrounds gender constructions, particularly in relation to violence and suffering. While some would argue that his work perpetuates stereotypes and caricatures of gender relations—without question, many scholars have sharply critiqued his work for this very reason[7]—others would say that in his work he captures with poignant brilliance the "national character." Either way, his enduring influence commands attention.

In Paz's foregrounding of gender, he elucidates the Mexican social imagination from the vantage point of the character and motives of the *macho*. While this elucidation of the *macho* is not necessarily his aim, he in fact paints a portrait of the Mexican patriarchal[8] worldview through his view of the dialectical relationship between men and women.

> Every woman—even when she gives herself willingly—is torn open by the man, is the *Chingada*.[9] In a certain sense all of us, by the simple fact of being born of woman, are *hijos de la Chingada*, sons of Eve. But the singularity of the Mexican resides, I believe, in his violent, sarcastic humiliation of the Mother and his no less violent affirmation of the Father. A woman friend of mine (women are more aware of the strangeness of this situation) has made me see that this admiration for the Father—who is a symbol of the closed, the aggressive—expresses itself very clearly in a saying we use when we want to demonstrate our superiority: "I am your father." The question of origins, then, is the central secret of our anxiety and anguish. We are alone. Solitude, the source of anxiety, begins on the day we are deprived of maternal protection and fall into a strange and hostile world. . . . The *macho* represents the masculine pole of life. The phrase "I am your father" has no paternal flavor and is not said in order to protect or to guide another, but rather to impose one's superiority, that is, to humiliate. Its real meaning is no different from that of the verb *chingar* and its derivatives. The *macho* is the *gran chingón*. One word sums up the aggressiveness, insensitivity, invulnerability and other attributes of the *macho*: power. It is force without the discipline of any notion of order: arbitrary power, the will without reins and without a set course.[10]

Yet his description of the Mexican social imagination falls seriously short, which many feminist theorists have noted, because he utterly dismisses and ignores the concrete expressions of women's subjectivity.[11] Nonetheless, his admittedly limited reading of the Mexican social imaginary bears attention in that it offers a glimpse of a tenacious, hegemonic worldview that keeps the notion of Latina suffering deeply rooted.

Paz offers us some explanation for what American Studies scholar Alicia Schmidt Camacho refers to as an "operative social fantasy." "Precisely because the feminicide exploits the social fantasy that some women are made to be abused, the movement seeking justice must radically alter the perception that poor women are not subjects who deserve the protection of the law."[12] Paz helps us to see this social fantasy. "His work reads like a historical justification for and anguish about violence against women, against the mother or wife who abandoned and/or betrayed the son or husband."[13] He shows us the social construction that Latin American scholars, like Argentinean Marcella Althaus-Reid,[14] and journalists, like Columbian Silvana Paternostro,[15] rightly and severely critique. And their work makes clear that his depictions are not peculiar to Mexico but shed light on the construction of extreme gender inequalities in various Latino/a communities.

Emilie Townes offers a much more insightful approach to the underside of imaginal social existence in her towering work *Womanist Ethics and the Cultural Production of Evil*. As part of her conceptualization of the deep structures of social legitimacy, she focuses her critical and analytical attention on how a society produces evil—and consequently misery and suffering. She terms this dynamic "the cultural production of evil."[16] More specifically, she examines in-depth the way particular images of black women (for example, Aunt Jemima, the Tragic Mulatta, Topsy, and others) have been used and continue to be used as "conductors and seeresses." These stereotypical images reveal much about how evil is "created, shaped, maintained, dismantled."[17] Her approach draws on "Michel Foucault's understanding of the imagination and Antonio Gramsci's use of hegemony," and shows how the hegemonic imagination generates "caricatures and stereotypes" of black women that insidiously reflect and further the cultural production of evil.[18] Analogously, Townes's work recommends that stereotypes of Latina femaleness are likewise used to legitimize socially the furtherance of evil and, consequently, to inform the active ways we envisage suffering in our social and personal imaginations. For as Townes rightly argues, structural evil is embedded not only in rational mechanisms but is also "maintained by more heuristic forces that emerge from the imagination as emotion, intuition, and yearning."[19] Stereotypes of Latina femaleness operate as these heuristic forces.

Yet stereotypes of Latinas, Townes's work would seem to suggest, ought not be reduced to freestanding portraits but rather should be understood in light of the narrative accounts by which each stereotype acquires its efficaciousness. These narrative accounts—hegemonic, sociocultural historical narratives—serve the interests of the most powerful and, accordingly, willfully exclude the interests of subjugated peoples. So much so that subjugated peoples, like Latinas, are little more than pawns or fixtures in someone else's story. To understand how these narratives designate Latinas as pawns is to understand how evil is structured and operative in society and in the lives of Latinas. This understanding of evil is further developed when we begin to recognize that "the story *can* be told in another way. It can be told in such a way that the voices and lives of those who traditionally and historically have been left out [can be] heard with clarity and precision. Even more, these voices can then be included into the discourse—not as additive or appendage, but as resource and codeterminer of actions and strategies. Yet this is not a crass teleological world. Rather, it acknowledges the intimate humanity of our plurality and works with as much precision as possible to name this plurality in its vicissitudes."[20] The structures that give rise to evil and thus social suffering are, in part, the product of the stories we tell ourselves about who we are and how we came to be. Typically, hegemonic power within society recounts history in a way that minimizes the atrocities that would detract from and call into question its "superiority," "goodness," and ascendancy.

A consideration of these cultural representations and their accompanying stories, in light of the feminicide, calls our attention to the perniciousness and insidiousness of this evil. By examining cultural representations, their narratives, and the messages they are made to carry, we learn something of how evil is produced by the power of seductive images and narratives that point us toward how we "ought to" think about human brutality. In the process, we come to see that evil is, in fact, banal and extreme but never radical. For as Hannah Arendt has so thoughtfully noted: "It is indeed my opinion now that evil is never 'radical,' that it is only extreme, and that it possesses neither depth nor any demonic dimension. It can overgrow and lay waste the whole world precisely because it spreads like a fungus on the surface. It is 'thought-defying,' as I said because thought tries to reach some depth, to go to the roots, and the moment it concerns itself with evil, it is frustrated because there is nothing. That is its 'banality.' Only the good has depth and can be radical."[21] Since evil is ultimately "thought-defying," we need to come to terms with the social imaginary and the potent cultural representations that keep it rooted in place.

Cultural-Symbolic Female Representations of Suffering

From the perspective of Latinas, a number of images and stories stereotype and caricature Latina womanhood, particularly the female binary of Guadalupe-La Malinche, the image of La Llorona, and the mythic account of Coyolxauhqui, among others. These images offer us an entry point for our discussion. They extend an appeal that has far too often been manipulated in a way that makes institutionalized violence, structural evil, and horrific suffering all appear legitimate. Accordingly, these images serve as conduits to advance how Latinas are to understand suffering from within a sociocultural hegemonic narrative. Yet some nuance is necessary. To explore these stereotypes and to suggest that they shape how we understand and appropriate suffering is *not* to suggest a subtle determinism. Rather, it is to make clear that they do map for us in a powerful fashion the terrain of the *possible*, which most of us take for granted. Obviously, this terrain does afford us some room for creative expression. Nevertheless, the hegemonic narrative defines the terrain in such a way as to prevent the undermining of the fundamental structures of society.[22]

Before turning to the various cultural representations, it is important to recognize that several U.S. Latino/a theologians have explored the theological meaning of Guadalupe and other Marian images. But far too few of these works have addressed the ways these images have been used to limit and reduce Latinas' humanity. If we want to reveal genuinely the liberative meaning and graced moment of the Guadalupe image (and other Marian images), then we must address transparently and directly how this symbol and others are manipulated to influence how Latinas are seen and how Latinas see themselves. Far too often, these cultural and religious symbols have been manipulated to detrimental effect, a development that warrants consideration, particularly by Latina feminist theology.

A closer examination of the stereotypes and caricatures, or false images of Latinas, raises several questions. What do the origins of these stereotypes and their narratives suggest to us about the relationship of Latina womanhood and suffering? How do these stereotypes mediate suffering as a social experience? How do the myths attempt to define and circumscribe the ways in which Latinas' view their experience of suffering?

Guadalupe-La Malinche: A Female Binary

Our Lady of Guadalupe has long been a potent, vital religious symbol. As such, theologians, among others, have developed a wide range of interpretations of her. Some portray her as a liberative symbol for women (and men), while others point out the ways she has been used to render women passive, silent, and obedient. Given the focus of this book, what follows is a consideration of Guadalupe and women's suffering, only one among many interpretations. Many women turn to her for consolation when they are suffering, but her connection to suffering involves more.

To understand Guadalupe and women's suffering, we need to appreciate her as part of a female binary along with La Malinche. This chapter is interested in the ways in which these two models of Latina womanhood endure as stubbornly tethered to one another, and as such, the ways this binary serves to further a patriarchal worldview. From the time of their birth, Mexicans and Chicanas/os,[23] women and men, have absorbed this binary pair into their psyches, which more specifically has furthered a particular view of women and suffering and how these are related. Both of these images have their origins during the time of the Mesoamerican conquest in the early sixteenth century.

The origins of the Guadalupe-Malinche female dualism reside in Mexico's nation-making (beginning in the sixteenth century) and thus in the development of a Mexican national consciousness. Shortly after the conquest, the religiously oriented Mexican mind begins to distort the story of an indigenous woman named Malintzín Tenepal. In the process, this woman becomes more widely and infamously known as La Malinche. Tagged as the ultimate traitor of Mexico, she comes to symbolize the "total negative essence of the Mexican woman."[24] Malintzín ("La Malinche") served as Hernán Cortés's translator, back and forth between the indigenous languages and Cortés's Spanish. Without her linguistic assistance, Cortés could not have conquered the Aztec nation and could not have assumed authority over numerous other indigenous tribes. She becomes his mistress as well, bearing some of the first mestizo children. Through her gift of speech and by virtue of "sleeping with the enemy," she is judged treasonous. Along with Cortés, Malinche serves as the sacrificial victim in the Mexican national consciousness and begins to be seen as a scapegoat of her people.

Concurrent with the vilification of Malinche came the emergence of Guadalupe, a Marian figure imbued with transformative powers and the hope of a brighter tomorrow. The Guadalupan Mary is said to have appeared to an indigenous, middle-aged man, Juan Diego, and through him assured the people of her enduring love and care for them. Analogous to the Virgin Mary, elevating and idealizing Guadalupe allows women to be " 'glorified' as more than human but still denied full Christian person-hood."[25] This idealization becomes manifest in the spiritual feminine (the Virgin Mary and Guadalupe) that elevates and transforms the soul yet readily fosters and makes more palatable the subordination of women.[26] Within such a religious climate, a relationship of male domination and female submission becomes normative because females are ultimately pegged as either "the virgin" (good) or "the whore" (evil) and are thus denied the complexity of their full humanity. In the process, women begin to see themselves as slaves to a script not of their choosing and, accordingly, come to believe that being born female is a condemnation to enslavement. One is either a "Guadalupe" or a "Malinche." Against this backdrop, suffering takes on a central role in the life of women irrespective of the pole of the female binary. This binary, codified in the ideology of "marianismo," idealizes suffering as integral to what it means to be a woman. Marianismo, which is the so-called veneration of the Virgin Mary, encourages women to follow the "example" set by Mary—that is, to model "self-sacrifice, self-effacement, and self-subordination"[27] and by so doing become "spiritually superior." Such a path to "spiritual superiority" inevitably cultivates in women a stance of passivity and endurance in the face of suffering. Through marianismo, a woman would ideally come to understand herself

> as a virgin, as a saintly mother, as a wife-sex object, as a martyr. . . . Church teachings have directed women to identify with the emotional suffering of the pure, passive bystander: the Virgin Mary. It is believed that through Her, [a woman] experiences a vicarious martyrdom in order to accept and prepare herself for her own oppressive reality. In order to be a slave or a servant, a woman cannot be assertive, independent, and self-defining. She is told to act fatalistically because "all comes to those who wait." She is led to believe it is natural to be dependant psychologically and economically, and she is not to do for herself but to yield to the needs of others—the

patron, her family, her father, her boyfriend, her husband, her God.
. . . [Marianismo portrays] the woman as semi-divine, morally superior, and spiritually stronger than her master because of her ability
to endure pain and sorrow.[28]

Conversely, women who speak on their own behalf, who articulate
their own needs and desires, who make their own decisions about when
and where to traverse the boundaries of cultural sexual norms, become
dubbed as "traitors," or "Malinches," to their families and their people.
So much so that the adjective *malinchista* is rather commonly used as a
label for those who "betray," for those who allow themselves to be used
and "seduced" by foreign interests and for those women who act out of a
self-referential mode of authority. Malintzín, that is, La Malinche, while
a historical figure is also much more. She represents an unresolved conflict in the Mexican imagination and sensibility. According to this conventional mindset, La Malinche deserved to suffer because she betrayed.

In short, the Guadalupe-La Malinche binary contributes to the ways
Latinos/as envision suffering socially and personally and thereby functions to keep Latina agency and behavior tightly circumscribed, particularly in the midst of significant personal suffering.

La Llorona: Suffering without Release

The image of La Llorona, the weeping woman, emerges from the weav-
ing together of Indian and Spanish tales and folklore dating from before
the time of the conquest. In the mid-sixteenth century, Fray Bernardino
de Sahagún records an account of Ciuacoatl, an Aztec goddess, who
appears at night crying out for her dead children.[29] Tales of La Llorona
are popular not only throughout the U.S. southwest and in Mexico but
also in many countries of Latin America, including Chile, Columbia,
Guatemala, Honduras, Nicaragua, El Salvador, and Panama, among others. She has endured as a strictly folkloric figure and a maternal female
symbol. Today, several interpretations of her legend live on in literature,
for example, in the work of Sandra Cisneros[30] and, in music, for instance,
in the work of Joan Baez.[31] While many different versions of her legend
endure, in almost every case La Llorona represents a woman whose children were murdered or who in a moment of madness murders her own
children, typically by drowning them. As a result, she roams the earth

unable to rest; she embodies a restlessness, a menacing fear, and a terrifying guilt. As Tey Diana Rebolledo explains, "La Llorona was a syncretic image connected both to Spanish medieval notions of *ánimas en pena*, spirits in purgatory expiating their sins, and to the Medea myth. She was also closely identified with pre-Colombian Aztec cultural heroes such as *Mocihuaquetzque*, valiant women who died in childbirth (and who were the only Aztec women to achieve afterlife in the place of the warriors). These women were held sacred by Aztec warriors, . . . [and] were believed to have supernatural powers."[32]

She symbolizes woman as one who endlessly suffers, whose suffering can slip easily into destructive madness aimed not only at herself but also at others in her path. She strikes fear. La Llorona is said to roam deserted roads, particularly those close to streams, rivers, and other bodies of water, and to appear so as to trigger fear in those who wander at night alone. Many Latinos/as associate her image with children who drown. "Today in New Mexico . . . there are signs with the symbol of La Llorona warning children to stay away from ditches." She embodies the negative mother image and is linked to "sexuality and the death or loss of children."[33] Arguably, she serves as a warning to mothers about the risk of tragedy that may befall their children, whether or not they are to blame. She signals that children may be "lost because of violence, neglect, abuse" or "because of their assimilation into the dominant culture" or for any number of reasons. She serves as a reminder of our "morality and obligations."[34]

The story of la Llorona plays a role in the hegemonic patriarchal worldview, argues Octavio Paz: "Who is the *Chingada*? Above all, she is the Mother. Not a Mother of flesh and blood but a mythical figure. The Chingada is one of the Mexican representations of Maternity, like *La Llorona* or the 'long-suffering Mexican mother' we celebrate on the tenth of May. The *Chingada* is the mother who has suffered—metaphorically or actually—the corrosive and defaming action implicit in the verb that gives her her name. . . . 'What is the *Chingada*?' The *Chingada* is the Mother forcibly opened, violated, or deceived. The *hijo de la Chingada* is the offspring of violation, abduction, or deceit."[35]

What La Llorona suggests to us is that women, particularly poor women, know suffering because they have been betrayed by men, typically economically and socially upper-class men. This story warns that the rather common experience of suffering, brought on by sexual and

familial betrayal, can lead women to destructive insanity.[36] The patriarchal context in which many Latinas find themselves must be destroyed at
its root lest women be continually relegated to a "long-suffering" life as
central to the female condition.

Coyolxauhqui: Dismemberment

The image of the Aztec[37] goddess Coyolxauhqui, while not as widely
recognized as images like Guadalupe, La Malinche, or even La Llorona,
is nonetheless a highly significant image and myth. The Aztec creation
myth, in which Coyolxauhqui plays a major role, reveals the foundation
of Aztec cosmology as well as a worldview that makes sacrifice and suffering, and gender roles, tangible.

This myth, explains Davíd Carrasco, was elaborately ritualized at the
center of Tenochtitlan (what is today Mexico City) for the purpose of
achieving this capital city's primary aim. "The capacity to control peoples, goods, relationships, meanings, and human lives was expressed in
the centripetal and centrifugal power of the capitals."[38] The monumental
rituals of human sacrifices set on a large stage find their origin in this
myth and functioned to orient peripheral societies to the center, to the
Aztec capital Tenochtitlan. These rituals were performed in the religious
precinct the Aztecs believed to be the center of the universe, at the Templo Mayor pyramid. The Templo Mayor rituals materially signified their
understanding of cosmic order and, to a degree, enacted the Aztec's sense
of political destiny. Human sacrifices "had profound and detailed political purposes as well, often dramatizing the tensions of center-periphery
geopolitical relations. . . . The flux of political history, fortunes, and
uncertainties was handled through the immense tribute system by which
nearby and peripheral communities demonstrated their dependence upon
and servitude to the capital by paying large quantities of goods on a regular basis, always threatened with the pain of human sacrifice or military
attack."[39] These larger social, indeed cosmic, rituals serve to contextual-
ize the weightiness of the symbol of Coyolxauhqui and the myth in which
she plays a significant role.

The Aztecs recorded this myth in a *teocuitatl*, that is, a "divine song,"
which Miguel Léon-Portilla refers to as a type of epic poem. For many
years before the Spanish conquest, the Aztecs honored "The Birth of Huitzilopochtli, Patron God of the Aztecs."[40] Aztec goddess Coyolxauhqui,

goddess of the moon, is the daughter of Coatlicue, the Mother goddess. Coyolxauhqui is sister to four hundred [male] gods of the South (the stars), and an older sister to Huitzilopochtli, the god of war and of the sun. Upon learning of their mother's pregnancy, Coyolxauhqui and her four hundred brothers decide that Coatlicue's pregnancy has dishonored them. Coyolxauhqui incites her brothers and leads them to the top of Coatepec Mountain in a plot to kill their mother who, according to Cherríe Moraga, represents patriarchal motherhood. But, while still in the womb, Huitzilopochtli, learns of the plot. At the moment of the attack, Coatlicue gives birth to Huitzilopochtli, a full-grown warrior dressed for battle and enraged at his sister. Huitzilopochtli takes a serpent made of fire and strikes Coyolxauhqui, cutting off her head and dismembering her body. Her body rolls down the mountain and in the process her limbs break off. Her arms and hands fall in one place, her legs in another, and her body in yet another. After decapitating and dismembering his sister, Huitzilopochtli proceeds to ravenously pursue and annihilate every one of his four hundred brothers. This myth is about the transmission of Coyolxauhqui's ferocity, and that of her four hundred brothers, to her brother Huitzilopochtli. As Carrasco explains: "The aggression of Coyolxauhqui and her four hundred siblings dissolved before this one great warrior who did more than defeat and kill them, he obliterated their existence."[41] This cosmic drama reflects the daily supremacy of the sun (Huitzilopochtli), which utterly obliterates the moon (Coyolxauhqui) and the stars (four hundred brothers).

The Aztecs regularly dramatized the myth of Huitzilopochtli and Coyolxauhqui. At the top of one of the two huge pyramids that constituted the Templo Mayor (built to image Coatepec Mountain) sat an exalted image and temple honoring Huitzilopochtli, and at the base of this pyramid's long majestic stairway rested a massive twenty-two-ton circular stone image of the dismembered Coyolxauhqui. As part of an elaborate ritual, Aztec warrior-priests took victims up to the top of the Templo Mayor. These warrior-priests would proceed to cut out the victims' hearts from their bodies and to offer the hearts to Huitzilopochtli, after which the victims' lifeless bodies were thrown down the long staircase at the front of the Templo Mayor. These bodies landed on the image of Coyolxauhqui, certainly an ominous warning. "This drama of sacrificial dismemberment was vividly repeated in some of the offerings found around the Coyolxauhqui stone in which the decapitated skulls of young women were placed."[42] Further, many of the body parts and artifacts found in close proximity to the Coyolxauhqui stone were those of victims who were enemies of the Aztec people.

No doubt, the elevation of Huitzilopochtli in relation to the obliteration of Coyolxauhqui represents a worldview where periodic ritual violence is deemed sacred. The contributions of Carrasco make clear that these rituals were a "dramatic cosmic victory of Huitzilopochtli and the Aztecs over celestial and terrestrial enemies," that about one third of the Aztec yearly festivals prescribed the ritual killing of women, and that while women were involved in the ritual killing of other women, ultimately these sacrifices were directed by male warriors and priests.[43]

The Aztec creation myth teaches that Huitzilopochtli (sun, male, warrior son) dominates and obliterates his sister Coyolxauhqui (moon, female, angry daughter), and constitutes a myth of redemptive violence. The larger community is believed to be redeemed through the reenactment of this cosmic drama. This Aztec creation myth has violence as the center of creation and violence as the force that brings order from chaos.

Parallels can be drawn, I would argue, between the Aztec creation myth and the Babylonian creation myth of *Enuma Elish*, which is dated from around 1250 BCE. In the Babylonian myth, with chaos reigning, Marduk agrees to establish order. As Walter Wink tells it (here he is following the work of Paul Ricoeur), "Creation is an act of violence: Tiamat 'mother of them all,' is murdered and dismembered; from her cadaver the world is formed. Order is established by means of disorder. Creation is a violent victory over an enemy older than creation. The origin of evil precedes the origin of things. Chaos (symbolized by Tiamat) is prior to order (represented by Marduk, god of Babylon). Evil is prior to good. Violence inheres in the godhead. Evil is an ineradicable constituent of ultimate reality, and possesses ontological priority over the good."[44]

The parallel between the Aztec and the Babylonian myths is significant because the glorification of redemptive violence at the heart of both of these myths is precisely what the Christian story subverts. Simply put, in these two myths, evil precedes the good, on the one hand, and when superseded allows for creation and remains integral to creation; while on the other hand, in the Christian story, all creation is inherently good, and evil comes second, corrupting creation.

Both the Aztec and Babylonian myths claim that violence is the center of creation, and both recount the story of a female goddess who is not only murdered but also dismembered. While, on the one hand, these two creation myths teach us to exterminate our enemies; in sharp contrast, on the other hand, the story of Jesus teaches us to love our enemies. As Wink explains, the biblical myth of creation in the first chapters of Genesis stands diametrically opposed to its Babylonian counterpart, and I would add, to its Aztec counterpart as well. Genesis teaches us that "a good God creates a good creation. Chaos does not resist order. Good is ontologically prior to evil. Neither evil nor violence is a part of the creation, but both enter as a result of the first couple's sin and the machinations of the serpent. A basically good reality is thus corrupted by free decisions reached by creatures."[45]

The parallels between these two myths matter, as does the sharp contrast between them and the biblical creation story. These ancient myths are far from defunct; in fact, they are thriving today in our popular culture. As Wink insightfully observes, "The myth of redemptive violence inundates us on every side. We are awash in it yet seldom perceive it." This myth influences popular culture through movies (*Jaws*, James Bond, *Mission: Impossible*, and others), cartoons (Teenage Mutant Ninja Turtles, Superman, Spider-Man, The Incredible Hulk, Batman, and others), and even our "foreign policy, nationalism, . . . militarism." If we follow Wink's argument that the myth of redemptive violence continues to reappear "as a religion dedicated to the support of the powerful and privileged through violence,"[46] then we can find evidence for this in our contemporary foreign policy of NAFTA, in the militarization of our international borders (especially our border with Mexico), and in the endless accounts of immigrant bashing that confront us regularly in our daily newspapers and on our nightly newscasts, to name a few. The central point here is that the myth of redemptive violence, in its Babylonian and Aztec versions, is alive and well in the policies of the United States and Mexico, in matters concerning their relationship to one another, and, no doubt, in the feminicide in Juárez.

With its account of female dismemberment, the Aztec myth created a symbolic, "sacred" link between violence against women's bodies and the supremacy of male divinity. Moreover, it idealizes male humanity as dominant over female humanity. One way this is made manifest is in the acute ongoing suffering of female humanity in the feminicide. Even though the creation myth of Huitzilopochtli and Coyolxauhqui may not be widely known today, it has helped to create a sustained and preeminent pattern of thought. Initially, this myth fostered terror in the imaginations of any would-be challengers to political and religious authority (initially embodied as Aztec supremacy). It defined "legitimate" gender relations and clarified the "inherent" relation between women and suffering. Perhaps the legacy of this myth can be found in the social-political unconscious, or said differently, the social imaginary worldview, that idealizes "Latinas and suffering" and makes this connection appear as somehow preordained by God. Indeed, Wink's work would support just such a claim. And of course, this connection is not unique to Mexico. Among many other peoples similar configurations of redemptive violence, women, and suffering have been tied to the "Christian" worldview, with disastrous results for women.

⌘ ⌘ ⌘

An exploration of these preeminent cultural representations suggests a hegemonic Mexican patriarchal worldview that legitimizes and idealizes the suffering of women, even as that suffering is destructive to women.[47] This is, of course, not unique to Mexico. These myths and archetypes of womanhood function so as to circumscribe and orient the societal imagination at a subconscious level in such a way that women and suffering become linked to one another. At times, these cultural representations and their myths are interpreted so as to make this "woman-suffering" relation appear wrapped in longing and legitimacy. Ironically, it is even made to appear desirable.

In her celebrated short story "Woman Hollering Creek," Sandra Cisneros captures this deeply felt socially imaginary world in her literary reinterpretation of La Llorona in the character of the young woman Cleofilas. When we are introduced to her, Cleofilas has a naive, romanticized view of the world and of her husband. After the birth of her first child and when she is pregnant with a second, she finds herself faced with an increasingly violent husband whose abuse threatens her life and that of her unborn child. Her two widowed neighbors on each side, Soledad ("loneliness and solitude") and Dolores ("sorrows"), embody the seemingly God-ordained link between women and suffering. Over time, painstakingly and with the help of others, Cleofilas takes steps toward self-awareness and critical awareness. This eventually leads her to resist and break free from the destructive situation in which she has been living.[48] Cisneros, through the figure of Cleofilas, enables her readers to appreciate the multilayered and monumental challenge involved in breaking the link between women and suffering.

While in his classic work *The Labyrinth of Solitude* Octavio Paz does not sufficiently critique this hegemonic worldview, he nevertheless sheds significant light on the other side of this dynamic, putting forward a penetrating description. Throughout, he presumes a "modern" perspective reflected in his Archimedean point of view, his view from nowhere. Indeed, he claims that the Mexican (read universal) regards women as essentially a passive conduit, a channel for what is universally needed within society, an instrument of the will and desires of men. Woman is not asked to consent to any of this; she is defined by a passivity that makes her the "repository" for what society wishes to preserve and transmit to the next generation. Her primary role is to provide social stability and continuity; she is of a lesser humanity and through her suffering moves beyond her condition and acquires the attributes of men. In sum, her suffering, borne in silence, enables "woman" to become more like "man."

Such a point of view affords woman no subjectivity, no desires, and no will of her own; her action in the world is the means by which society realizes its goals; her instincts are not portrayed as her own but as those of her people. Paz claims that women are prized when they are " 'long-suffering' in the face of adversity."[49] In his words:

> Despite her modesty and the vigilance of society, woman is always vulnerable. Her social situation—as the repository of honor, in the Spanish sense—and the misfortune of her "open" anatomy expose her to all kinds of dangers, against which neither personal morality nor masculine protection is sufficient. She is submissive and open by nature. But, through a compensation-mechanism that is easily explained, her natural frailty is made a virtue and the myth of the "long-suffering Mexican woman" is created. The idol—always vulnerable, always in process of transforming itself into a human being—becomes a victim, but a victim hardened and insensible to suffering, bearing her tribulations in silence. (A "long-suffering" person is less sensitive to pain than a person whom adversity has hardly touched.) Through suffering, our women become like our men: invulnerable, impassive, and stoic. . . . Thanks to suffering and her ability to endure it without protest, she transcends her condition and acquires the same attributes as men.[50]

Note what Paz is suggesting here, namely, that for women to be "long-suffering" is to give selflessly to society what it needs; to endure all manner of suffering passively, quietly; and to cultivate pain as a constant companion that elevates one's being. Above all, to be "long-suffering" allows women to become human, to resemble men more closely.

This idealization of suffering has another side. For in contrast, Paz describes a "bad woman" as one who is linked to the idea of "aggressive activity,"[51] which stands in contrast to passivity, like the "self-denying mother," the "waiting sweetheart." Within this worldview, as Paz reminds us, activity and immodesty are closely linked. Needless to say, this view destroys women.

In sum, these stereotypes and caricatures of Latina womanhood have been constructed to suggest a dangerous, inherent link between women and suffering, the acceptance of which is captured in the often repeated phrase, "long-suffering woman." It is, at times, used as a badge of "honor." Within the patriarchal worldview that generates these stereotypes, the suffering of Latina women is idealized in and of itself. The message is clear. If a Latina bears her suffering in silence, then she somehow becomes morally and spiritually superior. It is *as if* this is her calling by virtue of her sex and God's design. As feminist theorists have pointed out, this message is embodied in distorted but nonetheless pervasive patriarchal constructions of the Guadalupe-La Malinche female binary and in other myths like La Llorona and Coyolxauhqui. Arguably, the social imaginary world in which these constructions live and thrive may have subconsciously contributed to a mindset that, however reluctantly, tolerates the ongoing murders of young, poor Latinas like Sagrario González.

Since a social imaginary worldview largely functions at a subterranean level, it eludes straightforward explanation. An exploration of the feminicide would be incomplete without this particular angle on cultural representations inasmuch as they call our attention to the production of evil and, in so doing, in broad strokes begin to suggest how a tragedy like the feminicide could emerge. The preceding exploration rounds out a social-suffering hermeneutic because it affords us a glimpse beneath the surface of our analysis. A horror such as the feminicide cannot be fully analyzed. In the end, this feminicide eludes explanation.

The Drive for Release, the Quest for Salvation

Appreciating the more critical awareness of the feminicide that has emerged from a social-suffering hermeneutical reading, this last section asks the question: How does the feminicide, when viewed through the lens of a social-suffering hermeneutic, recontextualize the doctrine of salvation?

In order to appreciate how a social-suffering hermeneutic recontextualizes salvation, we need to recall in broad strokes how suffering has typically been regarded. According to Kleinman, most of the writing on suffering from the Western tradition reflects such an individualized perspective that pain is understood as utterly incommunicable. In other words, we cannot know how another feels pain. This isolates the sufferers and affords her or him alone the ability to know the pain that she or he is experiencing. Conversely, it means that when we ask another about their experience of pain, we do so from a position of some doubt; their pain is beyond our capacity to appreciate its existence. So much so that when with a friend in pain, to respond by saying "I know how you feel" is frowned upon and viewed as being an inappropriate response. "How could you know how another feels?"

This view of suffering breeds a kind of solipsism that accordingly eschews any moral dimensions of suffering. In contrast, a social-suffering hermeneutic sets this approach aside and instead focuses attention on "how such suffering is produced in societies and how acknowledgment of pain, as a cultural process, is given or withheld."[52] While our incapacity to imagine another's pain (the traditional preoccupation in Western tradition) may not readily lend itself to moral questions, our incapacity to acknowledge another's pain most certainly raises moral questions.

Far more often than not, the pain of others, particularly pain brought on by institutionalized power, remains sequestered from public view. We find numerous ways to keep this kind of suffering of our time at bay, distant. It slips in and out of our awareness with the passing stories we read in our daily newspapers. Undoubtedly, we realize that recognizing "social suffering" will be personally costly. It is far easier to view the pain of others as a misfortunate occurrence, the poor luck of the draw, rather than as a product brought about by unjust systems and structures. To label the suffering of others a "misfortune," of course, trivializes their suffering. Because we tend to view pain as incommunicable, we do not make a connection between the suffering in Juárez and the pain we experience in our own lives. We certainly feel pity for the other and moved to respond with charity, but seemingly, no further thought seems warranted. Indeed, as Lawrence Langer has argued, "We need a new kind of discourse to disturb our collective consciousness and stir it into practical action that moves beyond mere pity."[53] When we view suffering at a distance, when it is "not in my back yard," so to speak, we see our own society as somehow superior, as possessing greater moral status relative to the society experiencing the suffering. Ironically, this is so even when we are the perpetrators of the "distant" observable suffering.[54]

A social-suffering hermeneutic brings the absurdity of this situation into focus. Instead of allowing the social systems that give rise to suffering to remain hidden behind a veil of bureaucratic obscurity, and instead of relegating the experience of suffering to the realm of abstraction by labeling it a "necessary and unavoidable" by-product of society, a social-suffering hermeneutic maintains *in the fore* the integral relation between social systems with destructive fallout and the resulting personal stories of human tragedy. But its value extends further. It draws connections between the experiences of those who live in the *favelas* of northeastern Brazil, in the gang-ridden barrios of south-central Los Angeles, and in the *casas de carton* of Ciudad Juárez (México).

In all these settings, the desperately poor and powerless know a life utterly defined by questions of survival at its most basic level. These populations find themselves to be casualties of a global political economy far beyond their sphere of influence. Making connections among these geographically disperse communities neither reduces their varied stories of human tragedy to a collection of personal "anecdotes" of suffering nor allows suffering to remain a concern distant from present life. These connections reveal an embedded structural element within our globalized economic infrastructure that generates such groups of people in desperation and will continue to do so. A social-suffering hermeneutic makes transparent a picture of human tragedy that demands a response, social-political as well as personal.

In the face of this feminicide, the question arises: What is the social meaning of all these brutal assassinations of girls and women? Not only are young female lives completely destroyed, but also a reign of terror has swept over Juárez, one comparable to the repressive violence of the "dirty wars" of Latin America, with their "codes of urban violence and serial assassinations."[55] Not only has the government demonstrated its incapacity to provide a minimal protection for its female (and male) citizenry, but any vestige of a legitimate legal and political (governing) system has also been obliterated. Not only are vulnerable women subject to torture, sexual attack, assassination, and disappearance. Society itself has been destroyed, its rituals and ways of life.

Here is a society in a social vertigo marked by a dizzying free fall of confusion, an irrational, hellish whirl, an emergence of a clandestine brutish "authority" that rules by killing innocents, instilling extreme fear, and idolizing the most heinous forms of violence. As a result of the Juárez feminicide, we need to rethink our understanding of political authority and the ways religious substructure has been forged to legitimate that authority. Hannah Arendt captures this well in her observation (written long before the feminicide): "Nothing perhaps distinguishes modern masses as radically from those of previous centuries as the loss of faith in a Last Judgment: the worst have lost their fear and the best have lost their hope. Unable as yet to live without fear and hope, these masses are attracted by every effort which seems to promise a man-made fabrication of the Paradise they had longed for and of the Hell they had feared."[56]

While I have referred to the violence discussed herein as feminicide, asking the question of "social meaning" could suggest that this violence might also be called a "sociocide," the killing of society. The interrelatedness of feminicide and sociocide is significant. When we are faced with the breakdown and collapse of our social bonds, with the destruction of our sense of interrelatedness with other human beings and with the whole of creation, then we see ever more sharply how community must be a condition of the possibility of our knowing salvation. What we need to see, all of us, is the escalating destruction of society under the weight of the feminicide. So, what exactly does this mean? Analogous to the ways sociologist Keith Doubt argues that genocide serves as a means to sociocide, so too would I argue that feminicide is a means of sociocide. In an effort to explicate a clear understanding of sociocide—and drawing on the work of Tom Cushman and Stjepan Meštrović—Doubt contends:

> If genocide is a coordinated plan of different actions aiming at the destruction of the essential foundations of the life of a national group, sociocide in turn is a coordinated plan of different actions aiming at the destruction of the essential foundations of society. Jonathan Schell . . . indicates how genocide leads to sociocide: "When crimes are of a certain magnitude and character, they nullify our power to respond to them adequately because they smash the human context in which human losses normally acquire their

meaning for us." . . . What is the human context in which human losses acquire meaning for us? It is the social. When crimes against humanity are of a certain magnitude and character, they result in the murdering of the human context in which these losses acquire meaning for us. With the murdering of the social, crimes of a great magnitude can occur with impunity. Crimes assume a limitless character. The murdering of society necessarily accompanies war crimes, crimes against humanity and genocide; the murdering of society is not just an unexpected upshot, but a logical consequence. Sociocide goes beyond the evil of destroying individuals, no matter how large the number. Sociocide nullifies the human ability to respond to these losses in an appropriate way because it mutilates the lifeworld that has the power to redeem the human losses suffered.[57]

Feminicide, like genocide, directs us toward not only the destruction of individuals, female human beings, but also beyond the edge of our capacity to reason.

As poet and performance artist Guillermo Gómez-Peña has observed: "We are living in the age of pus-modernity, a blistering, festering present. And in these times, all known political systems and economic structures are dysfunctional. . . . Many see this as the era of *la desmodernidad*, a term that comes from the Mexican noun *desmadre*, which can mean either having no mother, or living in chaos. The Great Fiction of a social order has evaporated and has left us in a state of meta-orphanhood."[58] We are living in an era marked by a sociocidal dynamic. The border region, most notably now, has taken on the character of a festering wound that refuses to heal because of ongoing brutal attacks on all manner of community, all manner of civil society, all manner of what humanizes us. It is the idea that all that speaks of community, of civil society, of a more hopeful life, is being summarily destroyed.

In the face of feminicide and, finally, sociocide—overwhelming evil— the Christian understanding of salvation begins with the Christian's experience of release from this horrific evil, a sense of God's inexplicable healing in the midst of the evil.[59] The overwhelming experience of evil no doubt pushes the questions: Can someone, some power far greater than ourselves, release us from the bondage of this evil? Can some greater power bring relief? We must seek "a release from guilt by the forgiveness of sin, a release from the bondage of an anxious sense of radical transience, from anxiety in the face of death, from anxiety in the face of the seeming absurdity of existence, from the bondage of a sense of being trapped without hope of release in systematically distorted structures of one's individual psyche or of society and history or even from bondage to the contemporary fascination with evil."[60] As a dialectical experience, it is a release "from," while at the same time being an experience of "freedom for."

We likewise must seek "some new way of existing as an authentic human being; an experience of freedom for living in the world without ultimate mistrust of existence; a freedom for accepting the created world and one's own finitude as essentially good; a freedom for accepting the fact of one's own acceptance by God despite sin and guilt; a freedom for facing death as not the final world; a freedom for acting in solidarity with others in the trust that such actions ultimately do make a difference; a freedom for accepting experiences of peace, joy, and understanding as manifestations, however fragmentary, of the presence of God."[61] Our desire for "whole life" is our longing for salvation. Salvation begins here in this life, which includes all of us. God inaugurated God's saving presence among human beings at creation, gave it final expression through the person of Jesus the Christ, and continues it in the dynamic action of the Holy Spirit in history. The recontextualization of what salvation could mean necessitates an approach to salvation that presumes an integral relation between the history of salvation and the history of the world, and that presumes salvation to be the work of the triune God.

The feminicide further recontextualizes how we think about salvation by foregrounding four particular questions, each of which we will look at in turn: (1) What is the relationship between salvation and ethics? (2) What is the relationship between salvation and female humanity? (3) What is the relationship between salvation and history? (4) And what is the relationship between salvation and our image of God?

First, *what is the relationship between salvation and ethics?* As many scholars have argued, including Elizabeth A. Johnson, "Christian soteriology has basically a narrative structure . . . [one based on] the foundational narrative of Jesus as bringer of salvation."[62] As she further explains, a foundational narrative structure forges a world of meaning that interrelates past, present, and future; that takes into account the unpredictable, tangible realities of life; that breaks open the world beyond the visible and tangible; and, finally, that orients the human desire for meaningful living. Embedded within the telling of the story of "Jesus as bringer of salvation" resides an explanation for why we need salvation, how we are saved, and what the nature of salvation is and means. If the salvation story is told in a way that frames Jesus' life, death, and resurrection as a legal transaction that occurred "once and for all" and by which sinners' debts are "fully paid," then such a story creates a separation between this "transaction" (salvation) and the call to live a Christian life (ethics). In the process, ethics and salvation function as separate spheres in the context of historical, concrete human experience. Thus, salvation and ethics become neither antagonistic nor integral to one another. Within such a salvation story, "grace" is made to cover all ongoing sinfulness and failure. This makes for a slippery slope. When does the separation reach the point of accommodation to violence within the social order?[63]

Second, the feminicide foregrounds the question *what is the relationship between salvation and female humanity?* For decades now, feminist theologians and others have considered Rosemary Radford Ruether's celebrated question, "Can a male savior save women?"[64] Without question Ruether calls attention to much of what is problematic in Christologies that fail to confront and subvert explicitly the "patriarchalization of Christology."[65] The feminicide, however, asks that we extend our frame of reference to consider anew some of the ways that "the full dignity of women as christomorphic in the community of disciples" has been largely erased by androcentric Christology, thus placing "women's salvation . . . in jeopardy, at least theoretically."[66] One way of addressing this concern is by asking how salvation and female humanity are related, a question many feminist theologians have posed.

Implicit in this question is a fundamental critique. Far too often, and to great destructive effect, suffering has been viewed as "one's cross" and therefore to be endured as Jesus endured his suffering on the cross, forging "salvation" for humanity. The stereotypes and caricatures discussed in this chapter promote a falsely intrinsic women-suffering relation and thus directly feed into this death-dealing view. What results is the distorted notion that this is the way for women to secure salvation. This kind of thinking has been conveniently used to mask and deflect attention from gross injustices and preventable miseries. Missing is a critical distinction. We need a thoughtful and incisive way to distinguish between "suffering caused by the wrongdoing of others and that existential anguish present in every human life."[67] Ivone Gebara rightly observes that far too often "the message of Jesus on the cross leads us to believe that suffering that comes from injustice will lead us to redemption, to victory over our enemies. For women, the path to take us there is to contemplate the sufferings of this man on the cross and to accept our own crosses. The promises of the resurrection call us to bear our sorrows and humiliations and even to renounce our basic human rights. Through experience we can say how much, in practice, this theology accentuates the victimization of women and encourages them in domestic and familial martyrdom."[68] When the nexus of women and salvation points to the idealization of suffering, then we slip rather easily into an image of God that places redemptive violence at the center of Christian faith, utterly corrupting Christianity's life-giving message.

The third question posed by the feminicide is *what is the relationship between salvation and history?* Horrific evil on the scale of the feminicide brings to the fore the broken, disruptive, contingent, overwhelming, chaotic character of real history. Suffering on such a massive scale confounds reason. It is irrational. Such suffering may be described as an interruption, a massive chasm, a break that will always remain unbridgeable. To suggest otherwise would be to trivialize the suffering of the feminicide's victims. "And to allow that this event is part of an overall divine plan for the world would be to make god into a monster, no matter how much one talks about divine goodness and power."[69] The irrationality of the feminicide means that an account of hope in the possibility of salvation emerges from beyond the fissures of history.

If, as Gebara tells us, the "place of evil, of unhappiness, of often incomprehensible suffering carries within it a call to salvation or some provisional path to freedom,"[70] then we need to ask: How do we discover the "provisional path to freedom" in concrete history? Arguably, the exodus narrative offers significant clues, both communal and personal. This text (Exod 1–15) not only gives us a telling of Israel's salvation narrative but also is intended "to evoke and generate transformation in each new moment of its hearing."[71] Walter Brueggemann posits that three dimensions constitute the faith transformation of the people of Israel. Transformation begins with the disjunctive step of *critique of ideology*, namely, that the people of Israel's life and identity is conflictual, communally and personally, in that each knows that "*we do not belong to Pharaoh's world*," that our experience of enslavement "is not simply to a spiritual power" but also "to a historically identifiable agent which has demonic force," and that we are each creatures "*enmeshed but nonethe-less destined for freedom.*"[72] The purpose of this first step is to assault the dominant system that keeps some enslaved immorally and illegally, denying them freedom and justice.

The second dimension of this transformation process is the "*public processing of pain.*" This step consists of taking the private pain experienced as a result of enslavement by imperial power and expressing that pain in an intentional, social, and public act intended to delegitimate the dominant power and authority. Crying out in this public manner carries enormous risk because of its subversive intent. The public nature of the step is paramount in that "as long as persons experience their pain privately and in isolation, no social power is generated. . . . [The] moment of outcry in Israel is a moment of "going public" in an irreversible act of civil disobedience. . . . The cry of pain begins the formation of a counter-community around an alternative perception of reality."[73]

The final dimension builds on the first two and entails "*the release of new social imagination.*" It means the social practice of a "transformed sense of reality," through which energy is released, birthing courage, hope, and a new way of understanding what it means to be community. The Pharaohs of the world will, nonetheless, continue to assault this new way of being by putting forward other forms of social life, forms that want to "privatize and reduce" the new social imagination. Yet this new social imagination has a power. "The social imagination of liberated Israel is not only a *liturgic* act (The Song of Moses) or a *political* act (of changing sovereigns at Sinai). It is also a *legislative* act. . . . It may begin in dreams, but it leads to acts of public shaping . . . into concrete economic and political terms. This is the work of Torah."[74] For the Christian community, this third dimension is the "reign of God" of Jesus' imagination. It is the experience of the resurrection. These three dimensions of faith transformation represent the call to salvation, the "provisional path to freedom" in history.[75] They break open for us liturgically and politically the ways in which salvation was experienced by the people of Israel in concrete history and a clue about how it might be experienced today, about how today, "fragments of salvation . . . gain a foothold within history."[76]

And finally, the fourth question: *What is the relationship between salvation and our image of God?* More often than not, the doctrine of salvation has been and continues to be defined as the work of Jesus Christ.

To the extent that our doctrine of salvation reflects a Christomonism, we lose sight of the more fundamental claim that "salvation comes from God through Jesus by the power of the Spirit. It is the gift of the whole triune God acting *ad extra*."[77] Salvation cannot but become distorted when we forget that the doctrine of the Trinity precedes Christology rather than develops from it. Some theologians today have begun retrieving this more ancient understanding of salvation, namely, that it is the work of the triune mystery of God. Much is at stake in this choice. When we focus so narrowly on Christ that we eclipse God the creator and the Holy Spirit, we end up compromising what it means to be church and to live a committed Christian life. An approach limited to Christ has been readily and repeatedly used to legitimize imperial power that, perhaps inadvertently but nevertheless tragically, destroys lives.

Salvation is best conceived in the terms of the mystery of the triune God. Relatedness is primary to who God is. This understanding of God means that salvation has "the destiny of the human person to be that of living in authentic communion with God, with other persons, and with all God's creatures."[78] This understanding challenges the subordination of woman to man (patriarchy) and stands for equality between the sexes, a much needed worldview in the context of the feminicide. As Catherine Mowry LaCugna makes clear:

> The doctrine of the Trinity is iconoclastic toward all human political arrangements where one (superordinate) is in power over the man (subordinates). When the doctrine of the Trinity was "defeated" by the return to a concern for God's inner life rather than with God's life with us in salvation history, it was easy to bypass the radical philosophical and theological proposal contained in Trinitarian doctrine and instead embrace the idea of a God-monarch who rules over the world that is subordinate to God's will. . . . The divine monarchy was used to justify different types of hierarchy: religious, sexual, political. This was clearly the triumph of a patriarchal understanding of God, despite the theoretical possibility to the contrary contained in the doctrine of the Trinity.[79]

When the triune mystery of God plays a central role in the doctrine of salvation, then communion among persons becomes central to what salvation means, drawing all of us into ever more authentic relationships with one another.

Conclusion

Even though each one of these four enduring questions (What is the relationship between salvation and ethics? What is the relationship between salvation and female humanity? What is the relationship between salvation and history? What is the relationship between salvation and the image of God?) represents a major research project well beyond the scope of this book, they situate the question of salvation within the horizon of the horrific evil of the feminicide. For this book, their importance lies in the way they orient our consideration of one of the most successful theological constructs of the Christian tradition, namely, Anselm's interpretation of the satisfaction metaphor.

3

Anselm and Salvation

I n the foregoing critical reading of feminicide, a *social-suffering herme-neutic* made clear the brutal execution of female human beings precisely because they are female, the tragic and unintelligible dimension of this evil, the social vertigo that this evil unleashes, and the varied ways we are all caught in its vortex.[1] The question of salvation, in its origin just as today, begins with our awareness of our abiding need for God. We need release from evil. We need God; we cling to the power of God in hopeful anticipation of healing, of a salvation that can come only from God. Our awareness of our need is never more acute than in the battle with evil, such as in the confrontation with the horror of feminicide. This chapter turns to a towering figure within the Christian tradition, Anselm of Canterbury (1033–1109), whose *Cur Deus Homo* (hereafter *CDH*), published in 1098, has become an unparalleled contribution to the doctrine of salvation. To this day, this approach holds powerful sway in the imaginations of many Christian faithful.[2]

For almost half of the Christian tradition's history, *CDH*, together with the variety of interpretations of *CDH* written over the millennium, has served as a primary resource for believers trying to understand what Christian salvation can mean particularly in light of the brokenness and suffering that mark every age of human history. Today, many of those who have suffered feminicide seek this same end. They desire a union with

God. They want release from the evil they experience or, short of that, at least some assurance that their suffering and that of their loved ones is not in vain. Why examine *CDH* and not another construal of Christian salvation? Elizabeth A. Johnson captures well the overriding import of *CDH*:

> In the eleventh century the biblical and patristic pluralism so characteristic of the interpretations of Jesus and salvation began to recede in the West due to Anselm's brilliant restructuring of the satisfaction metaphor into a full-fledged, ontologically based theory. To wit: God became a human being and died to pay back what was due to the honor of God offended by sin. I sometimes think that Anselm should be considered the most successful theologian of all time. Imagine having almost a one-thousand-year run for your theological construct! It was never declared a dogma but might just as well have been, so dominant has been its influence in theology, preaching, devotion, and the penitential system of the Church, up to our own day.[3]

Anselm's contribution to this discourse has been critiqued, reshaped, and reinterpreted over the course of some nine centuries.

There are, of course, differences between what Anselm wrote (and intended), on the one hand, and how he has been interpreted, and sometimes misunderstood over the years, on the other hand. This includes the various popular appropriations of Anselm, including various satisfaction theologies popularly preached and practiced today. While other interpretations of the doctrine of salvation have been developed over the centuries, arguably many of these later contributions have been, in some form, commentary on Anselm's towering work. In the last four decades, in particular, Christian theologians have again engaged in the foundational spadework of questioning the presuppositions and implications of Anselm's teaching. Today, the ability of Anselm's interpretation to respond to the concerns of our own time is under scrutiny.

In light of the Juárez feminicide, this chapter argues that the paradigmatic, enduring, and overriding Anselmian construal of salvation becomes far more problematic and, accordingly, less defensible. By the end of this chapter, it will be clear that there is a need to rethink salvation.

In order to defend this claim, the first section situates Anselm's contribution within the world that he inherited. It does this through a brief analysis of the intellectual, sociopolitical, theological, and ecclesial context that set the stage for his *CDH*. This section lays out the argument of *CDH* and investigates some of the subtle points of Anselm's doctrine of salvation. The next section considers the import of the historic legacy of *CDH*. *CDH*'s "history of effect" is a constituent part of what it means. It has often been misinterpreted in various historical contexts in a manner that ends up supporting ongoing violence to disastrous effect. The final section probes the relative adequacy of Anselm's argument to illuminate the meaning of salvation as this question emerges in the context of the feminicide. What this probing reveals are inadequacies in how Latina experience is situated and the gaps in thinking with regard to what is pertinent to the quest for salvation in the context of the feminicide. This examination and critique paves the way for a new consideration of salvation.

Anselm's Context and the Argument of *Cur Deus Homo*

Since the beginnings of the Christian tradition, theologians have put forward various explanations for the claim that Jesus the Christ saves, saves humanity, saves all of creation. During the patristic period, a wide variety of soteriologies emerged and flourished. Some theologians have mapped this early pluralism by distinguishing soteriologies based on the emphasis given to a particular aspect of Christ's existence. "The four major points of reference are Christ's incarnation, public life, crucifixion, and resurrection, either alone or in some combination."[4] Other theologians have used Jesus the Christ's threefold office of priest, prophet, and king as a method of mapping distinctive soteriologies of early church history.

While the patristic period knew a plurality of soteriological images, the advent of the medieval period brought with it "a more rigorously reasoned theoretical account of Christ's salvific activity,"[5] particularly evident in the work of Anselm of Canterbury.

Anselm's Milieu

The contexts within which theologians write significantly shape their theological imaginations. While theologians in every age no doubt strive to speak theological truth, how they understand truth, the ways in which they organize the development of their ideas is nonetheless informed by the world in which they live. In this respect, Anselm is no different from any other theologian. To read him while ignoring his personal and historical circumstances is to misread him because it overlooks the concerns that preoccupied Anselm and oriented his claims.[6]

To appreciate and evaluate Anselm's contribution means understanding something of the world in which Anselm found himself when he wrote *CDH*. Why did his contribution emerge when it did? What ideas and concerns marked the intellectual, monastic, ecclesial, and sociopolitical milieu that made the eleventh century ripe for such a substantive contribution such as *CDH*? While much is rightly made of Anselm's intellectual prowess, even genius, certainly that alone cannot explain the significance of his contribution.

We first need to understand that as a young man the Italian-born Anselm learned from many peripatetic masters in a time when universities had not yet come to be. Later, as an educated monk, he taught many others and in the process developed his own intellectual capacity.[7] His contribution emerges as a number of social forces come together and make their mark at the dawn of the medieval period. We will look specifically at the following five: (1) the intellectual revival of the eleventh century; (2) the organization of society into a feudal hierarchy; (3) the social ferment that brought about the Crusades; (4) the christocentrism of the monastic prayer life; and (5) the inherited view of salvation as a transaction between the devil, humanity, and God.

First, the eleventh century was a time of great intellectual revival, with achievements being wrought across the spectrum from theology and philosophy to mathematics and the natural sciences, from literature and the arts to architecture and the law.[8] Without a doubt, this rich, erudite environment significantly influenced Anselm, so much so that he is not only attributed with inaugurating scholasticism but is also recognized as the father of Scholasticism. Scholasticism refers to the medieval approach to thought that took seriously the analysis of philosophical ideas for the purpose of developing systematic theological claims. These claims enabled growth in the church's understanding of itself, of the world, and of its engagement with the world.[9]

With rapped attention, Anselm voraciously set about the work of sorting out the relation of faith and reason in the endeavor to achieve understanding. As scholars have widely noted, he immersed himself in the Bible as well as the writings of Augustine, from whom he learned Platonism. These gave him freedom for his own intellectual work. However, their presence in *CDH* is not explicit. Anselm neither uses biblical quotations nor directly references Augustine or Plato. As Sir Richard Southern has noted, "He could not provide details of his borrowings: they were too extensive, too freely and deeply ingrained in his own thought and adapted to his own needs, to be capable of any exact enumeration as borrowings."[10]

Yet as David Brown details, there is much to suggest that Anselm took the notion of ideal "form," for example, from Augustine's Platonism and showed that atonement "is secured through us 'participating' in the perfect exemplar or 'universal' human nature that Christ came to offer."[11] Anselm lived in a thought-world that assumed a connectedness, a corporate personality that included all human beings, so much so that there was no need for him to explain how any given person might take on Christ's act, might follow Christ's example. The presumption was for this possibility. What this presumption of corporate personality makes clear is that Anselm used reason to bolster the credibility of Christian faith, particularly for Muslims and Jews. Belief in God was the presumptive point of departure for developing theological claims, which one then sought to understand.

Second, much has been made of the sociopolitical imprint of feudal society. According to some, the reigning concept of political and social authority was feudal hierarchy, and this hierarchy served as a model for Anselm's soteriological construct. As Flora A. Keshgegian observes, "Many critics of Anselm have . . . argued that God's justice wins out over mercy. Early on there was discomfort with the narrow legalistic categories that Anselm seemed to use and his reliance on images of Teutonic law and feudal social structures."[12] More recently, G. R. Evans writes that Anselm resisted becoming an archbishop, and that when he did it was clear that he had much to learn of how the world works. While he drew on the feudal framework of society for his notion of "right order" and for his "concept of divine honor," other sources were also key.[13] David Brown takes this pause even further, claiming that "in terms of Anselm's reliance on feudal imagery. . . . Such a grounding is much less plausible than is usually claimed."[14] Anselm viewed himself primarily as a monk and not as a feudal lord. Anselm's biblical and Platonist assumptions, Brown points out, offer us another explanation for what informed his notions of satisfaction, order, obedience, and honor. Feudalism for Anselm might best be thought of as the social imaginary that his argument not only reflects but also advances. This imaginary functions to support and legitimize hierarchies of power.[15]

Third, Anselm lived and wrote as the Crusades began. Arguably, his *CDH* and the Crusades grew out of the same soil. In 1095, three short years before *CDH*'s publication, Pope Urban II convened a Peace Council in France, which was a gathering of bishops, laity, nobles, and monks. He implored them to take up arms and avenge the "unspeakable degradation and servitude" to which Christians had been subjected in their own lands. With this plea, he stirred up hostility against the Muslims, launching the First Crusade. "The pope advocated 'righteous warfare' as a form of love, 'for it is charity to risk your life for your brothers.' "[16] Anselm and Urban were good friends, and at one point they camped out together in Italy to watch a Norman knight, Roger of Apulia, lay siege on Capua.[17] The connection between the two goes further, as Anthony Bartlett explains, "The cross-references between the genesis of Anselm's work and the context of a violent Christendom cannot be ignored. . . . Those who 'took the cross' in the First Crusade participated in the symbolic world that also produced the *Cur Deus Homo*, and their action and mind-set provide an illustration of background dynamics at work in this document. . . . Both the militarization of the cross and its interpretation as satisfaction arise via the figure of Christ as warrior-hero."[18]

As noted above, Anselm puts faith in Christ to a rational test. With the growing appeal of rational discourse, the church chooses to clarify its positions at the Fourth Lateran Council (1215), where the church not only puts forward the primary elements of Catholic practice and thought (sacraments, doctrine of transubstantiation, the seal of confession, the clerical discipline, and so on) but also writes and announces in the council's opening canon that "there is indeed one universal church of the faithful, . . . outside of which nobody at all is saved, in which Jesus Christ is both priest and sacrifice."[19] The effect of this was to render all non-Christians theologically "other"; primarily this meant Jews and Muslims. Even though these faiths believed in atonement, they did not claim that incarnation was necessary to secure it.[20] The point is that during this time the church claimed for itself unprecedented universal authority, which may have contributed to the justification of cruel violence against the theologically "other" (that is, Jews, Muslims, pagans).

Rita Nakashima Brock and Rebecca Ann Parker have drawn a tighter connection—while debatable—between Christ's ultimate sacrifice, vengeance against the "other," and belief in God's justice, claiming that in the Crusades the integration of these three found a sympathetic expression in the work of Anselm.

> Though Anselm insisted the atonement was a free and willing act of God, not dictated by necessity, humanity could not be saved from the curse of having dishonored God without the God-man's gift of death. Though he forbade his own monks from joining the Crusades, Anselm's doctrine of the atonement gave support for holy war. Christians were exhorted to imitate Christ's self-offering in the cause of God's justice. When authorities in the church called for vengeance, they did so on God's behalf. As Anselm wrote, "When earthly rulers exercise vengeance justifiably, the one who is really exercising it is the One who established them in authority for this very purpose." God's will must be obeyed, *Deus Vult!*[21]

This observation also, and importantly, suggests that Anselm's theology of the cross was designed to appeal to one's pietistic inclinations as well as one's intellect. Once the death of Jesus became *the* central saving event for Christians, as it did before Anselm began writing and as it came to a culmination in his writings, this idea was easily misused to justify a wide range of atrocities. Moreover, Christ's resurrection is never mentioned in *CDH*, further underscoring the centrality of Jesus' death.[22] All this said, Anselm's work bears the weighty concerns of his time and place.

Fourth, Anselm's work reflects his own monastic life of prayer,[23] as well as the influence of monastic writers and scholars of the tenth and eleventh centuries. These thinkers increasingly developed an understanding of Christ that has come to be known as "christocentrism." During the monastic period (900–1100 CE), christocentrism reached its high mark in the history of Western civilization. Indeed, monastic writers each attempted to outdo one another in their endeavor to promote an ever deepening love of Christ and "in extolling Christ as the source of all good."[24]

As the person and work of Jesus Christ became the all-consuming focal point of theological reflection, theological speculation concerning salvation grew as well. For monastic writers, "the plan of salvation, as defined and refined in this period, did not restrict itself to the theory of redemption in the narrow sense of that word. The 'picture of Christ' underlying it included not only the narrative of his suffering, death, and resurrection but the entire account of his life and work, his miracles and parables, as well as his crucifixion."[25] Accordingly, to be a disciple of Jesus meant to live a life that mirrored the discipline of Jesus in the whole of his human experience, to imitate Jesus daily in word and deed, to faithfully follow the will of God. This "discipline" was supported with the admonition found in Matthew 10:38 ("And whoever does not take up the cross and follow me is not worthy of me" [NRSV]) and grounded "the core of the Christian life of self-mortification, in which one died to the world."[26] In fact, to die to the world, even to the point of giving up one's own life, was elevated as the greatest expression of love.

Monastic writers emphasized Christ's teaching that through death we will rise again in the resurrection, the pinnacle of what we could aspire to. Some, like Cardinal Peter Damian, a monastic writer, expounded on "bearing the cross of Christ," which for him meant not simply imitating Christ's actions during his life but, more importantly, following the footsteps of Christ's passion. Jaroslav Pelikan recounts Damian's teaching: "An act of penance, such as fasting or flagellation, was, according to Peter Damian, 'truly a sharing in the passion of the Redeemer,' for by it the penitent was crucifying the allurements of the flesh in imitation of Christ on the cross. 'Christ has given himself over to death for us,' he admonished elsewhere, 'and therefore let us, for the sake of his love, also mortify in ourselves every desire for earthly pleasure. By his willingness to undergo the suffering of the cross, he has shown us the road by which we can return to our fatherland.'"[27] These ideas, all reflective of the uncompromising christocentrism of the time, were "in the air," so to speak, before Anselm wrote *CDH* at the end of the monastic period.

Fifth, and finally, Anselm inherited an understanding of salvation widespread among clergy and faithful alike that he found deeply flawed. During the tenth and eleventh centuries, the saving work of Christ on the cross was viewed as a transaction between the devil humanity, and God. Accordingly, Christ's crucifixion, death, and resurrection were liturgically commemorated as Christ's final victory over the devil and, in the process, lead to an identification of Christ with his suffering and death and with the image of sacrificial victim. As Southern observers:

> The strength of this account was that it conformed to recognizable norms of justice in human society, and in doing this it satisfied an underlying desire for justice in the universe. Moreover, it emphasized

the personal authority of Christ over the redeemed portion of mankind, and his right to lay down laws for those whom he would redeem. Further, it recognized the cosmic scale of Man's fall: he had fallen, after all, to the greatest enemy of God, and the recognition of the Devil's ensuing rights gave a certain dignity to the sinner, if not to sin.[28]

Further, this older account held a certain imaginative appeal in that it "was much more vivid and more easily accessible to ordinary people, and gave a more easily recognizable dignity to life."[29] Anselm took exception. He argued that the suffering, death, and resurrection of Christ could not and must not be viewed as a victory over the devil.[30]

If Christ's sacrifice of his very flesh paid the price for humanity's sin and thereby saved those who placed their faith in Christ, then to whom did Christ make the offering of his suffering and death? Clergy of this time used phrases like "make the offering" and "ransom for," suggesting that a debt was paid to the devil so that the devil would release human beings from his captivity. Once the devil was paid off, human beings became free of the devil's grasp. Advocates of such a line of thinking commonly defended their position because they thought it protected the immutability of God. For, they thought, if Christ's death paid a ransom to God instead of the devil, then this would imply that God changes God's mind, thus undermining God's immutability. Besides, paying a ransom to God would also suggest that God seeks revenge for sin, an idea contrary to belief in a just and holy God. In one of his notable Easter sermons, Peter Damian promoted this reasoning. In it he claimed that by Christ's cross and resurrection, Christ brought "the claims of the devil to naught and [restored humankind] to its place under God."[31] These ideas reflected one strand of thought dating back to the patristic period and championed by Origin. Recall that Origin suggested that Christ brought the devil's machinations to naught by deceiving the devil and thereby freeing humankind.

But Anselm recognized what others had not considered: to secure the salvation of humankind by means of deception would be unfitting for God, who is holy and just. Further, to imply any external constraint on God as suggested by a transaction with the devil would be inherently contradictory to the nature of God. The death of Christ could not be ransom paid to the devil. Therefore, this older proposal was impossible. As Southern explains,

> [Anselm] had too uncompromising and too unitary a view of God's dominion over the whole Creation to accept any view which diminished God's majesty in the smallest way. To allow the Devil, or any other rebel, a claim to justice against God was an unacceptable diminution of the divine majesty. Rebellion deserved nothing but punishment, and to have seduced the whole of mankind into rebellion only increased the punishment: it did not create an empire.
>
> Anselm's elimination of the Devil from the process of Redemption satisfies every rational instinct, and the direct confrontation of God and Man in the work of Redemption gives mankind a new kind of dignity which will appeal to later generations. But Anselm did not clear out the Devil's rights to replace them with the Rights of Man. On the contrary, he cleared out the Devil to enforce more completely the submission of Man to God. For Anselm, the only human dignity consists in submission to God's will; and it is this alone, strenuously pursued, which will lead to union with God.[32]

The death of Christ, his sacrifice, could not be addressed, said Anselm, either to the devil or to humankind but could be addressed only to God. In *CDH*, Anselm delineated both how this sacrifice was addressed to God and how God's immutability was preserved. He employed the concept of "right order" as the theological norm to orient the whole of his understanding of redemption.

The Argument

In *Cur Deus Homo*, widely regarded as his greatest work, Anselm begins with a question that he claims represents the thinking of the learned and unlearned alike who reject the Christian faith. Anselm's question is: "By what logic or necessity did God become man, and by his death, as we believe and profess, restore life to the world, when he could have done this through the agency of some other person, angelic or human, or simply by willing it?" (1.1).[33] This question orients the whole of Anselm's classic, which he framed as a debate between himself and Boso, who represents a devoted Jew who does not believe Jesus is the Christ and does not understand the necessity of the incarnation. Anselm intends to demonstrate that if the scriptures are not compelling enough to effect Christian belief, then reason will surely prove efficacious.

In crafting his response, Anselm organized *CDH* in two parts: the first deals with humanity's need for salvation, and the second delineates God's provision. God created human beings and the world for eternal blessedness, which comes about when human beings freely submit to the will of God for them. For human beings, freedom distinguishes their lives when they willingly submit to God and accept who they are in relation to God. Said differently, human beings and the world bear God's imprint of "right order." Right order characterizes the relation of human beings to the creator and orients the will and moral order of all creation. This right order, Anselm held, was ontological in that it concerns the most truthful essence of every being, including human beings, in relation to all that is, particularly in relation to God. It is human beings (and all of creation) who need this right order so that they can flourish in this life and know eternal blessedness. God as God does not have a need for right order.[34]

Yet human beings have refused to submit to the will of God; they have sinned. For Anselm, "Someone who does not render to God this honour due to him is taking away from God what is his, and dishonouring God, and this is what it is to sin" (1.11). Human sin corrupts the moral ordering and the justice of God. Through sin, humans disrupt the right order of the universe and thwart God's intention for the universe. Sin leaves humanity indebted to God and condemned to death. Due to sin, freedom has been lost.[35]

Human beings cannot restore the blessedness that they have lost through sin. Submission now to the will of God cannot make up for past sin because it gives God only what was due to God in the first place. The debt created by the offense against God is so great that the sum of all that is human would still fall short, making it problematic to secure a reconciliation that veritably covers the offense against God. Humanity and the whole universe are thus deprived of the blessedness for which God created them.[36]

Because of human sin, God's intention for humanity and for creation has been frustrated. However, this cannot be, since ultimately God's purpose must be fulfilled; therefore, there must be some means of securing salvation for humanity. God could not simply forgive human beings their sin by "mere fiat" or by eliminating the obligation of the offending persons. This "solution" was impossible because it would violate "the very order in the universe that God had to uphold to be consistent"[37] with

Godself and with God's justice. In Anselm's words: "If . . . sin is neither paid for nor punished, it is subject to no law. . . . Therefore, sinfulness is in a position of greater freedom, if it is forgiven through mercy alone, than righteousness—and this seems extremely unfitting. And the incongruity extends even further: it makes sinfulness resemble God. For, just as God is subject to no law, the same is the case with sinfulness" (1.12). Thus, to "render satisfaction," to forge a new reconciliation between God and humankind, meant that the right order, which was the essence of the universe, needed to be respected. For Anselm, the right order of the universe dictated either "satisfaction" or "punishment." Since through sin humans had violated God's honor, humankind would either be eternally punished or God would need to provide for salvation in some other way.

So that human beings could once again enjoy the eternal blessedness that God intended, an offering would be needed that was equal to or greater than the whole of human sinfulness. The reconciliation of sinful humanity to God required the effort of a being who was more than simply another human being. If the redeemer was only another human being, that person would already owe everything to God and therefore would have nothing more to offer that could compensate for the whole of human sinfulness. In addition, humanity would rightly be indebted as a servant to a being who was not God. A merely human redeemer would command humanity's obedience. Nonetheless, this cannot be, because humanity can only rightly be a servant to God alone (1.5). Thus, on the one hand, the redeemer had to be God. On the other hand, only a human being could represent humanity and offer satisfaction for human sin. The debt owed to God was humanity's debt. Therefore, this being had to know the frailty and vulnerability of a human being (1.19). Moreover, this human being had to be free of sin and free in his choice to surrender his life. "God the Father did not treat that man as you apparently understand him to have done; nor did he hand over an innocent man to be killed in place of the guilty party. For the Father did not coerce Christ to face death against his will, or give permission for him to be killed, but Christ himself of his own volition underwent death in order to save mankind" (1.8). It is the gratuitousness of Christ's offer that secures salvation for humankind, and not his obedient, sinless life. As David Brown notes:

> For Anselm even the God-man Christ is in no sense compensating for human misconduct in the perfect life he leads. He is merely fulfilling

the destiny of human nature which God made possible in creating it that way. Compensation or recompense must therefore, Anselm contends, lie elsewhere, and this he believes he has found in Christ's death. According to traditional Christian teaching, human nature is intended for eternal life and human beings die only because of the fall. Therefore a life voluntarily surrendered to death has nothing to do with the teleology of human nature. It is something returned to God that is not owed, a purely gratuitous act, and, because it is the life of a human being who is also God, an offering of infinite worth.[38]

Here rests Anselm's argument that only a being who was both God and human could secure salvation for humanity and creation.[39]

Anselm nuances his argument for the "God-Human" in some important ways. First, he wants to avoid any idea that the reconciliation or satisfaction, one and the same for him, effected by the God-Human serves the purpose of "placating an angry God," that somehow God, having been stirred to vengeful anger by human sin, is appeased by the punishment of God's sinless Son, Jesus.

This is an important distinction to make because some contemporary interpreters often project this idea onto Anselm. For Anselm, God cannot be wrathful because God is immutable. To assign wrath to God would be to undermine God's immutability, indeed, to completely misunderstand God's nature. So if God is not wrathful, then how are we to regard Christ's death as securing satisfaction? As Brown observes:

> The act [Christ's death] is entirely voluntary: it is not part of an established pattern where such conduct is expected, and where satisfaction is in one form or other simply assumed. Again, there is no gain on the part of the person receiving the satisfaction; God, Anselm insists, cannot be benefited in any way because divine impassibility means that God cannot have been hurt or harmed in the first place by human sin, the majesty of God requiring that nothing be outside His power (1.14-15). To suggest otherwise would be for Anselm to impugn the very meaning of the word "God."[40]

So for Anselm, at issue is not God's honor that must be assuaged but rather humanity's violation of its own nature as internally ordered to submit to God. The human situation is so marred by sin that reconciliation is a necessity, one that can be initiated only by the incarnation, which in turn makes possible a definitive reconciliation in the sacrifice of the God-Human. This sacrifice is gratuitous, thus not owed or expected, making reconciliation a possibility.

Second, Anselm resists the idea that humanity is passive in the work of redemption. Even though Anselm argues that only the God-Human can effect a true reconciliation, this reconciliation is not automatically applied to all humanity. In order to be saved, human beings must actively affirm that Christ's died for them; they must recognize Christ as acting in their stead.[41] Salvation demands that humans be in touch with their deepest desire and orientation toward God and that they open themselves to act in accord with this. The misconstrued notion of the "passivity" of humanity emerges from the distorted idea that a "substitution" transaction takes place between God and the Son. The Son, not himself needing to be reconciled to God, simply applies his sacrifice to humanity so that all are saved. Anselm's soteriological assertions, while significantly informed by the Letter to the Hebrews (2:9-18; 4:14-5:10; 10:10, 19-22), nonetheless guard against the idea that humanity plays a bystander role in its own salvation. In this biblical letter, human beings are delivered from sin and death when God's divine Son takes on human nature through the incarnation. As the divine Son, Jesus the Christ offers an acceptable sacrifice that nullifies human sin and makes eternal life with God possible for humanity.[42] While Anselm develops these biblical ideas, he nonetheless claims that the possibility of the application of salvation depends upon active belief (2.8).

Ultimately, Anselm offered a cogent argument for how Jesus' death on the cross was the redemption of humankind, an idea widely held, if little understood, during his lifetime. He took this conviction and interpreted it in a comprehensive, intelligent fashion superior to all other explanations of his time. His emerged as superior because he developed it in light of the larger body of Christian teaching, as well as in light of his conviction concerning the coherence of revealed truth. Coherence marked Anselm's explanations of the existence, nature, and being of God, and accordingly, his arguments concerning harmatiology, anthropology, eschatology, and of course, soteriology.

The Historic Legacy of *Cur Deus Homo*

If, in light of the feminicide, we ask the questions—What does Anselm's *CDH* mean? or How are we to understand *CDH*?—then a responsible and cogent response must take into account the consequences of *CDH* in history. In other words, the meaning of *CDH* cannot be rendered clear apart from the effects of this teaching in history. For if the purpose of thinking is to produce habits of action, and I believe it is, then we must consider the consequences of our ideas. The truthfulness of any claim must ultimately be measured in light of *all possible* consequences that could result from that claim.[43]

To understand what Anselm's contribution might mean in light of the feminicide, we must read *CDH* in terms of what Hans-Georg Gadamer calls its "history of effects." The term *history of effects* means that to interpret a text adequately we must take into account our own historical situatedness, and with regard to the text itself we need to appreciate the relationship "that constitutes both the reality of history and the reality of historical understanding."[44] The effect of a text in history is unavoidably and necessarily constituent of what that text means. Any given text acquires meaning through the course of history as various individuals put forward their reading of the indicated text, with each individual, naturally, situated from within their particular historical context. So when we stand at a historical distance from a text, we arguably have the possibility of understanding the text better than its author did. We have the benefit of the various readings that have further enfleshed the meaning of the text throughout history. As historically situated individuals, we cannot but engage the text from within our own situatedness. Indeed, as Gadamer claims, "history does not belong to us; we belong to it. Long before we understand ourselves through the process of self-examination, we understand ourselves in a self-evident way in the family, society, and state in which we live."[45]

Understanding *CDH* is not simply a question of understanding Anselm's context and the varied concerns of his time that informed his writing. Alone, such an approach would produce a romantic, distorted, and naive understanding of his contribution. We can and must also strive to understand the impact of his construction across the temporal distance that separates us from the writing of *CDH* in 1098.

Understanding a text is not merely a reproductive activity but a productive activity; in other words, in striving to understand a text, if we are to understand it at all, we come to terms with it in a fresh, different way. In a very real way, understanding is a work of translation. This must be so, says Gadamer, if a text is understood as not simply "a mere expression of life but is taken seriously in its claim to truth."[46] In the process, however, whatever we come to understand of *CDH* cannot be fully complete; it remains always to some degree deficient because of "the essence of the historical being that we are." Our particular, finite present necessarily has limitation, which unavoidably influences our ability to understand. Our own historical horizon both enables and limits our "range of vision," namely, "what can be seen from a particular vantage point."[47]

Moreover, we need to appreciate that reading a text is never an atemporal relationship between the interpreter and the text. Interpretation is simply not a dyadic (subject and object) process. As Josiah Royce insightfully noted, interpretation always entails not only the reading of a text but also "actively giving account (*logos*) of both the text and oneself to an other."[48] In Royce's words:

> Interpretation always involves a relation of three terms. In the technical phrase, interpretation *is* a triadic relation. That is, you cannot express any complete process of interpreting by merely naming two terms—persons, or other objects—and by then telling what dyadic relation exists between one of these two and the other. . . . An interpretation is a relation which not only involves three terms, but brings them into a determinate order. One of the three terms is the interpreter; a second term is the object—the person or the meaning or the text—which is interpreted; the third is the person to whom the interpretation is addressed.[49]

Significantly, interpretation is always directed toward someone or some body of persons, which means it always carries an ethical dimension. To foreground the ethical dimension of interpretation, as Royce did, calls attention to the worldview that the interpreter attempts to further through her or his interpretation, a crucial point as we consider *CDH*'s "history of effects."

The acclaim some scholars laud on Anselm seems to suggest that his achievement is so great that it stands on its own, that in his writing he somehow transcended the contextual and intellectual exigencies of his age. And, as the reasoning might follow, he can therefore be read without attention to his social, political, cultural, intellectual context. For example, according to medievalist David Knowles:

> Anselm, both as a thinker and as a personality, is one of the rare significant figures who belong to all time, one to whom philosophers

and historians and innumerable readers will turn for enlightenment and counsel irrespective of any attempt to fit him into his place in the history of thought. . . . There is nothing in Anselm's greatest work that derives from his own age or from his teacher: in this he is more original than Abelard or Aquinas. If we fix our eyes only on his own century, he is a sudden emergence, a Melchisedech without father or mother or genealogy. It is his achievement to stand forth as absolutely great in an age when others were only feeling their way towards thought and expression.[50]

Many share Knowles's adulation for *CDH*. Yet the legacy of this work is mixed.

History has taught us, time and again, that atonement theologies of the cross can be easily misinterpreted and misused to gloss over horrific violence perpetrated by Christians in the name of Jesus Christ. This reading of Anselm, albeit a distorted one, has been used to support and justify the tragic aftermath of the Crusades. As Brock and Parker have argued, Anselm's theology lent support to the crusaders who were promised that their sins would be wiped away and they would earn a place in heaven if they killed Jews and Muslims. Holy war ensured entry into heaven.[51]

Atonement theologies of the cross have contributed to a climate that tacitly permitted the Holocaust's atrocities. René Girard's work reveals the dangerous ambiguity of the rhetoric of sacrifice, that is, that the sinfulness of humanity must be paid for if the moral order of the universe is to be restored. Violence is implicit here. Indeed, the scapegoat mechanism can be used to read the history of the Jews in Europe for the last millennia.

Arguably, atonement theologies of the cross have likewise served to defend white supremacy in the aftermath of the U.S. Civil War. As M. Shawn Copeland has observed, "In fear and loathing, propped up by a version of fundamentalist Christianity, Southern whites conflated blacks with a 'satanic presence' that must be eliminated. Lynching was the instrument by which black bodies were to be purged from the white body politic. Then, in a mental leap of 'profound theological inconsistency,' whites deliberately associated the scapegoat sacrifice of blacks with the mocked, tortured, crucified Christ."[52] My point here is that we have many examples of atonement theologies of the cross being twisted to justify violence. Timothy J. Gorringe frames the problem well when he writes:

"The fusion of forensic and sacrificial images has exercised a unique power on the Western mind. Popular preaching, both Catholic and Protestant, urged guilt upon its hearers and then absolved it, resulting in a tangible sense of freedom or release. By his death Christ pays the cost of my sin. The believer is urged to reflect on this, and in particular upon the part he or she has played in that death. In this way the understanding of salvation has been individualized, and the connection of salvation with the kingdom has been lost."[53]

And in our own time, in far more pedestrian ways, a distorted Anselmian theology of the cross has been used to prolong, if not tacitly condone, situations of domestic violence and many other forms of violence—all under the banner of "carrying one's cross." In short, the legacy of this particular theology of the cross is troubled at best. Now I do not lay this at the feet of Anselm, because this troubled legacy manifests itself when Anselm is read in an ahistorical fashion, thus in a distorted way that he never intended. But it does highlight the need for a critical appreciation of how he has been misread in order to gain a more informed appreciation of his genuine contributions and limitations.

Cur Deus Homo and the Ciudad Juárez Feminicide

Context matters. It matters that we read *CDH* in a way that appreciates the world from which it emerged; it matters that we understand something of its history of effects. It matters as we consider how the feminicide recontextualizes the question of salvation. A number of questions posed at the end of chapter 2 identified some possibilities—how the feminicide situates those who have suffered because of it, which is, in the end, all of us, in relation to the quest for salvation. This section returns to those questions in light of atonement theologies, examining the relative adequacy of *CDH* and the gaps generated in its wake, that is, what we often do not consider and think through.

Salvation and Ethics

As we have seen, Anselmian satisfaction atonement argues that the brutal death of Jesus, gratuitously offered, secured human salvation by satisfying the requirement of divine justice. Ultimately, this interpretation of how human salvation is secured is based on an abstract theory, one that tends to narrow the ethical demands placed on believers in their day-to-day lives. The significance of Jesus is reduced to his death, and so to follow Jesus means to be willing to suffer and die. Satisfaction atonement, particularly as later interpreters of Anselm develop it, makes the ethical dimensions of one's decision making in daily life far less important. As a result of satisfaction atonement, the believer enjoys a life reconciled with God, a life that should reflect its now transformed state. However, whether a believer leads a transformed life or not, the earnest believer can be confident that she or he has secured reconciliation with God. Thus, identifying oneself as a believing Christian on the one hand and being concerned with how to live a Christian life on the other can be rendered distinct, even separate concerns.[54]

In the context of the Juárez feminicide, needless to say, the separation of salvation from ethics renders Christianity a passive presence in the face of horrific evil. Any in Juárez who would seek to dominate others for whatever reason—to gain greater corporate profit, to establish a drug cartel's territorial control, to make money through the illegal trafficking of human organs, to assert male supremacy, to further patriarchy, and the like—may find a religious world that, at best, poses no real threat and, at worst, enhances the pursuit of such desires. Passivity lends support to the status quo.

Anselm's satisfaction theory, by allowing a marked distinction between salvation and ethics, further enables adherents to ignore the way that this distinction supports an accommodation to violence. According to J. Denny Weaver: "The satisfaction motif given articulate form by Anselm does not assume nonviolence. It reflects the church that became fused with the social order, and it accommodates violence. It is not that the satisfaction motif promotes violence per se. Rather, this motif lends itself to easy accommodation of violence and projects little that specifically opposes violence."[55] In the context of women who know violence as a part and parcel of daily life, any accommodation to violence must be called out and denounced as evil and, therefore, as contrary to God's will. Anselm's theory does not help us here. If, as María Pilar Aquino claims, "theological discourse that begins from and speaks about the crucified majorities, the suffering peoples, the great masses or the poor is insufficient if it does not specify that these majorities are women,"[56] then plainly we need a soteriology that rethinks salvation from the experience of Latinas, particularly Latinas who live daily with the threat of violence.

As feminist theologians have pointed out, the problem is more than one of accommodation to violence. It is, rather, the passive submission to violence born of an all-too-common misreading of *CHD*. Atonement theories have far too often put forward a model in which God approves of violence against God's son, Jesus, and approves of Jesus' passive submission to the violence directed at him. Thus, passivity in the face of violence takes on a mantel of divine blessing and providence. For young, poor Latinas who live in Juárez, identifying with this depiction of Jesus would deepen whatever sense they have of themselves as victims and would foster within them a sense of *ajuante* ("endurance") as they face all manner of abuse and oppression. In Spanish, there is a popular expression, *que ajuante*, meaning "what endurance," and it is typically expressed with a sense of admiration for the one to whom it is directed since, as the thinking goes, they have borne their cross well and long. Regarding this sensibility, Ivone Gebara observes,

> The message of Jesus on the Cross leads us to believe that suffering that comes from injustice will lead us to redemption, to victory over our enemies. For women, the path to take us there is to contemplate the sufferings of this man on the cross and to accept our own crosses. The promises of the resurrection call us to bear our sorrows and humiliations and even to renounce our basic human rights. Through experience we can say how much, in practice, this theology accentuates the victimization of women and encourages them in domestic and familial martyrdom. For men, heroism for one's country is a must, while for women it is heroism for the home. In both cases the emphasis is on suffering and submission.[57]

This approach to bettering oneself constantly takes on the guise of "spiritual development"; yet it can lead to the slow destruction of a healthy sense of self. This is problematic. With victimization and passivity comes a loss of self, which does not lead to an experience of God. In fact, claimed Karl Rahner, as a human person grows and develops a healthy sense of self, a person concurrently develops in their experience of God. Conversely, he argued, a loss of self-identity means a loss in the experience of God.[58] If we accept Rahner's insight, then we have to question how the loss of self-identity can be seen as furthering salvation.

Salvation and Female Humanity

A consideration of the relationship between salvation and female humanity—and the Juárez feminicide demands nothing short of this—needs to begin with the way that *CDH*'s satisfaction atonement focuses all but exclusive attention on Christ's suffering and death as the source and summit of salvation for Christian believers. Idealized in this process is Jesus as a stand-in for sinful humanity; as the willing, innocent, sacrificial priest; as one for whom death is the preeminent act of faith. Rosemary P. Carbine has thoughtfully expressed this position:

> What do women in particular risk in imitating Christ, in patterning their subjectivity on the cross and its long-held theology of redemptive suffering? Interpreting the death of Jesus either to appease God's wrath or to show God's love may theologically sanction violence against women. In addition, substitutionary sacrifice theologies of atonement sacralize rather than stand against women's experiences of social, sexual, and other kinds of surrogacy. Women are put personally as well as theologically at risk when the death of Jesus is disconnected from its historical and theological context. . . . Identifying with the suffering rather than with the ministry of Jesus may undermine the full subjectivity of women.[59]

Time and again, womanist and feminist theologians have argued that to identify Jesus as the surrogate for a sinful humanity places women at extreme risk. No one has made this argument more cogently than womanist theologian Delores Williams.[60]

Ivone Gebara has addressed this problem through her critique of the "ideology of sacrifice." Horrendously, women are encouraged to sacrifice themselves to the point of erasure of their self-identity, that is, to the point where who they are is fully defined by the service others expect them to perform. This functions as a form of surrogacy, one in which the needs of society, of husband, of family, of church—and decidedly not personal hopes and dreams—defines the female human ideal. Indeed, that others hold up Jesus as the one who gave up everything so that others might live represents absolute self-denial, with disastrous consequences. As Gebara explains,

> The ideology of sacrifice, imposed by patriarchal culture, has developed in women a training in renunciation. They must give up their pleasure, thoughts, dreams, and desires in order to put themselves at the service of others or to live as others think they should. Women in many ways are made to serve others. At best they must accept

sorrow and suffering to make the scraps of pleasure acceptable. In Latin America women who do not live according to this logic are called "easy." They threaten the established order and arouse fear and envy in those submissive to the law of duty and sacrifice. . . . The ideology of sacrifice induces fear—fear of being separated from or abandoned by God; fear, too, of not being able to live up to the ideal deportment demanded by the culture; fear of not being accepted by men and recognized by other women. Fear of others leads inevitably to alienation from oneself. One does not become one's own person but what others expect. One loses a sense of self, often without even knowing it, and one conforms to the established models as if there were only one way of following our unique life and way to salvation. It is astonishing to hear women from Latin America and Africa say that in their countries women are brought up primarily "for men."[61]

When the dominant forces of society reduce Jesus' redemptive significance to his suffering and sacrifice, then suffering and sacrifice in turn function as the central means by which women finally obtain redemption. Suffering and sacrifice are held up as unambiguously "good." Accordingly, women and those who are economically poor end up having to make the greatest sacrifices in order to realize their salvation. In turn, the suffering of Jesus on the cross is used to "validate their suffering and [give] meaning to their lives,"[62] further reinforcing the idealization of suffering.

Since satisfaction atonement theories, CDH's and others, understand "reconciliation" as the product of a transaction that "functions outside of and apart from history,"[63] then the particularities of who Jesus was as a historical human being hardly matter, if at all. So, the constitutive dimensions of Jesus' personal identity, including his maleness, are rendered irrelevant theologically.

Ironically though, as Elizabeth A. Johnson and other feminist theologians have pointed out, "The fact that Jesus was a man is used to legitimize men's superiority over women in the belief that a particular honor, dignity, and normativity accrues to the male sex because it was chosen by the Son of God 'himself' in the incarnation. Indeed, thanks to their sex, men are said to be more conformed to the image of Christ than are women."[64] All of which places women's salvation in a precarious position, "at least in theory." Drawing on an early Christian axiom developed by Gregory of Nazianzus ("What is not assumed is not redeemed, but what is assumed is saved by union with God"), Johnson argues that "if maleness is essential for the christic role, then women are cut out of the loop of salvation, for female sexuality is not taken on by the Word made flesh. If maleness is constitutive for the incarnation and redemption, female humanity is not assumed and therefore not saved."[65]

Nowhere are the stakes around this question higher than in the feminicidal context of Juárez. It matters greatly where we stand theologically on women as christomorphic. Unless we claim that women bear the capacity to image Christ as fully as men, the dignity of female humanity remains secondary, lesser. The subordination of female humanity, in turn, contributes to, rather than resists, a climate in which violence against women can become commonplace. Women have, then, less reason to place their hope in the power of God to save them. To claim, however, that women are not only *imago Dei* but also *imago Christi* means affirming that women, along with men who confess Jesus as the Christ and who experience the power of the Spirit, then participate "in the living and dying and rising of Christ to such an extent that they can even be called the body of Christ. . . . Their own lives assume a christic pattern."[66] Thus, the possibility of salvation and resurrection becomes more real.

Salvation and History

As we have already discussed, in *CDH* the transaction between God and Jesus to secure humanity's salvation occurs outside of history yet results in a shift in sinful humanity's legal standing before God. In this view, the historical dimensions of Jesus' life, namely, his efforts to bring about and exemplify the reign of God throughout his ministry, remain at best secondary. Since this view of salvation is ahistorical, no clear tension emerges between the believing church and the world. "The point is that if one wanted to construct an ethic for the church of how the church looked in contrast to the world, Anselm's atonement imagery would be of little help. It simply does not supply the specifics of Jesus that would guide the church in posing a significant contrast to the world."[67] For those who reap the benefits of the world as it is, this view of salvation has marked appeal. For those on the underside of history, like the women in Juárez, it does not.

To this day, atonement theologies informed by an Anselmian view remain strong in the religious imagination of many Christians. For example, in the Roman Catholic Church on every Good Friday liturgy, the priest presents a large crucifix to the gathered faithful and sings or proclaims, "Behold the wood of the cross." The faithful respond with, "We adore you, O Christ, and we bless you because by your holy cross you have redeemed the world." For many worshipers, this practice can be interpreted as an affirmation of Anselmian atonement, an occasion in which Catholics lift up the death of Jesus as redemptive, leaving all else in a secondary position. Mel Gibson's recent film *The Passion of the Christ* (2004) enjoyed wide appeal even as many critiqued its depiction of Jesus' crucifixion. The film holds up Jesus' brutal suffering and death as the substitutionary offering to God for human sin and, in the process, reduces Jesus' significance to his crucifixion. This view of salvation continues to carry deep and enduring authority.

Precisely because the "salvific" transaction occurs outside history, it leads to the exclusion of insights pertinent in the context of feminicide. Anselmian atonement does not address the question of oppression and structural injustice, because his understanding of right order stays focused on directing the human will to God. Right relation refers to individual human beings' covenantal relationship with God. While sin, for Anselm, is the cause of *all* suffering and death, he did not consider how the sin of some results in the oppression of the many. It simply was not his concern. Suffering was not a distinct problem but was subsumed into sin. As Flora A. Keshgegian delineates this problem:

> A concept of justice defined as rendering each his or her due is based in a distributive notion of justice and a concept of restoration that suggests that losses can be recouped. Indeed, the "banking" categories of debt and merit imply that any negative balance is wiped out by the God-human. Those who do suffer oppression and abuse, however, teach us that there are losses that cannot be recovered. There are wrongs that cannot be righted. An appropriate theology of redemption must acknowledge such "unreconcilable accounts." In these ways, Anselm's theology does not address the situation of victimized women and others. There is little room for the tragic in a universe that God created as fundamentally good and which God restores to this original intent.[68]

Since this view does not consider questions of structural injustice and social sin, transformation at a social level remains beyond the boundary of Anselmian atonement. This atonement theology has the potential to call into question the human grasp for power, yet more often than not, it tends to have the opposite effect.

This atonement theology leaves us wanting. It does not provide a necessary role for the resurrection in salvation. It emphasizes judgment in the condemnation of human sin and, in so doing, critiques the "old age," which is governed by the power of sin. But it remains incapable of proclaiming the coming reign of God in history and of inaugurating the "new age" ushered in by the power of resurrection. Salvation in Anselmian terms offers no vision of the proleptic presence of God in the midst of our broken world.[69] In short, it lacks an eschatological orientation. M. Shawn Copeland turns our attention in this direction when she writes:

> If the cries of the victim are the voice of God, then the faces of the victims are the face of God, the bodies of the victims are the body of God. The anguish of the victims of history and the demands of authentic solidarity plead for the presence of the supernatural in the concrete. The history of human suffering and oppression, of failure and progress, are transformed only in light of the supernatural. If humanity is not an abstraction but a concrete reality that embraces the billions of human beings who ever have lived, are living, or will live, and if each and every human person is a part of the whole of interpersonal relationships that constitute human history, then we, too—each one of us—shall be transformed.[70]

In light of the feminicide, a theology of salvation needs to affirm and confirm the ways in which we anticipate eschatological healing in the here and now. A theology of salvation needs to anticipate resurrection. As discussed in chapter 2, Walter Brueggemann's threefold description of the faith transformation of Israel suggests as much.[71]

Salvation and the Image of God

When God's omnipotence is understood as a benevolent "power over," as "power to control" for the benefit of all, and when Jesus the Christ is depicted as the great almighty lord before whom all must surrender, when these are the primary images of divine power, they tend to lend support to the human impulse to unilateral power that asserts itself with force against any would-be challengers in the interest of some "greater good." This has meant that the "saving message that was once shared with people through life and praxis became codified into a stick with which to beat those who would not agree with the power brokers. This supreme lord has devastating effects globally, but it is true to say that where the colonial Christ has beaten men, it has crucified women. This understanding of [divine] power is not salvific."[72]

Anselm frames God's justice as primarily "concerned with the restoration of divine-human hierarchy,"[73] such that God's power is understood unilaterally and that relationality is an accidental and thus not a constitutive attribute of God. Anselm does, however, make clear that it is humans who need "satisfaction," and that satisfaction is not necessary for God and is not for the purpose of God's benefit.[74] Accordingly, Anselm does not consider that relationality might be constitutive of the very nature of God, or that a relational understanding of God would encourage not only right relations between human beings and God but also right relations among human beings and right relations between human beings and the whole natural world. Rather than unilateral power being the model, as in Anselm's *CDH*, relationality in the being of God might better serve to effect right order in all relationships. Moreover, such a model of God would more substantively support resistance to violence against women and resistance to acts of unjust aggression.

If we assume the relational nature of God as God's supreme characteristic, as Catherine Mowry LaCugna has argued, then we have a solid basis for understanding salvation as essentially "living as persons in communion, in right relationship . . . [and as] the ideal of Christian faith."[75] Again, the context of the feminicide would encourage this line of thought precisely because of its prophetic and liberative possibilities. As LaCugna avers:

> The starting point in the economy of redemption, in contrast to the intradivine starting point, locates *perichōrēsis* not in God's inner life but in the mystery of the one communion of all persons, divine as well as human. From this standpoint "the divine dance" is indeed an apt image of persons in communion: not for an intradivine communion but for divine life as all creatures partake and literally exist in it. Not through its own merit but through God's election from

all eternity (Eph. 1:3-14), humanity has been made a partner in the divine dance. Everything comes from God, and everything returns to God, through Christ in the Spirit. . . . There are not two sets of communion—one among the divine persons, the other among human persons, with the latter supposed to replicate the former. The one *perichōrēsis*, the one mystery of communion includes God and humanity as beloved partners in the dance.[76]

For those living in conditions of violence, the possibility of salvation takes on greater meaning, the coming reign of God appears more vivid, when the doctrine of the Trinity is the leading image of God in our consideration of salvation.

❧   ❧   ❧

Context matters, and in many respects Anselm's brilliant, towering work, *CDH*, while still widely influential and dominant nonetheless responds less than adequately to the extreme suffering of the women of Juárez. To situate theological questions in a context carries risk. Does the particular context frame the parameters of the theological discussion? Does this approach to theology simply universalize the context in question? Yet there is, I believe, an even greater risk in ignoring context. If we ignore it, theology can be more easily manipulated for destructive ends rather than enabling greater life. Most often, those who struggle daily against "sexual violence, dehumanizing poverty, or any other form of exclusion"[77] suffer most.

Conclusion

The foregoing analysis of Anselm's *CDH* has made clear the need to reconsider what salvation means. David Tracy once astutely observed that "in the contemporary fascination with evil, as in so many important theological issues, the religious sensibilities of religious peoples—especially oppressed and marginalized peoples in their songs, their endurance and protest, their struggles for justice, their forms of prayer and lament, their liturgy, their laughter, their reading of the scriptures—are often wiser, not only religiously but also theologically, than the carefully crafted theodicies of the professional theologians."[78] Tracy's point is well taken.

4

Responding to Social Suffering— Practices of Resistance

iven the enduring success of Anselm's theological construct, the contemporary tragedy of the Juárez feminicide makes clear the need to consider salvation anew. As Edward Schillebeeckx teaches us: "One of the tasks of theology is to safeguard belief in and this hope for a liberating, saving power which loves men and women and which will overcome this evil."[1] In no situation is such belief under a more acute assault than in the brutal sexual trauma that has cut short the lives of girls and young women. It affects not only victimized families and friends but also the wider community of Juárez, in which no poor woman can feel safe.

If belief in God means "belief in God's absolute saving presence among men and women in their history,"[2] then we must ask how the context created by this feminicide reorients or recasts our understanding of salvation. For insight we again return to the experience of those victimized by this ongoing horror and the courageous resistance they offer in the face of it. While the temptation may be to continue to gaze voyeuristically in disbelief upon the evil wrought here, it is the religious sensibilities of the victimized that must command our attention. Their songs, rituals, laments; their use of religious symbols; their anguished cries for justice;

their marches demanding a more just world—all these bear theological wisdom that sheds light on the nature of God's saving presence.

The victimized have created practices of resistance that demonstrate how individual persons and the community have identified the evil in their midst, have faithfully endeavored to subvert it and to dismantle it, and have used collective religious symbols as a means of entering into the living mystery of life, thereby ensuring their community's survival. These practices of resistance "claim a space" that enables those who suffer to be "present to" but not "consumed by" their experience of suffering. As such, the claiming of a space enables the victimized to realize some release from their experience of evil, and in that very release they come to know a healing presence, God's saving presence.

This experience calls attention to the social dimension of salvation. Here we will explore the practices of resistance and clarify the ways in which they are emancipatory, the ways in which they offer a release. The practices of resistance that have arisen in response to the feminicide forge a new, emancipatory political, social, and religious space and thus point to the primacy of a social dimension in our understanding of salvation.

In order to establish that our understanding of salvation, when considered in light of the feminicide and its aftermath, must privilege the social dimension, we begin with several examples of how many of the victimized have sought to resist and protest ("practices of resistance"). They have done so primarily through public actions using religious symbols (the cross, exodus) and using national and international days designated to honor women. Next, an analysis of these practices of resistance in light of popular religious practices as they are described by U.S. Latino/a theologians reveals the distinctive approach of the Juárez women. Finally, we will see that, through the practices of resistance, the surviving witnesses claim a space for the public processing of pain, for the subversion of the status quo, and for affirming, in the most radical way possible, the full humanity of girls and women. In so doing, they are birthing a new social imagination, one that makes visible the universal community of humanity and of creation and one that makes viable a more just world. By reclaiming the Christian symbols of exodus and the cross, the surviving witnesses of the feminicide go well beyond how Anselm and traditional theologies of atonement have interpreted salvation.

Tilling the Soil: Practices of Resistance in the Midst of Suffering

Ever since Juárez activists began picking up a pattern in the growing number of murders of girls and young women, in about the mid-1990s, they inaugurated networks of protestors who, ever since, have resisted the alarming violence against women. These networks have demanded public accountability and insisted that the feminicide end. These efforts accelerated sharply toward the end of 2001. Since then protestors have increasingly turned to "performance activism,"[3] namely, to marches, rituals, and dramas scheduled on seasonal days such as the *Dia de los Muertos*[4] (November 1), International Women's Day (March 8), International Day for the Elimination of Violence against Women (November 25), and Valentine's Day (February 14) as well as on the occasions when new bodies have been discovered in the desert, on the streets, or in fields around the city.[5] During these marches and protests, activists have frequently used large crosses painted either black or pink to honor girls and women who have been murdered.

A feminist group already in existence when the feminicide began, the *Ocho de Marzo* (8th of March), was the first group to "actively document and denounce the violence against women in Ciudad Juárez."[6] Esther Chávez Cano, founder and director of *Ocho de Marzo*, turned the group's attention to the abductions and disappearances of young girls and women when a pattern began to emerge. In 1995 this group began painting utility poles pink throughout the city and then attaching black ribbons to them,[7] a precursor to the more widely noted pink telephone poles with black crosses that were to come later.

Within a few years, mothers of the murdered victims were forming other groups, each with distinct aims and strategies for bringing the feminicide to the public attention and demanding that it end: *Voces sin Echo* ("Voices without Echo"), *Mujeres de Negro* ("Women in Black"), *Nuestras Hijas de Regreso a Casa* ("May Our Daughters Return Home"), *Mujeres por Juárez* ("Women for Juárez"), *Justicia por Nuestras Hijas* ("Justice for our Daughters"), along with many others. In 1997 Astrid Gonzalez founded *Citizens Committee against Violence*, which publicly denounced the killings by writing an open letter to then Chihuahua Governor Francisco Barrio Terrazas demanding that resources be put in place to bring the violence against women to an end and to prevent any further violence. He famously dismissed the brutal rapes and murders, claiming that the number of victims was not out of the ordinary or worthy of attention, that the girls and women killed were to blame for dressing provocatively and walking in poorly lit areas.[8]

In 1998 the murder of seventeen-year-old María Sagrario González Flores prompted her mother, Paula Flores, and the mothers of several other victims, to create another group, *Voces sin Eco*, to pressure authorities to investigate the murders, to take action against their perpetrators, and to offer support to all families directly touched by this violence.[9] In March 1999 black crosses painted against a large pink background began to appear on electrical poles throughout Ciudad Juárez. Members of *Voces sin Eco* created these symbols to honor the memory of the murdered girls and women by claiming public space for them and to protest the depravity of justice manifested by the ongoing feminicide. Every time another girl or woman was killed, *Voces sin Eco* painted a new cross, ensuring that these girls and women were not forgotten even though most civil authorities have repeatedly ignored, ridiculed, botched, or otherwise destroyed any attempts at a rigorous investigation. Even when *Voces sin Eco* disbanded in 2001, the former group's members decided to continue to "paint new crosses and freshen up old ones that had faded."[10] One woman "explained that black stood for death and pink for the promise of life and youth."[11]

While many of the practices of resistance entail a dramatic public display in the form of marches, installations, the erection of crosses, and the like, other forms of resistance also emerged. Most notably, *Ocho de Marzo* founder Esther Chávez Cano also founded *Casa Amiga* in 1999 in Ciudad Juárez. It was the first crisis center for women confronting domestic violence, victimized by the feminicide, or victimized by rape or any other form of sexual assault. This center strives to address the social trauma left in the wake of the feminicide and respond to the needs of victims of "rape, domestic violence, sexual abuse, and incest."[12] It supports women's journeys toward healing and wholeness by means of consciousness-raising workshops and feminist therapy as well as by generating a microculture of respect and community building within the center itself.[13] It advocates that "political authorities [be held] to account for femicide and other forms of violence and . . . all members of society [be held] to account both as individuals and as a *community*."[14] The center represents a practice of resistance in at least two senses: it is committed to creating a community that respects women in a context that threatens women's existence, and it takes public positions critical of the government's handling of this atrocity and demands accountability.

In 2001 there came a turning point. First, on February 14, Valentine's day, seventeen-year-old Lilia Alejandra García Andrade was kidnapped. Six days later, her nude body was discovered wrapped in a blanket and dropped in front of the plastics plant where she had been employed. "She had been choked, savagely beaten in the face, and parts of her breast had been removed."[15] An autopsy showed that when her body was found on February 20, she had been dead only a few hours.[16] Her mother, Norma Andrade de García, along with the mothers of six other victims, founded *Nuestras Hijas de Regreso a Casa* to demand justice. A couple of weeks later, on March 8, International Women's Day, several women from Juárez and El Paso carried wooden crosses and life-size photos of the murdered girls and women with them as they marched to and stormed the office of the "Special Prosecutor for the Investigation of the Homicide of Women." They demanded that justice be served.

Second, on November 6, 2001, five bodies were discovered at the intersection of two busy streets, *Ejército Nacional* and *Paseo de la Victoria*.[17] The very next day, three more bodies were found at this same intersection. Eight bodies had now been brazenly dumped in the heart of the city; perpetrators saw no need to conceal their murder victims in the deserts on the outskirts of Juárez. The following day, several protestors gathered in front of the Juárez special prosecutor's office; all were dressed in black, and they carried a large pink cross that they erected just outside the government building.[18] The discovery of these eight bodies served as the final catalyst for several local grassroots groups, NGOs, as well as national and international groups to join forces to stop the violence against women in Mexico. Finally, in mid-December, a candlelight vigil was organized where the eight bodies were found. Organizers expected about ten thousand people, and an estimated twenty-five thousand people came.[19]

By early 2002 these groups, some three hundred in all, came together under the umbrella *Campaña Alto a la Impunidad: Ni Una Muerte Más* ("Stop the Impunity: Not One More Death Campaign"),[20] better known as *Ni Una Más*. The leadership of this transnational coalition organized several demonstrations to call attention to the feminicide, to demand that it end, and to ensure that women in Mexico enjoy full rights as citizens.[21]

In March 2002 the large *Ni Una Más* coalition along with Chihuahua City–based *Mujeres de Negro* ("Women in Black") organized a dramatic, emotional march from Chihuahua City to the Paso del Norte International Bridge in Ciudad Juárez, naming their campaign *Éxodo por Vida* ("Exodus for Life").[22] This 230-mile march began on International Women's Day (March 8) and ended many days later. Participants wore long black dresses and pink hats, the symbol of women in a perpetual state of mourning for Juárez's daughters. The marchers included "elderly women, campesinas, housewives, factory workers, students, professionals."[23] According to Diana Washington Valdez, when the marchers reached the city limits of Ciudad Juárez, they were met by a group of "political thugs" who attempted to intimidate the women by pushing some of them to the ground and denying them the right to march into the city of Juárez. "Several men who accompanied the women intervened. They created a physical wedge between the two groups, and that permitted the marchers to continue into Juárez without further problems." As the marchers processed down major streets toward the center of the city, their numbers grew to thousands, defying Chihuahua's then "Governor Patricio Martinez's alleged attempts to stop the procession."[24]

The marchers eventually arrived at their destination in downtown Juárez, the Paso del Norte Bridge, where cars, trucks, and people cross from Juárez, Chihuahua, into El Paso, Texas. As Diana Washington Valdez tells it:

> When the protesters arrived . . . several of them climbed off a truck that had transported a large and impressive cross from Chihuahua City. They hooked up power tools and began to install it at the foot of the international bridge. The wooden cross was attached to a large metal panel, about twelve feet high, and which glistened with metal spikes. A sign at the top of the cross proclaimed "*Ni Una Más*" (Not one more). Other ornaments, including a plastic torso of a woman at the bottom of the cross, gave the new border fixture an eerily abstract quality. Tags with the names of victims, some labeled "unknown," were affixed to the metal spikes.
>
> Mexican bridge officials and armed police officers wrote down the names of the speakers. They asked people in the crowd questions about the leaders. Because of their connections, the organizers had obtained permission from federal officials to install the cross

and block bridge traffic for several hours. Using a bullhorn, Samira [Itzaguirre, a Juárez radio show host,] challenged anyone to take down the cross and told a cheering crowd: "If they take it down, we'll be right back and put up a bigger one in its place."

The Chihuahua City pilgrims said several men from their city who were temporarily out of work wanted to contribute in some way to the protest. One of them, Jaime García Chávez, had come up with the idea for the cross. With a deep sense of purpose, he and the others got to work, using their skills and tools to fashion the cross out of whatever scrap materials they could find.[25]

This cross installation has become a shrine for grieving family, friends, and others who demand that the violence end. It serves as a public symbol of protest against the violence that as of this writing has still not ended. It sits on one of the most significant and public locations on the border. Over one hundred thousand people cross the border daily between the two cities, and the Paso del Norte Bridge is one of only three bridges linking the two cities.

Not surprisingly, a countercampaign emerged to challenge the *Ni Una Más* coalition's work. According to Melissa W. Wright, this countercampaign, named *lucrar* (to be lucrative), is accusing the *Ni Una Más* coalition's leadership of using the pain and suffering of the victimized mothers and other women to the advantage of *Ni Una Más* organizers, enabling them to make money internationally and to advance their political stature. The discourse of *lucrar*, which is promoted by the government, claims that *Ni Una Más* has used the horrific stories from the feminicide to sell periodicals and to facilitate political campaigns that support liberal and feminist causes. In short, the accusation is that organizers have sold the pain and suffering of the mothers on the global market. Further, the government has manipulated the discourse of the *lucrar* campaign in order to silence all nongovernmental initiatives critical of the government's handling of the violence against women and the related investigations. In its discourse, *lucrar* has sought to undermine the legitimacy of women exercising their democratic rights through public actions in which they demand a government more attentive and responsible to the needs of all its citizens. This same discourse also serves to exacerbate any divisions or potential divisions among various groups protesting the feminicide. The countercampaign is, in part, a reaction to the financial support that

Ni Una Más has received from international sources, which has allowed *Ni Una Más* to forge a new political space that continues to confront local politics in Juárez.[26]

Nonetheless, protestors continue to erect pink crosses, raising one where the body of Lilia Alejandra García Andrade was found, her name written on the crossbar.[27] Eight pink crosses, each standing more than four feet tall, were erected where the eight bodies were found in November 2001. Ever since, in addition to painting telephone poles black with pink crosses, protestors have erected wooden pink crosses throughout Juárez to mark the location where a body was found, the name of the victim written on the crossbar. As these crosses have become increasingly numerous, they undoubtedly signal the growing social and physic nightmare that grips Juárez. They likewise signal a stubborn will to keep the memory of these tragic murders alive and to confront the city, state, nation, and international community with their own complicity in this abomination.

The symbol of a cross operates in the imagination of the mothers. One mother described her experience of being involved in the mothers' movement as a "calvary," in that participating means operating against your more immediate interests as well as those of your family. She and the other mothers have less time to spend as workers, mothers, wives, and so forth.[28]

Not everyone victimized by the feminicide chooses to participate, or feels that they are able to participate, in the public expressions of grief and protest. One mother, Bertha Marquez, remarked some ten years after her daughter's murder, "I never joined any of the advocacy groups that marched in the streets, or went to see officials like the president to demand justice. In my heart, I knew from the beginning that the authorities were never going to do anything to solve my daughter's murder."[29] Understandably, such a comment may reflect a sense of despair. It is, after all, truthful on one level, in that after launching multiple investigations the authorities by and large have neither solved the murders nor made a rigorous, committed attempt to do so. As Mark Ensalaco has observed: "The Mexican authorities' failure to investigate, prevent, and punish the crimes in Ciudad Juárez constitutes a form of gender discrimination. That failure has compelled the women of Juárez to mobilize in defense of their own rights."[30]

The foregoing practices of resistance have yet to effect the change that the women of Juárez seek. By any measure, these practices serve as a testimony to the enormous courage and unwavering determination of many, many women (and men). While the identity of the perpetrators is not entirely clear, many of those who have stood up to them have been threatened and, in several cases, killed. Certainly this is true for the women who choose to resist in such a public manner. These practices of resistance possess a kind of elasticity in that they can be created and shaped to bear constructive, life-giving possibilities, which give hope. They are also fragile in that they can be manipulated for good and for ill, and they almost invariably carry a measure of both. Nevertheless, they bear potential as portals, as occasions in which we might catch a glimpse of salvation.

Popular Religious Practices and Practices of Resistance

An analysis of these practices reveals that through them practitioners claim a space in which they further their political subjectivity, their religious subjectivity, and by so doing enable "fragments of salvation to gain a foothold within history."[31] To develop this claim, it is important to understand what it means to identify these public actions as "practices" and more specifically as a form of popular religious practice. While in some respects these "practices of resistance" are consonant with the ways U.S. Latino/a theologians have defined popular religious practice, they also suggest a fresh approach.

Since Latino/a theologians began writing theology in the U.S., they have examined Latino/a's religious practices and identified them as a *locus theologicus*—in other words, as a preeminent source or font for the development of theological discourse. While the practices delineated above did not emerge on U.S. soil, scholars who have studied the feminicide and the ensuing protests make clear that it is a binational phenomenon and requires a binational response.[32] It serves as an ideal opportunity for considering popular religious practices anew.

Before examining what these practices of resistance may suggest, what follows is a delineation of some of the more prominent characteristics of those practices that many U.S. Latino/a theologians agree constitute popular religious practices. For decades now, U.S. Latino/a theologians have sought to describe and define this phenomenon. As Orlando Espín and Sixto García observe: "In general terms, popular religiosity can be defined as the set of experiences, beliefs, and rituals which more-or-less peripheral human groups create, assume, and develop (within concrete socio-cultural and historical contexts, and as a response to these contexts) and which to a greater or lesser degree distance themselves from what is recognized as normative by church and society, striving (through rituals, experiences, and beliefs) to find an access to God and salvation which they feel they cannot find in what the church and society present as normative."[33]

This description must be further developed. First, the term *popular* does not refer to common, widespread, in vogue, and the like. *Popular* means that the "symbols, practices, and narratives are *of the people*."[34] "Popular religion is 'popular' . . . because its creators and practitioners are the people, and more concretely, the marginalized people in society (i.e., those social sectors pushed against their will to the 'dispensable' or 'disposable' margins of society)."[35]

Second, even a cursory reading of the history of Latinos/as in the United States reveals a long narrative of rejection by and exclusion from society as well as the church (both the Roman Catholic Church and mainline Protestant churches). For centuries, popular religious practices have remained a primary way Latina/o believers take on and sustain their Catholic identity, the way they appropriate their Christian beliefs. To a lesser degree, this holds true for Protestant Latinos/as as well. Through these practices, symbols, and rituals, practitioners affirm, explain, and defend the uniqueness of their encounter with God. Accordingly, the appropriation of faith and the encounter with God for many includes indigenous and African elements; in other words, it is not exclusively Western European in origin. Michelle A. Gonzalez, in fact, makes a point of clarifying that popular Catholicism is a form of popular religion. Popular religion is the term that explicitly recognizes elements from non-Christian religions and non-Western European histories.[36]

Third, on a related yet distinct point, popular religious practices are neither created by official representatives of the institutional church or any other specialists in religion, nor are they developed in opposition to "official" or "institutional" church teaching and practice. These practices most often emerge parallel to the institutionally promoted religious rituals and continue along on a parallel path. Latino/a popular religious practices, while not intending to subvert official practices, can nevertheless have this effect in that they most often grow out of the marginalized experience of Latinos/as in relation to the official church.[37] Put another way, Latina/o Catholic believers understand their own beliefs to be dialectically linked to those of the ecclesial elites.[38] Yet the distinction in this dialectic remains ambiguous. Some Latino/a theologians, rather than highlighting the differences between popular religion and official religion, point to the significant ways in which the two coalesce.[39]

Fourth and finally, popular religious practices are one way that Latinos/as come to terms with life's struggles. Alejandro García-Rivera observes that "partakers of popular religion may be seen as putting their faith 'on the line.' Disease, family unrest, or even social conflict may be typical motivation for popular religious practice, but they also happen to be challenges to faith, a struggle where faith is at stake. The result of that struggle is a reinterpretation or reevaluation of that faith . . . which is then willingly, consciously, made one's own."[40]

The above description does not take into account the ways that gender functions in popular religious practices. While many U.S. Latino scholars do include the experience of women in their descriptions, for the most part they do not provide an analysis of how these practices structure power hierarchies in terms of gender, not to mention the intersection of gender, class, race, and ethnicity.[41] María Pilar Aquino has certainly suggested as much. She makes the argument that popular religiosity (and therefore popular religious practices) remains an ambiguous arena for women because these practices too often bear the stain of the patriarchal worldviews out of which they emerge. Not much work has been done to sort out the patriarchal elements present in these practices. She observes, "Although popular devotions express liberating impulses that have helped the poor masses in their struggle to survive, especially when they are expressed in the language of resistance, it is also true that this same popular religiosity contains elements that legitimate submission to the oppressor. Because this environment has been basically patriarchal and *machista*, it is not surprising that women's religious expression also contains these elements."[42] This observation suggests that popular religious practices are endeavors fraught with complexity, particularly for women.

For example, many women have encountered well-meaning church leaders, family members, and friends who have encouraged religious practices as a way to "deepen" faith, yet they have found that these "practices" have turned out to be ossified rather than life-giving. These practices are ones that have become stale and that embody a rigid traditionalism rather than an emancipatory message. Regrettably, various Marian devotions have often been used to keep women in subordinate positions. Such practices have been designed to hold up the Virgin Mary as the ideal model for women; however, "with all her glory she is always obedient, she is not 'ordained,' she is the busy but submissive, patient, and suffering auxiliary who can intercede but not decide."[43] As I have argued elsewhere, the idealized portrayal of Mary has meant for a growing number of women a widening rift between the typical Christian images of womanhood they are offered and their deep longing for a God-centered life.[44]

However, the practices of resistance that have appeared in Juárez offer a distinct angle of vision on what U.S. Latino/a theologians have described as popular religious practices. We can see this complexity by way of five points. First, both may be described as "of the people" in that they emerge out of the imagination of a socially marginalized body of people. But their respective aims differ. While the primary aim of U.S. Latino/a popular religious practices has been to appropriate and sustain Christian faith in the face of rejection, the primary aim of the practices of resistance has been to use religious symbols to come to grips with horrific tragedy and extreme loss. In their selection of the cross and of exodus as their primary religious symbols, they recognize their own need for a kind of "language" that speaks of ultimate reality, of their confrontation with an unexplainable evil.

Second, and on a related point, most U.S. Latino/a theologians would not describe popular religious practices as intentionally subversive. In the words of González: "In and of itself, popular religion is not intended in any way to be subversive, yet in refusing to be silenced, rejected, and ignored, it becomes so."[45] Some have described popular religious practices as inadvertently subversive but not intentionally so. Or some attribute their subversive character to their emphasis on an "aesthetic affirmation of life." For example, Roberto S. Goizueta argues: "An aesthetic affirmation of life as an end in itself, popular Catholicism takes root most firmly in those lives that are, in every way, most 'useless' to our society, i.e., most economically and politically superfluous. The very emphasis on beauty, aesthetics, and celebration then—and only then—becomes, *de facto*, a subversive act in a society geared toward the accumulation of economic and political power."[46]

But what happens in a situation of extreme violence? Does it or should it change how we think about popular religious practices? The practices of resistance in Juárez explicitly and overtly intend to be subversive, politically as well as religiously. Through their use of religious symbolism and in the dramatic character of their actions, they aim to transform society. The practices of resistance are a means toward an end, the end being a society that deeply values and prizes the full humanity of its poor, female members. The practitioners fully intend to be radically subversive of all that renders poor women secondary, of all that judges female human beings to be of a lesser nature. Indeed, these practices overtly seek to dismantle everything that generates and sustains patriarchy as the social, political, and religious norm. In short, the creators of the practices of resistance understand and appreciate the subversive possibilities of dramatic action and religious symbols; these can be powerful and crucial tools in the endeavor to transform society.

Third, these practices of resistance reflect a sharp critique of the complexity and interlocking character of oppressive systems of domination. The feminicide is about more than the brutal murdering of women, as Rosa Linda Fregoso has noted. She writes: "Although the murdered women were indeed targeted for their gender, perhaps even more significant are the racial and class hierarchies that constitute their identities as women. As one of the mothers, Mrs. González, so aptly phrases it, 'For the poor there's no justice. If they'd murdered a rich person's girl, they'd kill half the world to find the murderer. But since they've only murdered poor people, they treat us like dirt.' "[47] So to label these practices as "feminist," a claim this chapter makes, does not mean that they are only interested in what is for or about "women" but rather that the emancipatory vision that informs them calls for the dismantling of all interrelated systems and structures of oppression, and then for the creation of new systems that more fully enhance the life of all. Drawing on the work of Elisabeth Schüssler Fiorenza, María Pilar Aquino pointedly specifies what a critical feminist framework advances: "While conventional studies sum up the multidimensional processes of the contemporary world in the term *globalization* or *neoliberal globalization*, a critical feminist analytical framework exposes the *kyriarchal* characteristics and interstructuring of those processes as they evolve within what I have been calling a *kyriarchal globalization* that validates and multiplies *kyriarchal relationships of domination*. Because of the kyriarchal articulation of the current neoliberal globalization, the patterns of social disparity and of sexual violence against women are bound to be repeated and multiplied again and again in every society, culture, and religion of the world."[48] In the creation of their practices, the practitioners have advanced a critique of the kyriarchal relationships of domination and, in turn, defended the lives of poor females and the radical equality of all human life.

Fourth, the creators and practitioners of these practices of resistance, while arguably dialectically linked to the larger Christian tradition, as evidenced by their choice and use of religious symbolism, may not see themselves as connected to the contemporary institutional church and its leadership. The larger Christian tradition and contemporary institutional church leadership do overlap in important ways, but they are by no means synonymous. The distinction here is not without problems. The larger Christian tradition endures in significant measure because of the leadership of the contemporary institutional church, that is, its bishops, priests, pastors, pastoral ministers, theologians, and so on who dedicate themselves to its continuity and vitality. By and large, U.S. Latina/o theologians have pointed out the ways in which Latina/o popular religious practices run parallel to institutionally promoted religious rituals. In contrast, the creators of the practices of resistance have developed their practices in a manner critical of the institutional church's conventional interpretation of its core symbols. For example, the practices of resistance consistently link female humanity with crucifixion, a revolutionary reordering of conventional understandings of crucifixion. Indeed, practitioners have recognized the radical nature and efficacious potency of Christian symbols, turning to them in the hope of making sense of their confrontation with evil.

Fifth, the practices of resistance spotlight what I call the *elasticity* of popular religious practices. By elasticity I mean the ability to mediate credibly an experience of the divine through the use of traditional Christian symbols in a manner that takes seriously God's active presence in the midst of extreme suffering. The elasticity of popular religious practices reveals the enduring viability of Christian symbols and ideas to speak deeply in diverse cultural and religious settings. Indeed, several theologians have described elasticity in their discussions of how the varied cultural roots of popular religion find expression in practices, particularly with regard to several indigenous cultures and African cultures.[49]

However, with the practices of resistance, elasticity takes on an added meaning. These practitioners are overtly linking Christian religious symbols with public civil days designated to honor women. For example, over many years, practitioners have staged International Women's Day (March 8) marches that employ the Christian cross. They have painted the Christian cross pink as a way of associating it with women's experience. Because popular religious practices can be said to thrive in the borderlands of the faith, similar to any borderland experience, they hold open the possibility of fresh, invigorating interpretations of the faith. This is of course complicated. When does a popular religious practice cease to be Christian? When does it go too far? While these questions are of vital importance, engaging them would take us far afield from the task of this chapter.

In brief, the creators of these practices of resistance offer a distinctive angle of vision on popular religious practices by their endeavor to process publicly the pain brought about by the horrific tragedy of the feminicide; by their intentionally subversive approach that demands that female life be valued and protected; by their attention to the interlocking systems of domination; by their radical interpretation of Christian symbols; and by their appropriation of the elasticity of popular religious practices, linking Christian symbols to publicly designated days honoring women.

Claiming Space, Processing Pain, and Social Imagination

While these practices of resistance transform our understanding of popular religious practice, the effect of this transformation bears much further consideration. With these practices, practitioners both claim space and in that claimed space confront the horror of their pain, which eventually allows them to create a transformed world. This process ultimately refuses to allow this collective trauma to have the last word. In this transformed space, practitioners forge a new consciousness, a visible *communal* consciousness. In the end, their practice suggests that community is the condition for the possibility of salvation.

Claiming Emancipatory Space

To appreciate the import of the practitioners' commitment to a communal vision and its theological significance, we need to recognize that Juárez's sociocidal onslaught has implications for all of us. Juárez is confronted with a demonic force. It expresses itself spiritually as well as politically, and one of its primary aims is the destruction of community. Goizueta tells us that "only two things can destroy community: apathy (lack of feeling), or the destructive expression of human feelings (through, for instance, violence)."[50] Both are at work. The conflict is over the struggle to control territory, and women's bodies have been the means toward this end. As social anthropologist Rita Laura Segato explains:

> The killers used the women's bodies to mark their territory and demonstrate their power. In some cases, it seems the deaths make no sense. They do not appear to be connected, but they are. . . . The fact that the deaths continue serves to reinforce the pact of silence that exists within this co-fraternity of brotherhood. . . . The violence serves as a system of communication among those who share in this code of power, which continues to unfold and becomes more complex each time. But, its motive is to produce and exhibit impunity as a mark of territorial control and of the vitality of the groups. You cannot have these kinds of crimes go on for such a long time and with this degree of impunity unless there is a second state, with a power that is parallel to or of greater force than the power of the state.[51]

The forces behind this feminicide recognize that any affirmation of women's humanity poses a real threat to their sociocidal objectives. So when forums or public discussions of the murders were scheduled to take place in Juárez, the "community of activists [knew] to expect a woman's murder during such events."[52] The killers hope that by creating a reign of terror, city residents will be so overwhelmed that they will grow affectively numb and thus apathetic. We all must see in this that a threat to women's lives in Juárez threatens all human beings everywhere. Our humanity is at stake.

Just as the tortured and murdered bodies of the victims have been strewn throughout the city to mark territory, on the most overt level practitioners have marked and reclaimed territory by painting telephone poles pink with black crosses throughout the city, one for each murdered victim. They have erected a pink cross at each location where a body was found. They have marched across the state and through the city of Juárez to erect a twelve-foot cross at the Paso del Norte bridge. They have physically marked the city and reclaimed every locale where a killing occurred. And when the practitioners act, they act on behalf of us all.

The practitioners have recognized and resisted the ways in which women's bodies themselves have been used by the murderers as territory marked through mutilation, violation, and ultimately destruction. When practitioners act in public, placing their bodily selves at risk, they reclaim their subjectivity and self-possession as embodied, female human beings who demand that public space be emancipatory space for women. Their own female bodies serve as the starting point for remaking community, for the in-breaking of a new social imaginary, one that forges a world in which women can independently, confidently, and freely move in public without fear. Rather than acquiesce to a social imaginary that presumes an integral link between women and suffering, these women (and men) through their actions in public subvert this link and forge another in its place, one that releases energy on the side of life. By overtly reclaiming Juárez through their use of crosses, marches, and the like, practitioners elevate the fight they are waging against feminicide and against sociocide to the level of the supernatural. Those who engage in the fight are creating a "we"; in other words, they are creating a new social imaginary, because through their practices they assert, "*We do not belong to Pharaoh's world.*"[53] In the ongoing struggles between the powerful and the poor, Michel de Certeau distinguishes two levels of discourse.

While one is the powerful's account of their victories, the other is the poor's religious stories of a "utopian space." This utopian space reveals that the injustice advanced by the powerful is both ubiquitous (synchronic) and historical (diachronic). It continually serves as a space of resistance and nonacceptance of the established unjust order. It subverts the fatality of dependency. In this utopian space, the poor come to see that meaning is no longer confined to the given facts of the situation. Meaning emerges from a larger context. In the following description of utopian space, de Certeau provides insight into this dynamic. Even though he is writing about the peasants of Pernambuco, he could just as well be writing about those publicly resisting the Juárez feminicide.

> In order to affirm the non-coincidence of fact and meaning, another scene was required, the religious scene that reintroduces, in the mode of supernatural events, the historical contingency of this "nature" and, by means of celestial landmarks, creates a place for this protest. The unacceptability of an order which is nevertheless established was articulated, appropriately enough, as a miracle. There, in a language necessarily foreign to the analysis of socioeconomic relationship, the hope could be *maintained* that the vanquished of history—the body on which the victories of the rich or their allies are continually inscribed—might . . . rise again as a result of the blows rained on its adversaries from on high.[54]

Practitioners, by claiming space in the city and by creating a utopian space, assert that this is a much bigger fight than the killers realize.

Moreover, practitioners through their claiming of space engage in a practice of foregrounding women's stories of suffering and struggle by linking them to two core biblical stories, the story of Jesus' death and resurrection and the story of the exodus. Drawing on their own experience, they are, in effect, writing the story of the killing of Juárez's women into these two biblical narratives.

They are lifting up the contemporary stories of women's crucifixion as well as enslavement and signaling the presence of women's suffering throughout history inclusive of the biblical period. They are claiming historical space by insisting that the stories of the victims will not be forgotten. Through their employment of biblical stories, they draw on an external power, a religious authority, one that they have made their own by means of the practices they have created.

All the practices of resistance creatively and transparently link Christian symbols and stories to symbols and stories associated with women. The crosses painted on telephone poles and erected throughout the city are pink in color, a shade of pink commonly associated with female humanity, youth and vitality, the season of spring, and the hope of a bright future. Pink crosses invite us to confront the irony in the killings of these young women. The march *Éxodo por Vida* began on March 8, International Women's Day, making a clear association between women's pursuit of justice, the tragedy of the feminicide, and the exodus story. The 230-mile march gestures toward the Jews' wandering in the desert for forty years in search of the promised land. Like the Jews who were threatened by the Egyptians chasing them, these women were threatened at the city limits by those who did not want a march through the city streets of Juárez. Marches with practitioners carrying pink crosses have also occurred on November 25, the International Day for the Elimination of Violence against Women, signaling connections between Jesus' crucifixion, the killing of Juárez's women, and the brutal executions of the Mirabal sisters of the Dominican Republic, in whose honor the United Nations General Assembly named the day. Patria Mercedes Mirabal, María Argentina Minerva Mirabal, and Antonia María Teresa Mirabal (the Mirabal sisters) all spoke out fiercely against the dictatorship of Rafael Trujillo. On several occasions, Trujillo had two of them incarcerated, where they were repeatedly tortured and raped.

Eventually, on November 25, 1960, he had the three of them executed.[55] Theirs too exemplifies a story of female crucifixion.

It is telling that the surviving witnesses to feminicide have chosen *crosses* to reclaim territory in Juárez, overtly associating crosses with female humanity by painting them pink and writing the name of the girl or woman victim on the crossbar. What does this say? To be sure, it signals an assault on patriarchal ideology, which has left its imprint on Christianity, not to mention on the culture and society of the Americas (and beyond). Through their use of crosses, the practitioners issue an indictment against the complicity of the church and state in the evil of feminicide. They reveal a link between crucifixion and female identity. Further, the crosses take us to a place that Anselm and his soteriological progeny could not have imagined, to a new social imaginary. While for Anselm the cross signals the suffering and death of Jesus Christ as his ultimate sacrifice offered out of love for humanity, for the witness survivors of feminicide, the pink crosses signal a loud and public *no* to feminicide, *no* to the brutal terror waged against women, *no* to all forms of misogyny, *no* to all forms of patriarchy from the most benign to the most brutal. Even more, they signal that the witness survivors have not succumbed to hurling their anger and outrage violently against others but have instead chosen to cry out *against* death and to cry out *for* life. They have chosen community. They have chosen to bring the crucified down from the cross.[56] *Pink* crosses mean that life can be and must be wrenched from death through solidarity that is built among those who have suffered feminicide and with others who insist on hope even in the face of terror.

"Public Processing of Pain"

The practices of resistance not only claim space but also make the private pain of countless families and community members a public, intentional, social act. When private pain is no longer an experience of the isolated many but becomes something socially and publicly expressed, it begins to generate social power. As Kathleen Staudt has observed: "At the border, anti-femicide activists have communicated, silently and loudly, with the use of symbols and colors: pink and black crosses. They painted names and colors on crosses, dresses, and public signs. Activists mourned silently in public, setting symbolic political stages for anti-violence activities. Victims' mothers and activists repeated stories, showed pictures, and gave personal testimonies at rallies, creating vivid memories with personal names and faces attached to them."[57] The *Exodo por Vida* march, the large cross installation at the Paso del Norte bridge, all of these have transformed the private suffering of victimized families into a public discourse that makes evident the absence of public standing and civil rights for the economically poor in the borderlands.

As Reinhold Niebuhr once remarked, power is never given up willingly. When the women in Juárez lay claim to their standing in the polis, that claim provokes a harsh, negative reaction. The Mexican government's reaction to the women's public expression of their pain has been sharply negative. They have employed one of oldest strategies in history to discredit the women involved. They have referred to each of these women as a "public woman," a term intended to cause damage. By sharp contrast, being a "public man" carries a highly positive connotation. A public man is generative of the economy, the culture, the democracy, and so forth, in short, an ideal man. A public woman is analogous to a prostitute. Being labeled or identified as a "public woman" (participating in the public marches and protests organized by *Ni Una Más*) is dangerous not only because it advances the supremely undemocratic position of excluding women from participation in public life in the polis but also because it serves to justify violence against and the killing of women who are out in public.[58] This warped mindset claims that women who are victimized or disappeared have brought it upon themselves because they were out in the streets unaccompanied by a male guardian/protector and thus are "bad women."[59] The visceral conflict concerning the value of public man in contrast to public woman illustrates the potency of the social imaginary of our common lives, its power to shape our perception of legitimate behavior and belief.

Through the public processing of pain, women practitioners risk much because it aims to delegitimize dominant power, to estrange the basis of the dominant discourse's authority, to reject the rules of the game. It is subversive. "Gender practices are regulated through social norms and . . . common practices normalize behaviors and interactions. Violence against women is all too 'normal' in gender interactions. Anti-violence activists challenge the normalization of violence, reframing it instead as abnormal and no longer (if it ever was) legitimate."[60] In the struggle to delegitimize violence against women, the creators of the practices of resistance have been hard pressed to identify institutional allies, even among those with similar commitments. As Kathleen Staudt observes: "Although faith-based communities espouse principles that seem compatible with life and safety, they do not necessarily respond to human rights discourse. At the border, religious leaders have been latecomers or absent from the anti-femicide and anti-violence movements, despite activists' use of . . . crosses and crucifixes to dramatize and legitimize their cause. When clergy speak and write about violence against women, new constituencies become aware and potentially involved, thus reaching beyond the human and women's rights base of the movement."[61] The practitioners, in this instance, bear acute risk because even the institutions where they might expect support are far too often enmeshed in the dominant power structure and will not risk their own resources and stature.

The women practitioners exemplify radical courage by publicly drawing connections among the young women being crucified today, the crucifixion of Jesus, and God's presence with them in their processing of pain. Their practices challenge everyone who calls themselves Christian to recognize that the crucifixion continues in our own time and that those being crucified today are poor, young, brown, and female. Typically, Christians paint crosses somber colors—browns and blacks—but not pink. A pink cross creates dissonance. Pink is not a color associated with horrific tragedy; yet pink was chosen by the practitioners to agitate us. The victims, practitioners are telling the world, must be counted among the crucified peoples. By going public, practitioners challenge everyone to consider: What does it mean to speak of a *crucified people* when the crucifixion is a feminicide? Their practices represent a glaring refusal to be silent, intimidated, or private in the face the terror.

Yet in tying the suffering caused by feminicide to Jesus' suffering on the cross, I do not intend to further a link between women and suffering. In fact, just the reverse. By going public the women practitioners are seeking another end. Disastrously, the women-suffering link served to legitimize women's suffering as integral to their nature, which led and still today leads to the destruction of women's personhood and humanity. Undoubtedly, in the case of the Juárez feminicide, most of the women practitioners have suffered greatly and, by engaging in public practices of resistance, do risk further suffering. However, in many instances, their personal decision to engage in practices of resistance and thus to risk suffering may reflect an informed commitment to act on behalf of a better world.

Such a decision, then, does not destroy them but rather enables them to grow more deeply into who they are. This growth is the case when a person has a sufficiently integrated life, one in which they have come to own who they are and what they are about in the world. In other words, first they are self-possessed and have made a decision to act, with some consciousness of the consequences. Second, the decision to act must be freely chosen and not a reaction to coercive force. And third, the decision to risk further suffering can bear meaning in light of the network of relationships that a person values and wants to uphold. These relationships may be tangible, that is, with people in one's life today, or they may stretch beyond the bounds of one's life span with, say, great-great-grandchildren or perhaps with figures long past. Women practitioners have chosen to act on behalf of a better world, even at the risk of suffering.

Due to the subversive nature of these practices of resistance, they generate social power. They serve as an occasion during which social anger is released, when those gathered cry out against any ideology that functions "by cover-up, whitewash, and denial."[63] Indeed, the women have confronted as much in the sexist lies associated with the label of "public woman" and in the civil authorities' refusal to seriously investigate the killings of Juárez's daughters, despite all manner of pretense to the contrary. None of this has discouraged the women from public action or weakened *Ni Una Más*'s work. Rather, it has served to invigorate many women, encouraging them to exercise their birthright as citizens by participating in public action in the streets.

Accordingly, these women have played an important role in democratizing the country and in reinterpreting the meaning of Christian symbols. They are "re-signifying the subject of the public woman and in the process turning around the hierarchies within the family, the economy and the political sphere, which have depended upon the reproduction of a feminine subject excluded from public space."[64] "Power is the ability to take one's place in whatever discourse is essential to action and the right to have one's part matter."[65] Conducting practices in public, as *Ni Una Más* has done, has created a new mindset within the public arena and has launched a process of transformation.

Birthing Social Imagination

The public processing of pain generates social power, which pushes forth a "new social imagination."[66] These practices of resistance thoughtfully and vigorously support another consciousness; they enable all gathered to experience a transformed sense of reality, one in which the creators and participants together become subjects who help create a new world.

The practices enable the birthing of a social imagination because they first offer a critique of ideology and then an opportunity for the public processing of pain. They critique the reigning ideology of patriarchy and kyriarchy by making public connections between, on the one hand, the cross and exodus, which are both male-centered symbols, and on the other hand, female humanity. By and large, the cross and exodus undergird the Christian social imaginary in a way that does not disturb the notion of God as male or the notion of Christian leadership as predominantly male (and seemingly legitimately so). Obviously womanist, Latina feminist, and Euro-American feminist theology all call this male-centeredness into question, as do the writings of female mystics like Julian of Norwich, among others. Suffice to say, there are other exceptions. The practices of resistance also call this male-centeredness into question. The practices, by publicly linking female humanity to crucifixion, destabilize a male-centered Christian social imaginary. For many, linking female humanity to crucifixion disturbs, and not simply because feminicide concerns brutal killings. The ideological critique is unmistakable.

Social power is generated by the practices because they publicly hold together the numerous murders of women and unimaginable suffering. The practices make possible the processing of this pain on a large, social scale. They likewise raise doubts about the legitimacy of dominant power and authority, which public officials nervously recognize. As I have already discussed, several local, state, and national officials have already and repeatedly tried to explain why they are so impotent in bringing the perpetrators to account and the feminicide to an end. In April 2009 the Mexican government was put on trial in front of the Inter-American Court in Santiago, Chile, for its ineptness in handling the feminicide cases. While the practices are not solely responsible for generating this public attention, they nonetheless direct international focus to the horrific tragedy of the feminicide.

A new social imagination is being born because the practitioners have insisted on an alternate view of reality and have begun to realize their view in both time and space. They have claimed territory with the pink crosses erected throughout Ciudad Juárez and with the public marches they have organized. They have also claimed time. Through their use of Christian symbols, they refuse to be isolated in their own time but have made a temporal connection between their tragedy and the crucifixion of Jesus Christ, between their tragedy and the journey from slavery to freedom that occurred in the exodus many millennia ago.

This birthing of a social imagination is analogous to what Schüssler Fiorenza points toward with her "hermeneutics of creative actualization," which, she tells us, "seeks to retell biblical stories from a feminist perspective, to reformulate biblical visions and injunctions in the perspective of the discipleship of equals, to create narrative amplifications of the feminist remnants that have survived in patriarchal texts."[67] This feminist vision, of course, includes men and women in a discipleship of equals; the emphasis is on women's experience as a corrective to patriarchy and kyriarchy. This new community is one where women and men both take their place in public and private. What is being birthed entails both a new understanding and a new experience. The knowing and the being community are integrally related, and this comes to birth through the practices of resistance.

These practices of resistance reveal the emergence of a social imagination born at the nexus of reason, desire, ethics, and ritual practice, an insight U.S. Latino/a theology has been exploring for some time. For example, Goizueta significantly develops this insight through the course of his *Caminemos con Jesus*. In his discussion of popular religious practices, he claims: "The liberation of the poor has not only an aesthetic dimension, not only an ethical-political dimension, not only a socioeconomic dimension, but also a rational dimension."[68] This is a communal reality, he tells us. Along a similar line of thought, feminist scholar of religion Amy Hollywood argues that feminists have not sufficiently explored the interrelation of reason, desire, ritual, and practice. She focuses on the notion of *habitus*, the daily bodily practices that make up our lives and through which our beliefs become deeply inculcated to the point that they appear natural. Thus she tells us, "our deeply embedded disposition and beliefs" can be transformed only through new practices that break open new ways of being. Our most deeply held beliefs are not only a matter of reason, emotion, and desire but also a matter of the "embodied nature of the *habitus*." *Habitus* matters significantly in ways we too often overlook.[69] Those who create and participate in the practices of resistance understand that publicly practicing a new social reality is integral to its coming to birth.

Conclusion

These practices of resistance afford us a glimpse. They point toward the insight that salvation cannot be understood as only a future reality that lies beyond this lifetime. "Salvation must be something that can also be experienced now. Salvation has to be formulated as a symbol pointing to a reality that is existentially actualized in a person's life."[70] These practices also reveal to us that salvation must be interpreted socially as well as individually. We are made to be in relationship with others, with creation, with ourselves, and with God.

5

On the Possibility of Salvation

The horrific suffering brought about by the feminicide, the depth of its underlying roots, the limited ability of Anselmian atonement soteriology to respond, and the practices of resistance that have grown from the ashes of this tragedy lead us to our final topic: how the practices created by those who have lost loved ones to the feminicide carry theological insight into the meaning of salvation.

Through the practices of resistance, we discover that two dimensions of salvation take on increased importance. First, salvation is necessarily actualized in history, albeit not fully. Second, salvation necessarily entails making visible the elemental social relations of all humanity and all creation. We must clarify what these two aspects of salvation might mean and how they come to the fore through the practices of resistance. The meaning of salvation cannot be reduced only to these two aspects. However, we must examine the "the salvific character of historical acts," the ways in which particular historical acts bear the presence of God more fully, "and how that presence is actualized and made effective in them."[1]

As God's salvific presence is actualized more fully in history, this salvific presence makes the social, spiritual unity of all humanity and creation more visible. If salvation means being released from the clutches of evil, if it means being released from guilt and sin, if it means being freed from anxiety no matter the form this freedom takes, then surely these practices, as a resistance to and subversion of that which fractures social relations, reveal a vision of a transformed humanity, a humanity that sees more clearly, that embraces more fully the fundamental spiritual unity of all creatures.

While suffering in and of itself is not salvific, our response to suffering, our own and that of others, matters nonetheless. Through the example of the women in Juárez, we learn that community is the condition for the possibility of salvation. "Community" as developed here embraces and includes the two dimensions of salvation: history and relationality. Those who have suffered the feminicide teach us that community is born and sustained by commonly held decisive events that we claim as significant to us whether they date from a long-ago past or point toward an anticipated, far-off future. These events are recognized, interpreted, and celebrated as decisive in the life of the community. Those who have suffered teach us also that community is forged by a commitment to others, particularly to the most vulnerable, and from a commitment to see our lives as inherently connected to those who live now, those who lived long before our lifetime, and those who will live long after we are dead. They teach us that community comes into being through a process whereby we understand our present moment in light of the past, with an eye toward the future, and in relationship to others. In so doing, these practices of resistance point toward the fundamental spiritual unity of all humanity and creation, and in this way they serve as a portal to God's saving presence in history.

To develop the claim that community conditions salvation, we examine the existential and theological challenge presented by *social suffering*, such as that found in the example of the feminicide. What do those who have suffered the feminicide suggest to us by their *response* to it? What lies in the balance of their response to the feminicide? What kind of response affords us a glimpse of the "salvific character of historical acts"?[2] What kind of response does not? In other words, how does the primacy of community come to the fore in the practices of resistance? What constitutes community? Finally, we will see that these practices of resistance, more than revealing the primacy of community, direct our attention toward the claim that community is the condition that makes salvation possible.

On Matters of Suffering and Response

Many feminist theologians, among others, develop the claim that suffering in and of itself is not salvific. As Elizabeth A. Johnson argues:

The depth of suffering Jesus experienced on the cross, the wretched suffering as such, is not *in itself* salvific. Indeed, speaking from the historical point of view, numerous theologians today do not hesitate to call his execution a tragedy, disaster, fiasco, an unmitigated failure. Rather than being an act willed by a loving God, it is a strikingly clear index of sin in the world, a wrongful act committed by human beings. What may be considered salvific in such a situation is not the suffering endured but only the love poured out. The saving kernel in the midst of such negativity is not the pain and death as such but the mutually faithful love of Jesus and his God, not immediately evident.[3]

Just as Jesus' execution can be regarded as "a strikingly clear index of sin," so too the brutal murders of Juárez's girls and women serve as a contemporary index of sin. Just as Jesus' suffering is not salvific, their suffering cannot be regarded in any way as salvific either for themselves or for others.

Yet today the notion of redemptive violence (or salvific violence) dominates, as Walter Wink has amply shown.[4] Even though Anselm's celebrated contribution and the varied satisfaction theories of atonement it spawned do not promote suffering per se, they have been widely and consistently used to encourage a passive response to suffering. They do little to support the dismantling of the suffering brought on by unjust social institutions. Proponents of these theories judge Jesus' death as a substitutionary sacrifice for human sin, which in turn furthers the sanctification of violence, reinforces the idea that we worship a divine sadist, encourages victims of all manner of abuse to submit passively, and thus "separates salvation from ethics."[5]

When salvation means to have one's debt paid that was owed to God, salvation is understood apart from any effect or impact that it has on the subsequent life of the saved individual. Salvation in terms of a legal transaction is salvation separated from ethics involved in the concrete, historical life of the saved individual. In fact, it might even be argued that this motif assumes the ongoing sinfulness (failure) of the sinner and provides an understanding of atonement where grace covers the penalty of that sin. This approach to atonement reflects a church that has reached accommodation of violence within the social order.[6]

Suffering brought on by horrifically unjust social structures, then, becomes a social norm to which believers accommodate themselves. With an Anselmian understanding of salvation, Christian discourse has far more often than not given license to a passive response to social suffering, if not actually conflating suffering and salvation. We realize salvation not in suffering itself but rather in the context of our *response* to suffering.[7]

Social suffering brought on by structural evil presents us with more than the problem of how to rid the world of evil. The experience of all serious suffering, most certainly social suffering, evokes a response. In our response hangs the question of salvation. Without a doubt, absolutely and unequivocally, we must work toward the elimination of the causes that further structural evil and that generate tragedies such as the feminicide. However, evil at the root of social suffering is not entirely transient but "is a reality and a deep rooted one."[8] This evil presents us with "more" than the problem of how to eliminate or destroy the cause that furthers social suffering. This "more" demands attention.

While evil may be manifest to a greater or lesser degree, the very character of evil, as is found in the feminicide, makes its absolute abolition impossible. We cannot view the world merely as an experience of the present nor merely as an experience external to ourselves; rather, we must realize that it lives within us and within our communities. Evil arising out of unjust political and social structures becomes ubiquitous and produces a context in which we carry the historical memories of the effects of evil. We carry within us the "irrevocable past."[9] Even if we regret our own past moral failings and, in the present, strive to realize a life committed to a higher moral standard, we still carry within us all that we have done in the past along with our present choices. We can neither shed nor erase decisions made in our past. Nor can we erase our memory of the evil we have experienced. Indeed, neither our individual nor our collective experience of past evils can be eliminated, whether we consider the evils we have committed or those perpetrated against us. To say that the only problem that evil—in this case the feminicide—presents to us is the problem of how to get rid of it is to ignore one of the greatest moral challenges we face.

Irrevocable deeds, precisely because they cannot be undone, press upon us the inerasable problem of evil. As Josiah Royce observes, "One of the central facts about life is that every deed once done is *ipso facto* irrevocable. That is, at any moment you perform a given deed or you do not. If you perform it, it is done and cannot be undone. This difference between what is done and what is left undone is, in the real and empirical world, *a perfectly absolute difference*. The opportunity for a given individual deed returns not; for the moment when that individual deed can be done never recurs."[10]

History provides abundant examples of the challenge presented to us by our irrevocable past, and these blatantly teach us that our experience of past evils cannot be eliminated. For example, post–World War I Germany endured economic sanctions exacted by the Allies. This in turn, among other things, contributed to an internal climate that eventually led to the rise of fascist Nazism and the scapegoating and murdering of millions of Jews. Many Jews who live in Israel today trace their family history to the Shoah, and to some degree this history fuels some aspects of the resistance to granting the Palestinians full rights as citizens of the state of Israel. The memory of past evils can and does shape decisions we make in the present. While to some degree the reality of evil inevitably endures, we must nonetheless resist it. We must respond. Our response must remain devoted to the furtherance of a community that values the common good above all else. We begin to realize salvation when we hold fast to this commitment, particularly when we know suffering—in other words, when we experience evil.[11]

It is in how we respond to the irrevocable past, particularly to the tragic consequences of evil, that we either cooperate with God's salvific presence among us or we do not. Salvation from God takes root and grows in history.[12] It is within history that humans are called to communion with God and with each other, and the historical practice at play is the challenging of evil and the advancement of the common good. Edward Schillebeeckx advances this notion when he writes:

> Salvation from God comes about first of all in the worldly reality of history, and not primarily in the consciousness of believers who are aware of it. The cognitive sense of this is, of course, itself a separate gift, the significance of which we may not underestimate. But where good is furthered and evil is challenged in the human interest, then through this historical practice the being of God—God as salvation for men and women, the ground for universal hope—is also established and men and women also appreciate God's salvation—in and through acts of love. Human history, the social life of human beings, is the place where the cause of salvation or disaster is decided on.[13]

Indeed, no experience more sharply confronts the possibility of salvation in history than the experience of evil and the response it evokes.

What can be the experience of salvation for the families who already know the horror of the feminicide in the loss of their loved ones? And for the Juárez community that already knows the experience of living daily life amid social trauma? And for all of us, who, whether we know it or not, are affected by this evil? In the feminicide, all of us confront the problem of the irrevocable past and in the process squarely face the question of the possibility of salvation.

To situate the question of salvation this way presumes salvation in history. The historical destiny of humanity consists not in a positivistic claim, with its optimistic understanding of human progress, but rather in a claim that in the midst of history's irrational, contingent character some actions mediate God's self-giving more intensively. Humanity comes to know its own destiny in these proleptic moments, on the occasions of its own greater openness to God's self-giving. In contrast, another long-standing and commonplace approach that has proven problematic in our own time is a theological construct that distinguishes between, on the one hand, "salvation history" as identified with *the supernatural* and, on the other hand, human history as identified with *nature* or *the natural*. This theological construct "has deformed Christian praxis and undermined the relevance of our theology,"[14] according to Ignacio Ellacuría, who rightly critiques this construct because it leads to the separation of salvation from ethics. It implies that human beings in and of themselves remain extrinsic to the world and history. These are simply the stage upon which humans express the essence of who they are, an essence only tangentially touched by the world and history. In the process, God and human persons likewise tend to remain more extrinsic to one another. If "salvation history" is distinct from "human history," God participates in history but only in a partial way; God communes with humans in nature, but this too is limited.[15]

This construct is woefully inadequate because human history utterly needs God for its sheer existence. We recognize God's gratuitous self-gift as freely moving within history and expressing itself in distinct ways. God finds expression with varied levels of intensity. While the free decisions of human beings play a role in the level of reception of God's self-giving, "even in the case of sin we are fully in the history of salvation; sin does not make God disappear, but rather crucifies God, which seems like the same thing but in fact is profoundly different."[16] When sin crucifies God, we have an occasion of an extreme rift—humans cannot exist without God's constant self-gift, yet in sin humans utterly deny God.

In contrast, the practices of resistance, in their unreserved affirmation of the value of female humanity, occasion an openness to God in the face of evil and human sin. In them we find an example of a heightened intensity of God's self-giving. When we take the transcendentality of history as a given, as Ellacuría has suggested, then we may discover an openness to God in actions that strive to mediate God's self-giving more fully. Such is particularly the case in places and on occasions that seem most God-forsaken.

To develop this idea further, we begin with an admittedly simple distinction. As Exodus and the other historical and prophetic books show, within history some actions favor God and the people, and some oppose God and the people. This tangible, historical reality carries revelatory significance, either by further revealing or further concealing God's nature and salvific intent. This revelatory significance, of course, raises questions. What does it mean to take seriously the historical nature of salvation? If we claim that salvation history necessarily means salvation in history, then it follows that this salvation in history will be worked out differently depending upon the given historical context, its time and place. It likewise follows that salvation in history will be somehow realized in the concrete reality of both human history and our "membership" in a group of people. Drawing on the work of twentieth-century scholars of Hebrew scripture, Ellacuría delineates how we might understand salvation in history:

> It is the history of a people with concrete problems of a political nature that God's revelation and salvation take on flesh and blood. Moving from political experience to religious experience, they wait and look for Yahweh's revelation to interpret and resolve the problems of their nation as a public totality. God's revelation belonged to the chosen people. Membership in this people, which was the overall object of salvation, is the thing which permits each individual to hope for his [or her] own salvation. And the salvation of the individual relates to his or her life here and now. In and through this here-and-now salvation, the Israelites gradually come to learn about a higher salvation. . . .

Christians must admit that the socio-political version of the Jewish religion and that of their own political praxis are very primitive.
They must insist that the presence of God in natural and historical
reality is not the presence of a demiurge who miraculously rewards
or punishes the religious behavior of individuals and nations. On
the theoretical level *they must seek a line of action that will transform the world and human society*; then they must implement it in
their praxis. It will serve as the essential sign, without which man's
[*sic*] transcendent salvation cannot be rendered present. Christians
must insist that history is the locale of God's revelation, and that
this revelation is meant to show us here and now that God is revealing himself [*sic*] in history.[17]

Two points are significant here. First, salvation concerns the transformation of the world in history, without which the fullness of salvation, its
transcendent character, cannot be realized. Second, while salvation may
be realized in history in a range of ways, it is made evident in our response
to suffering. Salvation invariably involves a new way of seeing the world
and what is possible in the world, in other words: conversion. By "conversion" I mean letting go of an old way of seeing the self, God, the world,
and others and being open to a radically new way of seeing.

Nevertheless, two particular responses to suffering—namely, despair
or egocentrism—undermine the possibility of our acting in accord with
God's will. They cannot be described as conversion because in the end they
represent a refusal to let go of the old way of seeing. To give into the temptation either to despair or to egocentrism flattens the historical praxis of
salvation. In other words, to give into a "radical pessimism" or to a "corrosive form of ethical individualism"[18] takes one down a path that destroys
the self, the community, and the furtherance of the process of salvation.

Radical pessimism grows when those who suffer the feminicide
develop an attitude of resignation in the face of this evil, not seeking
"a line of action that will transform the world and human society."[19] It
means withdrawing from the world and resigning oneself to the world
as it is. It is a form of self-denial in that it idealizes passivity not only in
relation to the world but also in relation to the self. Accordingly, it means
the absence of a purpose in life, which is in effect the denial of the self.
While such an attitude stifles hope, it also distorts the historical process
of salvation by denying the possibility of the material, social ascendency

of the good. It is a denial of the resurrection. Movement against evil in history is constitutive of salvation.

Second, a corrosive form of ethical individualism emerges when those who are suffering choose to make themselves the center of the world, viewing everyone and everything else in the world as extensions of themselves. Here their purpose in life so determines everything in the world that other people are merely a means to an end. In this case, those who suffer move through the world with the expectation that their own personal loss and pain orient the world of everyone with whom they come into contact.[20] While this attitude overwhelms and kills hope in others and in themselves, it likewise distorts the historical process of salvation by stripping it of the possibility of a social moral vision. It corrupts resurrection by making it the exclusive purview of a single individual's deliverance and vindication.

A distinctive third kind of response furthers God's saving action and contributes to the fulfillment of the self, of humanity, and of history. Conversion is at the heart of this third response because it entails a radical change of our social imagination. This response, namely, the "subordination of evil through the pursuit of the greatest good," represents a radical fidelity to God's reign in our time and recognizes that the poor themselves are the favored locus of God's love and are thus the locus by which we come to see clearly God's saving action in history. For it "is not those innocent of evil who are fullest of the life of God, but those who in their own case have experienced the triumph over evil."[21] Salvation can be realized only when it is in question. Indeed, we can never fully rid the world of evil, but we can subordinate it. "The knowing of the good, in the higher sense, depends upon contemplating the overcoming and subordination of a less significant impulse, which survives even in order that it should be subordinated."[22]

When we experience evil, that is, when we suffer—particularly when we suffer unjustly—our initial inclination tends to be to destroy the source of our suffering, for example, killing the person who has caused grave harm. In the face of the Holocaust, attempts were made on Adolf Hitler's life. However, if our *only* response to evil is to destroy what we judge to be the source of evil, then we have not realized the greater good.

But if our response to suffering includes using our experience creatively toward some greater purpose, then we have thwarted evil in pursuit of a greater good. Through their practices of resistance, the practitioners advance this higher end. Their response contributes to the ongoing work of transforming our world so that it is more just and more humane. Their practices of resistance make such a contribution because they squarely face the real situation of ongoing crucifixions and demand that the crucified . . . peoples of our time be brought down from the cross.[23] The transformation of this world is realized when those who are most vulnerable among us, in this case the feminicide victims and their families, strongly desire and actively work to bring about a realization of the reign of God that is greater than what they have known. Many of those who have suffered the feminicide have used core Christian symbols (cross and exodus) to facilitate the transformation of society for the better.

Most importantly, the practices of resistance affirm the primacy of community. Community is fundamental to the human condition and to the condition of all of creation.[24] As these practices instantiate the communal dimension, they likewise resist and subvert sociocide and ideally direct attention to the marks of salvation in history.

On the Primacy of Community

What does it mean to suggest that these practices of resistance, as they denounce the horror of the feminicide, instantiate and announce anew the primacy of community? We begin with the claim that salvation has to do with the survival of community, a hallmark in U.S. Latino/a theology, one noted in the writings of Miguel H. Díaz. He posits that

> the notion of salvation as survival of community lies at the heart of Latino/a theologies and, more specifically, is a central theme in Latina/o popular Catholicism. To date, the theological interpretation of various symbols and narratives associated with Latino/a popular Catholicism exemplify how survival is understood as a kind of communal preservation, liberation, and "healing" (to us the most basic term associated with Augustine's soteriology) essential for the mediation of salvation. It is not by chance that some of the great voices in European and Latin American theologies have argued for the integral relationship between salvation history and human history on the basis of the experience of popular Catholicism: "The affirmation of God's history as the true history embracing everything that happens in history . . . come to us through popular religion and also through pre-Christian religious traditions."[25]

But salvation concerns not only the survival of the Latino/a community but also the survival of the larger, universal human community and of a flourishing creation.

Many U.S. Latino/a theologies, feminist theologies, womanist theologies, and other liberationist theologies have argued for the interrelated and communal dimension of all humanity and creation, and virtually all have explored at length the implications of such an assertion. Many of these theologies would be strengthened if they more explicitly attended to the philosophical presuppositions of a social understanding of reality.

To claim that salvation must be a communal reality situates salvation inside an understanding of the universe as suffused "through and through" by social categories. Accordingly, based on Josiah Royce's work, the category of "community" serves as the intellectual foundation for the assertion that only a life lived in pursuit of spiritual unity is both meaningful and is a furtherance of salvation. All other orientations to life are, in the end, nonsensical.[26] In Royce's words: "All experience must be *at least* individual experience; but unless it is *also* social experience, and unless the whole religious community which is in question unites to share it, this experience is but as sounding brass, and as a tinkling cymbal. This truth is what Paul saw. This is the rock upon which the true and ideal church is built. This is the essence of Christianity."[27] Christian theology has presumed salvation to be individual and personal, and without question this is so. But it is far more challenging to explain in what sense salvation is social and is a communal reality.

If community is to be understood as central to salvation, then it must take on a much more precise meaning. Here the term *community* does not refer to a colloquial notion of a group that gathers together but does not necessarily have a shared history or vision of itself. Rather, a body of people becomes a community as a result of particular processes of *interpretation*. Interpretation is *the way* community is formed and sustained.[28] Ultimately, salvation in history is actualized through a particular kind of community. So we need to first understand the nature of community, and then we can turn to how community is central to the meaning of salvation.

As human beings, we are inherently social creatures and are thus given to be in relation with one another. But we find ourselves frustrated by the estrangement that marks the difference between our ideas and purposes, and those of the others. We likewise see a similar frustration in others. Essentially, interpretation seeks to create a vision that enables us to bridge our experience of estrangement. Processes of interpretation allow distinct selves to enter into communion with one another.[29] In Juárez, through the practices of resistance, creators and participants interpreted their experience, forged a communion with one another, and signaled the primacy of community for their lives and for the lives of us all.

Three central dynamic processes illustrate the principal role of interpretation in the formation and sustenance of community.[30] First, a community exists when its members claim at least some identical events as significant for them. Even though all members agree that particular events are central, each member will interpret the meaning of the events differently. Second, a community comes into being when individual members extend their lives in time well into the past and the future so that each claims events as their own that exist beyond the span of their lifetimes. These ideally extended selves are not simply a collection of past and future events or experience but are an interpretation of those events and experiences. Third, a community comes into being through a time process whereby it bears a consciousness of its past, present, and future. It interprets its past toward the future in the present. These three dynamic processes make community possible. We will look at each of these three in turn.

Shared Events

Participants in the practices of resistance forge a community because they individually and collectively claim particular identical events of a long-ago past, or of a hoped-for future, that they hold to be meaningful for themselves now. On the occasions when the participants commemorate these shared events, they sustain and invigorate their communal life. Participants must recognize the event not only as central in the life of the community but also as central to the life of each individual community member. Community depends for its very existence upon its members, believing that specific events, which occurred long before and will occur long after their lifetimes, bear meaning in their lives now. Individual members must interpret these common events as constitutive of their lives now, and by so doing they constitute a community. While each participant may understand the events differently, they nonetheless hold particular events in common.[31]

No Christian symbol is more ubiquitous during the practices of resistance in Juárez than the cross, almost always painted pink. The cross signals a past event, the execution of Jesus, that participants claim holds meaning for them now. It is a central symbol in the life of this gathered community. Undoubtedly, the cross does not mean the same thing to each, yet the event of the execution of Jesus and the contemporary execution of Juárez's daughters are linked in the use of this symbol. Perhaps the use of the cross signals that the crucifixion continues as an evil hurled against the innocents of today, the daughters of Juárez. Perhaps the cross is meant to signal an event that cannot be dismissed as commonplace but rather bears transcendent significance in some mysterious way. Perhaps the cross implies that even though human beings have failed in the extreme to bring the feminicide to an end and its perpetrators to account, another judge—namely, God—will render the ultimate judgment in the case of this evil. Perhaps the cross intends that death cannot have the last word and resurrection will come.

While the cross is found everywhere in the practices of resistance, the Christian symbol of Guadalupe is found only sporadically. Given that Guadalupe is the central Mexican religious female image, her lesser role is notable. Understandably, in the context of the feminicide, the shared event of the crucifixion of Jesus resonates at a deeper level. To put this resonance in theological language, perhaps the practitioners are identifying female humanity with *imago Christi*, that is, claiming that female humanity as female is called to "be conformed to the image of Christ."[32] This claim would mean, of course, that the historical Jesus does not exhaust the meaning of Christ. While practitioners presumably would not describe what they are doing in this manner, their practice orients us toward the affirmation of woman as *imago Christi*. In this particular case, for the practitioners to claim Guadalupe as a shared event would not make as radical of a statement.

The symbol of exodus serves as another shared event. By laying claim to exodus in their 230-mile march from Chihuahua City to one of the international bridges in downtown Juárez, the practitioners interpret as their own the passage from bondage to freedom. Some might even claim that their march has its own Pharaoh figure in the person of Chihuahua's then Governor Patricio Martinez and his attempts to stop the march at the Juárez city limits. His attempt served as a no to the women's affirmation of female humanity, to their pursuit of a more democratic Juárez that welcomes female voices in public discourse and honors the dignity of female humanity. Perhaps for some, their lengthy march reflects a pilgrimage, a journey with not only political significance but theological significance as well. Perhaps this march is waged in the hope that God will listen to prayers and pleas for an end to the tragedy of Juárez.

We find another series of shared events in the selection of days commemorating women and honoring women's contributions for marches of protest. For example, marches have regularly taken place on November 25, the International Day for the Elimination of Violence against Women. By scheduling a march on this day, practitioners link the violence against women in Juárez to the violence against the Mirabal sisters of the Dominican Republic.[33] Perhaps the association drawn between these two horrific experiences will elevate concern for the women in Juárez and will link this tragedy to the long history of tragic acts of violence against women. Likewise, such an association may suggest that women have courageously and repeatedly worked toward a more life-giving society throughout the course of history, even when it would likely cost them their lives, as in the case of the Mirabal sisters. To make this association suggests that the Juárez feminicide, disastrously, is *not* an historical aberration. To march on November 25 may build, in the imagination of participants, a solidarity across the course of history with others who have resisted violence against women and with others who will do the same in the future.

By holding up particular shared events, practitioners forge a community among themselves and with others who find their vision compelling.

Ideal Extension of the Self

Community comes into being when individuals not only claim particular shared events as meaningful but also when they ideally extend their own lives so that the work they do together, along with its past, present, and future, represents for each participating member her or his life writ large. When those who suffer feminicide gather for practices of resistance and protest, they draw a connection between their lives and the lives of women and men who have long since died, as well as between their lives now and the lives of those who will be part of generations yet to come. This ideal extension of their lives means that they understand their lives in a fashion that takes on past glories and future promises. Thus, these practitioners join their resistance to past efforts to denounce and dismantle atrocious evil and to any future resistance to assaults on female dignity and the dignity of us all.[34]

Practitioners are making a judgment that by extending their lives far into the past and far into the future they enter more deeply into the gift of life today and enhance it. So when the practitioners march in the Exodus for Life or when they paint crosses pink, they extend their lives back in time to the exodus event and to the crucifixion of Jesus, as well as forward in time to the future promise that each of these events carry, to life as members of the chosen people of God and to the promise of resurrection. An individual who understands their life as extended in this way sees their legacy and significance in a manner larger than what can be contained in their own brief lifetime and earthly existence. Thus, practitioners are interpreting their life span in the context of a much longer temporal trajectory.[35] This ideal extension of the self necessitates an interpretation. One must develop some sort of reason, which can be drawn from any of several realms of human experience, for taking on or resisting past glories and future promises. Thus, one must make a judgment concerning the extent to which the ideal past and a hoped-for future enter into one's life and provide direction. Needless to say, when individuals see their lives as extended in this way, it means that they are conscious of their collective life as a community.

The practices of resistance affirm the lives of Latinas in Juárez yet to be born. Through these practices, women are affirming and pursuing the creation of a city radically different from the one they inherited. They are saying that we know we can create a city more in keeping with God's reign, one that more fully respects its female citizens. The use of religious imagery and resources furthers a demand that the heinous sociocide transpiring gives way to a liberative and humanizing society. The practices affirm that a more humanizing society is possible. What the practitioners demonstrate for is not utopia but rather a society that is more democratic and more just than the current body politic of Juárez. By their practices, they are asserting that a more humane society is possible.

By ideally extending their lives in time, the practitioners constitute a community in solidarity with those who have defended human dignity in the past, particularly female human dignity, and with those yet to be born.

Time Process

Most significantly, a community comes into being through its consciousness of both its history and its hope for the future. "A true community is essentially a product of a time-process."[36] A community is formed and sustained when each member interprets the community's past toward an ideal future that its members envision in the context of present experience. This interpretation reflects, at least roughly, a coherency. It is through a complex and lengthy process that a community develops some consciousness of its past, whether real or ideal, and generates intentions for its future. Obviously, memory and narrative play central roles. A community's "time process" serves an integrating function in which a community reads shared events, past and future, in the present in a manner that allows each individual to extend their lives ideally and well beyond their life span.

Community is not a "compounding of consciousness." If it were, it would become synonymous with a crowd, amorphous and lacking stability. To equate a community with a crowd would imply that the individual consciousness of each participant is absorbed, even if only temporarily. A crowd is not a community because, even though a crowd has a mind, it has "no institutions, no organization, no coherent unity, no history, no traditions." A community, Royce tells us, is not what William James understood as a blending of several consciousnesses or "a sort of mystical loss of personality on the part of its members."[37]

Rather, just as individual lives are constituted by stories, stories likewise constitute and unify communal life. The stories that members of a community tell themselves about their community reflect the community's consciousness of itself. In many respects, selves and communities are similar. At any one moment in time, the self is conscious to only a fragment of the self. For the self is, "by its very essence, a being with a past" and given to the "pursuit of its own chosen good." Thus I can recognize myself as historical continuity, as made up of the goals that I sought out yesterday and still seek today. Over time I continue to pursue an idea of myself. "In brief, my idea of myself is an interpretation of my past—linked also with an interpretation of my hope and intentions as to my future."[38] The self is a community, and so are many members who together share an awareness of themselves through time. As Royce observes:

> When many contemporary and distinct individual selves so interpret, each his [or her] own personal life, that each says of an individual past or of a determinate future event or deed: "That belongs

to my life;" "That occurred, or will occur, to me," then these many selves may be defined as hereby constituting, in a perfectly definite and objective, but also in a highly significant, sense, a community. They may be said to constitute a community *with reference* to that particular past or future event, or group of events, which each of them accepts or interprets as belonging to his [or her] own personal past or to his [or her] own individual future. A community constituted by the fact that each of its members accepts as part of his [or her] own individual life and self the same *past* events that each of his [or her] fellow-members accepts, may be called a *community of memory*. Such is any group of persons who individually either remember or commemorate the same dead—each one finding, because of personal affection or of reverence for the dead, that those whom he commemorates form for him a part of his [or her] own past existence. A community constituted by the fact that each of its members accepts, as part of his [or her] own individual life and self, the same expected *future* events that each of his [or her] fellows accepts, may be called a *community of expectation*, or upon occasion, a *community of hope*.[39]

The practitioners in Juárez have formed a community because through their actions they have interpreted a *past* they have claimed (for example, the cross and exodus) toward the *future* promise of these two historical events in the context of the *present* experience of feminicide.

On a public, collective level, these Latinas have engaged in a communal time process by developing a narrative of their own, one in which they see themselves as moral agents and subjects of their own history. They recognize what Ada María Isasi-Díaz has observed: "large-scale social changes that make liberation possible necessitate changes of heart and mind that are not possible on the grounds of reason alone. People need a story."[40] For these practitioners to develop their own story carries enormous import, because in doing so they "conceive a new and just world order but also because [their stories motivate all participants to] remain faithful to the struggle to make this a reality."[41]

Perhaps nothing manifests the communal time process more strikingly than the way in which the practitioners have integrated two distinct symbol systems in their practices. As already mentioned, on the one hand, they draw on two Christian symbols, the cross and exodus, and on the other hand, they make use of days commemorating and honoring women (March 8, November 25, February 14) and use the color pink to paint crosses—pink being a color traditionally associated with women and girls. What matters here is the integration. Perhaps this integration calls into question Christianity's traditional patriarchal mindset, an often operative presumption on the part of most believers that maleness and divinity are essential to one another in a fundamental way. By integrating female representations into the core symbols of the Christian social imaginal world, these practitioners are in effect calling Christian believers to conversion, to critically question the ways in which patriarchal as well as kyriarchal thinking and practice have seriously compromised and distorted Christianity. Indeed, these practitioners invite believing Christians to recognize the utter radicality of the gospel message, a message that affirms women as *imago Christi*. Now, the practitioners would likely not express the message of their practices as I have done—they create their practices based on their intuition. Notwithstanding, their insight into the gospel message is a profound articulation of community driving toward salvation.

Perhaps this integration also invites the women who have known the searing pain of losing a daughter and the endless trauma of living in irrational, chaotic violence to greater intimacy in their relationship with God. To bring their feelings of rage, outrage, madness, numbness, despair, and perhaps even hate before God. In the mystery that is God, one cannot anticipate what awaits.

Through the communal time process, a community comes to know itself more deeply by laying claim to history and time on a large scale. As practitioners interpret symbols, be they Christian symbols or symbols of female humanity, they give an account of who they are today in light of their reading of the past and the future.

⊠　　⊠　　⊠

Significant here is the cohesion of these three conditions of community: namely, that participants all concur that certain shared events bear meaning for each of them both individually and collectively; that individuals see the meaning of their lives as extended beyond the limits of their lifetimes; and that participants recognize the ways in which they are part of a time process. These three conditions together deepen the communal vision of participants by furthering a social coherence and visibility.

Furthering the Realization of Salvation

Community comes into being and is sustained through the practices of resistance. These practices, because they are fundamentally an interpretation, create community. An interpretation invariably has some purpose or aim orienting it, and in the process, an interpreter through her or his interpretation strives to create a unity of consciousness with those who find the particular interpretation compelling. This in turn forms and sustains a community.[42] But the practices of resistance do more than point to the primacy of community: they (ideally) suggest that salvation in history is furthered to the degree that the spiritual unity of the world is made more visible. What the practices (ideally) reveal is that salvation is realized through the forging of a particular kind of community, one that reveals clearly the interrelatedness of all humanity—past, present, and future— and the interrelatedness of humanity with the whole of creation.[43] Obviously, even at their best, the practices of resistance offer us only a glimpse of salvation in history, a glimpse that is necessarily fleeting and fragile.

We must appreciate that when we affirm the communal, interrelated nature of all that is, it implies that the purview of salvation concerns all of humanity and all of creation. The human condition invariably entails a conscious longing for salvation, a longing for a reality greater than the fragmentary, chaotic, at-times-irrational experience that is our experience of living. We are social creatures. We need turn no further than our system of internment for an example illustrating this point. It is no surprise that solitary confinement ranks at the apex of punishment. We depend upon one another for our psychological development, for our social well-being, for our very survival. Our need for one another comes more sharply into view in the experience of evil. This experience encourages us to realize that only some form of communion, or community, can possibly save us. It is a particular form of community that furthers salvation in history. And the church at its best, that is the church actively discerning the outpouring of the Holy Spirit, mediates the birth of this new community.

What does it mean that a salvific community is one that makes the spiritual unity of the world more visible? Three marks distinguish the spiritual unity of the world. First, a salvific community must be oriented toward the widest possible communal vision, one extensively inclusive; and because it inclines this way, it must have the most vulnerable at the center of its vision. Second, its orienting vision must not be a synthesizing vision but rather one that reflects a "unity-in-difference," meaning one that safeguards the integrity of each distinct self while seeking an expanded unity of consciousness. Third, this vision must actively discern the work of the Holy Spirit, who guides all humans and all of creation (past, present, and future) toward a realization of the spiritual interrelatedness of the whole. This realization comes clearly into focus through the subordination of evil, even though the endeavor to subordinate evil remains inevitably fragile. We will now look at each of these three.

Toward the Widest Possible Communal Vision

The salvation of human persons essentially comes about through devotion and dedication, initially to a particular community. In the experience of devotion to a particular community, ideally human persons learn to dedicate themselves to a purpose that stretches well beyond their own personal gain. And, ideally, their given community itself strives after the greatest good for all, in terms of both individual members and the community itself. The community orients itself toward the greatest good through ongoing processes of its own ethical transformation. So while human persons learn to love a very particular community, the discipline of loving a particular community can open human persons to others so radically that their openness ultimately includes the universal community of all human beings and of creation. Our love of community, then, should extend beyond our own group; beyond all humans living now; and even beyond all humans that have ever lived, are living, or will live. So while every interpretation that sustains community is situated and particular, if it is to further salvation, it must point toward the widest possible communal vision.[44]

If we are to emerge from the ravages of this feminicide with some measure of our humanity, it will only be because those who have lost the most in this tragedy nonetheless desire a more reconciled and just human community than the one they came to know in the feminicide. And while their practices of resistance are directed at the authorities in Juárez, these same practices, understood in the best possible light, are directed well beyond Juárez. The practices of resistance signal that those who have suffered the greatest loss—the senseless, brutal execution of their beloved daughters—have chosen not to allow their suffering to devolve into a destructive rage aimed at others or themselves but have chosen instead to prevail over the effects of evil they know only too well. This perspective demonstrates not an easy optimism but rather a sober hope. As those who reflect on history know, humanity in every age has seen the wreckage of many failures. Human tragedies appear regularly on the stage of life. The courage of those who suffer to prevail in the face of evil is no sure thing, yet when they do prevail they create a space from which we may offer an account of hope, and we may rest assured about the possibility of salvation.

Salvation is realized when we make visible the most expansive understanding of community. The poor play a preeminent role in this process because they feel materially and acutely the effects of collective sin. Their vulnerable situation means that they are less able to cushion themselves against the impact of the world's heinous evils. Moral evil and failing, as in the feminicide, reflects sin as a collective reality, a reality that makes possible and much more likely the occurrence of individual sins. It is the collective sin "that destroys history and hinders the future that God wanted for history; this collective sin is what causes death to reign over the world, and hence, we must be freed from our collective work of death in order to form once more the people of God."[45]

The work of salvation concerns concurrently both the political liberation of the people as well as their turning to God. Jon Sobrino captures well the confluence of these ideas when he writes, "In historical language, the poor have a humanizing potential because they offer community against individualism, co-operation against selfishness, simplicity against opulence, and openness to transcendence against blatant positivism, so prevalent in the civilization of the Western world. It is true, of course, that not all the poor offer this, but it is also true that they do offer it and, structurally speaking, in a form not offered by the First World."[46] Generally, the poor are more receptive to God's presence in their lives and more willing to turn to God. Their vulnerability can and often does afford them a readiness.

What those who have suffered the most desire, express, and realize through their practices of resistance is a vision for the world that deeply affirms the dignity of all human beings but especially the most vulnerable among us, which in this case means poor, brown women. The realization of this vision is all the more precious in light of the irrevocable and horrific past that those who suffer know. In many respects, their vision for the world mirrors the vision that Jesus lived and died defending. "In being condemned personally, Jesus had to learn the road to definitive salvation—a salvation . . . that was essentially a matter of the coming of God's Reign and not a personal resurrection separate from what had been his earthly preaching of the Reign."[47] Analogous to Jesus, many who suffer feminicide have come to see that salvation entails not only a personal release from the horror of the feminicide but rather, and more significantly, a deliverance that is collective, social in nature, and, in other words, a deliverance that makes the reign of God more socially real[48] as well as more personally real.

At their best, the practices of resistance also undermine the trajectory of sociocide brought on by the brutal killing of women. The practices stand for the proposition that we all have a stake in what happens to poor, brown women in Juárez. As such, they invite conversion. They invite us to change the way we view ourselves, God, the world, and others. The practices subvert the evil of the feminicide and, in so doing, encourage us to see our communion with one another in a more transparent, active, and coherent manner. Thus, we come to know more deeply our own desire for final wholeness and reconciliation. When practices of resistance point toward the largest possible community, when they honor and respect differences while furthering spiritual unity, and when they provide us with a glimpse of divine mystery, all these confirm for us that in spite of the chaotic, irrational, terrorizing evil of the feminicide, we can know a God who saves, a God who responds to our deepest desire for healing and wholeness.

A Manifestation of "Unity-in-Difference"

Salvation in history is realized through dedication to a particular community that, at its best, strives after the widest possible communal vision. However, this raises the question of how love of a community that furthers salvation does not lead to a synthesis that compromises the uniqueness of each member. Why would the all-encompassing vision not reduce or eliminate the particularity of members?

Interpretation, which sustains community, seeks out the meaning of a given distinct idea *in light of others* so as to invent a "realm of conscious unity."[49] This can come about only when the interpreter so genuinely understands the motivation, value, and contribution of each distinct idea that the interpreter makes each of those ideas his or her own. Obviously, the value of distinct ideas can vary enormously, making judgment integral to interpretation. The ultimate interpreter is God. Furthermore, this understanding of interpretation is a credible response to the classic philosophical problem of the one and the many, in that the integrity of each distinct self is honored while a unity of consciousness is sought. Thus, the unity sought and ideally achieved exists in a much larger consciousness. The integrity of the formerly estranged ideas is not compromised in the process because the integrity of each takes on new meaning. In the practices of resistance, because core Christian symbols (for example, the cross and exodus) are interpreted in light of representations of female humanity (for example, pink crosses or the various days commemorating and honoring women), each can be understood *in light of the other* and, in the process, the particularity of each is enhanced and deepened.

This dynamic engagement means that this feminicide can be interpreted as a crucifixion of female humanity. Indeed, the proliferation of pink crosses would suggest nothing less. Yet historically, the crucifixion has been associated with maleness in the person of Jesus. María Pilar Aquino has consistently argued that "theological discourse that begins from and speaks about the crucified majorities, the suffering peoples, the great masses of the poor is insufficient if it does not specify that these majorities are women."[50] In the context of the feminicide, Aquino's claim takes on greater poignancy. The feminicide in Juárez demands that we begin to understand crucifixion not only in terms of the poor (of which women and children number in the majority) but also in terms of women as women. Through their reinterpretation of the Christian symbol of the cross, the creators of the practices of resistance shine a spotlight on the relationship between female humanity and the possibility of salvation. As Elizabeth A. Johnson avers:

> The Christian story of salvation involves not only God's compassionate will to save but also the method by which this will becomes effective, namely, by God's plunging into sinful human history and transforming it from within. The early Christian axiom "What is not assumed is not redeemed, but what is assumed is saved by union with God" sums up the insight that Christ's solidarity with all of humanity is what is crucial for salvation. "*Et homo factus est*," "and became a human being": thus does the Nicene creed confess the universal relevance of the incarnation by the use of the inclusive *homo*.

But if in fact what is meant is *et vir factus est* (became a man) with stress on sexual manhood, if maleness is essential for the christic role, then women are cut out of the loop of salvation, for female sexuality is not taken on by the Word made flesh. If maleness is constitutive for the incarnation and redemption, female humanity is not assumed and therefore not saved.[51]

Indeed, then, we can read these practices of resistance to affirm that female humanity is assumed in the incarnation and thus can be saved. The use of the cross in these practices suggests parallels between the murder of these girls and women and the murder of Jesus. Both were victims of the unjust practices of the state and of the reputedly compromised complicity of their local religious leaders. Both knew the horrific angst of feeling abandoned by God and allowed to perish. The horrific executions of both were intended as public billboards. Jesus' crucifixion served as a warning and threat to anyone who would dare challenge the Roman Empire's authority. The dead bodies of these girls and women were often left in public places, flaunting the fact that poor females could be brutally killed with impunity, ultimately a warning to any woman of modest resources who sought to stand up for herself. She could be killed and no one would be held accountable. Implicit here is the message that, like Jesus, poor girls' and women's bodies are disposable and have no standing before the state or, apparently, in the eyes of church authorities.

What is more, the practices turn our attention to the gendered[52] nature of this contemporary crucifixion. As a "crucified people," the victims of this feminicide are among "a vast portion of humankind, which is literally and actually crucified by natural oppression and especially by historical and personal oppressions."[53] The victims exemplify a group "from whom the sin of the world continues to take away all human form, and whom the powers of this world dispossess of everything, seizing even their lives, above all their lives."[54] However, because the feminicide is a crucifixion of females as females, it fundamentally transforms the meaning of a crucified people. The feminicide provokes a Christian iconoclasm in that it shatters what comes to mind when we use the term *crucifixion*. For example, in the following passage, Jon Sobrino describes the high price paid by the crucified people themselves and those who speak out on their behalf. He writes: "As long as [the crucified peoples] suffer patiently, they are regarded as having a certain goodness, simplicity, piety especially, which is unenlightened and superstitious, but none-the-less surprises the educated and secularized people from other worlds. Yet when they decide to live and call on God to defend them and set them free, then they are not even recognized as God's people, and the well-known litany is intoned. They are subversives, terrorists, criminals, atheists, Marxists, and communists. Despised and murdered in life, they are also despised in death."[55] However, in the case of the feminicide, the well-known litany intoned must now include the labels of "prostitutes," "women of a double life," "women who invite violence into their lives by 'dressing provocatively,'" and so forth. Female *crucifixion*, for Christians, changes the terms of the discourse.

This extended analysis shows that the particularity of Christian symbols is enhanced when they are interpreted in light of representations of female humanity. This creates an expanded unity of consciousness, inviting love of a more universal human community while respecting the integrity of particular experiences. The focus here is on women as a collective, but the principle at play applies equally to their respective experiences as individual victims of the feminicide.

Toward an Understanding of Divine Nature

If we hold that to be salvific, interpretations must direct us toward the spiritual unity of all humankind and the whole of creation, then perhaps we need to rethink how we understand God's salvific action in the world. The practices of resistance, in my judgment, reflect the richly dynamic presence of the Holy Spirit and suggest that we look in the direction of the triune God. They affirm what Elizabeth A. Johnson once observed:

> The very framing of the subject at hand as "Jesus and salvation" is too narrow. Salvation comes from God through Jesus by the power of the Spirit. It is the gift of the whole triune God acting *ad extra*. To concentrate on Jesus alone in a kind of Christomonism has led historically to many dead ends for understanding as well as to imperialist action toward those who do not believe in Christ.
>
> In particular, the Spirit has received short shrift in our understanding of salvation. But as history goes on after the historical Jesus, salvation is primarily a pneumatological phenomenon. It is Spirit-Sophia-Shekinah who provides the connection between the

historical Jesus and the present community, and who empowers the present experience of salvation. The whole triune mystery of God, with Jesus as the concrete sacrament, needs to be rewoven into the narrative of salvation.[56]

By situating the question of salvation in the context of the "whole triune mystery of God" and by attending to the work of the Holy Spirit, we open up new ways of understanding how God responds to our longing for wholeness and reconciliation, particularly if we take this one step further. More precisely, if we conceive of God's action in the world as essentially an interpretive dynamic, then we can more decidedly affirm and honor not only the uniqueness of each person but also the interrelatedness of all.

This approach would further suggest that in and through our relationship to God we most authentically know ourselves and others, and are known. For in God our personal and our social nature is fully transparent, since, as Royce argues: "How better can we conceive [divine nature] than in the form of the Community of Interpretation" (a term of art for the triune God), "and above all in the form of the Interpreter" (a term of art for the Holy Spirit), "who interprets all to all, and each individual to the world, and the world of spirits to each individual."[57]

Conceiving God in this way could be richly suggestive for understanding salvation and for engaging Christology.[58] This approach would foreground the Holy Spirit as the active guide of the universal community of humankind and as the one who pushes forward our understanding of Jesus the Christ. It is *in* the symbol of the Spirit that we are loyal and we are one. When we love a community as we would love another person, only then do we participate in the ongoing revelation of the world as a realization of the spiritual unity of the whole.[59] "The core of the faith is the Spirit, the Beloved Community, the work of grace, the atoning deed, and the saving power of the loyal life."[60] Salvation comes about through devotion to a cause, through an expanded self-consciousness converted by our love of community. Ultimately, our cause is the reign of God. Salvation requires the dynamic work of the Holy Spirit to deliver us and to stir us to unity. The action of the triune God prods us to become part of the endless process in which salvific interpretations emerge out of an ongoing contest with evil, that is, with all that would impede and disrupt the emergence of the unity of the universal community.

Catherine Mowry LaCugna's work points in this direction with her assertion that communion is the meaning of salvation.

> *Living as persons in communion, in right relationship, is the meaning of salvation and the ideal of the Christian faith.* God is interactive, neither solitary nor isolated. Human beings are created in the image of the relational and gradually are being perfected in that image (*theōsis*), making more and more real the communion of all creatures with one another. The doctrine of the Trinity stresses the relational character of personhood over and against the reduction of personhood to individual self-consciousness, and also emphasizes the uniqueness and integrity of personhood over and against the reduction of personhood to a product of social relations. Thus it can serve as a critique of cultural norms of personhood, whether that of "rugged individualism" or the "me first" morality, as well as patterns of inequality based on gender, race, ability, and so forth.[61]

To frame salvation and the image of God in this manner enables us to claim that without the realization of the reign of God in history, which necessarily has political and ethical dimensions, salvation cannot attain its fulfillment. Its fulfillment entails a reflection of the Trinity. To be made in the image and likeness of God who is trinitarian means that we are inherently social. Thus, the social dimension of salvation, made manifest when the spiritual unity of the world is most transparently visible, reflects an image of God as Trinity.

Even so, a social approach to salvation affirms the transcendence of God in that it views salvation—while realized in history, while including the political, and while involving the ethical push/pull of human decision making—as more than all of these.[62] Jesus models for us the pursuit of the reign of God. While he did not seek the reign through the acquisition of political power, neither did he pursue it in a manner divorced from historical embodiment. What we come to see in Jesus is that the reign of God does concern the political order wherein human beings live in fidelity with God.[63]

What does this line of thinking suggest to us about Jesus Christ's role in the realization of salvation? The salvific role of Jesus must be centered on his ministry, which included healing, table fellowship, forgiveness, and insistence on a just world. It is Jesus' ministry in relation to the paschal mystery that must be at the forefront of the doctrine of salvation. Further,

Jesus' role must be understood in the context of the triune mystery of God. "Salvation comes from God through Jesus by the power of the Spirit."[64] By the power of the Spirit and through Jesus' ministry, cross, and resurrection, Jesus subverted evil, making the salvific community—that is, the reign of God—more visible in this world. Anselm's contribution fails to take into account that we cannot adequately understand salvation apart from the ministry of Jesus. It is the whole of Jesus' life that reflects the dynamic presence of the Spirit and makes visible the reign of God.

The practices of resistance can be read as an expression of love for the community of Juárez and as an attempt to seek out the Holy Spirit. They pursue a larger truth. They embody what Roberto S. Goizueta observed when he wrote: "To know the truth is to become a participant in the life of the crucified and risen Christ, which in turn implies a participation in the lives of those peoples who are themselves crucified victims, those whose wounded bodies are the mirrors of our souls."[65]

We can see the Holy Spirit's role through a consideration of how the practices mediate participation in Christian truth by taking participants to the space of the "empty tomb."[66] Analogous to the ambiguous space of the empty tomb, the practices invite participants to enter into the liminal character of their efforts to come to grips with this tragedy, and to do so in the company of others attempting the same and in the company of God. Through the practices, participants negotiate the place in between despair and hope; in between the tragedy of crucifixion and the hope of vindication, the promise of a resurrection. Through their practices, the practitioners issue a challenge to theological discourse to "take seriously the space of the brutal victimization of women and other nonpersons and at the same time claim wo/men's agency in either collaborating with or transforming such spaces of death."[67]

In the "empty tomb" tradition, as developed by Elisabeth Schüssler Fiorenza, we discover a space "for affirming the vindication of the Crucified Ones and their agency of possibility for becoming the Living Ones." This tradition can serve as a means "to develop and adjudicate our own christological meaning-making in the face of violence and killing today."[68] In some real measure, the practices create a space for the feminicide's resistors to hurl their anguished cries, "My God, my God why have you abandoned me? Why have you abandoned your daughters of Juárez?" Are not such cries akin to a call to God and a call upon God to act so that the historical trajectory within which the women of Juárez find themselves does not simply continue into the future but rather that their cries lead to a "break [in] the process, and that [the hoped-for] break in the process is where something more than history becomes present in history"? The something "more" than history is recognition of the possibility of novelty within a given historical situation that "breaks into the normality of the experience. . . . History is the arena of novelty, of creativity; God's self-revelation comes by making 'more' history, that is, a greater and better history than existed in the past."[69]

Ambiguity abounds in the space of the empty tomb. As Schüssler Fiorenza explains, "The texts of the empty tomb tradition take suffering and death seriously but do not see them as having the 'last word' or a religious-theological value in themselves. Since G*d was absent in the execution of the Just One, the women's presence under the cross is a witness to this absence. The tomb is the brutal final reality that eclipses G*d and vitiates all possibilities for the future. But the 'tomb is empty!' "[70] Like the tradition of the empty tomb, the practices encourage a candid and openhearted reckoning with the feminicide's unimaginable violence and social trauma. Many of the practices lay claim to particular places, locations in Juárez to remember the murdered, to demand that these murders stop, and to infuse and inhabit these places with a more egalitarian, democratic, and life-giving spirit in keeping with belief in a God who unceasingly loves and demands justice. The tomb is empty, which means that the Spirit of God is here in our midst making resurrection and salvation possible in the here and now. Death does not have the last word. A new life in the embrace of God is possible.

To whatever degree the practices of resistance further our communion with one another and with God; to whatever degree they subvert evil; to whatever degree they reveal the visibility and vitality of the spiritual unity of the world, they nevertheless everywhere retain a vulnerable existence. They are vulnerable to human failing. We are fallible. Our commitment to community cannot be coerced. The fragility of our efforts toward community is nowhere more apparent than in the midst of tragedy and in our confrontation with evil. Salvation in history depends primarily on the difficult endeavor to love again in the midst of tragedy, to act on our love for community while in the midst of our experience of evil.

⌗   ⌗   ⌗

For the spiritual unity of the world to become visible, and thus for salvation to be partially realized in history, we need a compelling vision and a lived experience that foster a love for community that extends to all, an expanded consciousness that fully respects the integrity of each individual self, and an understanding of God that foregrounds the triune mystery and the work of the Holy Spirit. The Christian claim that salvation comes through Jesus the Christ must be considered in light of the doctrines of Trinity and of the Holy Spirit.

Further, we realize salvation when we seek the greatest good through the subversion of evil, which the practitioners exemplify through their practices. Salvific interpretations stand for the proposition that some ills, when faced and used to create some greater good, afford us a glimpse of the spiritual ascendancy of the good because the spiritual unity of the world comes into sharper focus.

Conclusion

We can understand salvation only through our communion with one another, with God, and with creation. Without a love for community, without an active drive to make more visible and vital the many ways we are interrelated, salvation is impossible. We need to interpret salvation through a personal and individual lens, but when we reduce salvation to no more than this, it is not Christian salvation. To interpret salvation socially is to bring the crucified peoples down from the cross; is to further the reign of God in our midst; is to know God's self-gift of healing, reconciliation, and wholeness. Through their public actions, those who have suffered feminicide in Ciudad Juárez have laid claim to their religious birthright, revealing community driving toward salvation. They have made it known that the grotesque execution of Juárez's daughters is not, cannot, and will not be the *last word* on their lives. The victims' struggle for life does not end in their execution and death. The practitioners have tilted the community of Juárez and all of us toward the possibility of hope and salvation.

Notes

Foreword

1. Irving Greenberg, "Cloud of Smoke, Pillar of Fire," in *Holocaust: Religious and Philosophical Implications*, John Roth and Michael Berenbaum, eds. (St. Paul: Paragon, 1998), 331.

Introduction

1. Karl Rahner, "History of the World and Salvation-History," trans. Karl Kruger, in *Theological Investigations*, vol. 5, *Later Writings* (Baltimore: Helicon, 1966); Edward Schillebeeckx, *Church: The Human Story of God*, trans. John Bowden (New York: Crossroad, 1994); Rosemary Radford Ruether, *New Woman, New Earth: Sexist Ideologies and Human Liberation* (Boston: Beacon, 1995); Rosemary Radford Ruether, *Women and Redemption: A Theological History* (Minneapolis: Fortress Press, 1998); Gustavo Gutiérrez, *A Theology of Liberation: History, Politics, and Salvation*, trans. Sister Caridad Inda and John Eagleson (Maryknoll: Orbis, 1988).

2. Philip Gourevitch, *We Wish to Inform You That Tomorrow We Will Be Killed with Our Families: Stories from Rwanda* (New York: Picador, 1998).

3. Rosa Linda Fregoso and Cynthia Bejarano, eds., *Terrorizing Women: Feminicide in the Americas* (Durham: Duke University Press, 2010); Diana Washington Valdez, *The Killing Fields: Harvest of Women* (Burbank: Peace at the Border, 2006), 255–63.

4. Linda Alcoff and Elizabeth Potter, eds., *Feminist Epistemologies* (New York: Routledge, 1993), 3.

5. Ignacio Ellacuría, "The Historicity of Christian Salvation," in *Mysterium Liberationis: Fundamental Concepts in Liberation Theology*, ed. Ignacio Ellacuría and Jon Sobrino (Maryknoll: Orbis, 1993), 253–54.

6. Mary McClintock Fulkerson, *Places of Redemption: Theology for a Worldly Church* (New York: Oxford University Press, 2007), 14.

7. David Tracy, "Saving from Evil: Salvation and Evil Today," in *The Fascination of Evil*, ed. David Tracy and Hermann Häring (London: SCM, 1998), 114–15.

Chapter 1: Suffering—A Social Reality

1. I use the words *we* and *our* throughout this text to situate the reader as active and responsible in the context of the argument I am advancing.

2. For a sustained discussion, see Susan Sontag, *Regarding the Pain of Others* (New York: Picador, 2003).

3. Rosa Linda Fregoso and Cynthia Bejarano, eds., *Terrorizing Women: Femicide in the Americas* (Durham: Duke University Press, 2010), 2.

4. As quoted by Fregoso and Bejarano, *Terrorizing Women*, 2. The original is published in Brook Sari Moshan, "Women, War and Words: The Gender Component in the Permanent International Criminal Court's Definition of Crimes Against Humanity," *Fordham International Law Journal* 22 (1998): 155.

5. According to Rosa-Linda Fregoso and Cynthia Bejarano, "While the English-language use of femicide dates back two centuries, [Diana E. H.] Russell . . . [in her 1977 "Report on the International Tribunal on Crimes against Women" *Frontiers* 2, no. 1: 2] first used the concept in testimony before the first International Tribunal on Crimes against Women in Brussels in 1976, where she drew from the *Oxford English Dictionary*'s definition of femicide as 'the murder of women and girls by men.'" See Fregoso and Bejarano, *Terrorizing Women*, 37n21.

6. Fregoso and Bejarano, *Terrorizing Women*, 4.

7. Ibid.

8. Ibid., 5.

9. Johanna Ikonen, "Feminicide: The Case in Mexico and Guatemala" (Background Paper for European Parliament, April 19, 2006), http://www.europarl .europa.eu/meetdocs/2004_2009/documents/fd/droi20060419_h_backgroundnote _/droi20060419_h_backgroundnote_en.pdf. See also Monica A. Maher, "Daring to Dream: Faith and Feminicide in Latin America," in *Weep Not For Your Children: Essays on Religion and Violence*, ed. Lisa Isherwood and Rosemary Radford Ruether (Oakville, Conn.: Equinox, 2008), 187–213.

10. Diana Washington Valdez, *The Killing Fields: Harvest of Women* (Burbank: Peace at the Border, 2006), 363; Teresa Rodríguez, Diana Montané, and Lisa Pulitzer, *The Daughters of Juárez: A True Story of Serial Murder South of the Border* (New York: Atria, 2007), 38.

11. Diana Washington Valdez, "Mexico on Trial in Murders of Women," *El Paso Times*, April 30, 2009.

12. Rodríguez, Montané, and Pulitzer, *Daughters of Juárez*, 41.

13. Ibid., 39–41, 199–203, 211.

14. The following represent some of the contextual factors that led to the feminicide. It is taken from Rodríguez, Montané, and Pulitzer, *Daughters of Juárez*. All page numbers in parenthesis refer to Rodríguez's book. A number of social, political, and cultural factors contributed to the emergence of this feminicide. Beginning in the middle of the 1960s, the Mexican government authorized and implemented the Border Industrialization Program (BIP), with the goal of lessening the high unemployment rates in the northern border states of Mexico. U.S. corporations participated in this program by building factories all along the border. The 1982 devaluation of the Mexican peso prompted an increase in the number of factories built on the southern side of the border such that by 1991 there were 700 maquiladoras along the border, three hundred of which were in Ciudad Juárez. When then President Bill Clinton signed the North American Free Trade Agreement (NAFTA) in 1993 and began its implementation in 1994, he created a marked increase in the number of maquiladoras in Ciudad Juárez once again. Tijuana's growth meant that among Mexican border cities it had the largest number of new factories. However, Ciudad Juárez had the largest maquiladora workforce, a workforce in excess of 200,000 by 1994. For much of the 1990s, Juárez attracted tens of thousands of workers each year, all in search of a better life. The population in Juárez grew so rapidly that it was impossible for the public works infrastructure to keep up. For example, in 1995, Juárez had more than 6,000 cantinas but only 624 schools. During this period, estimates of greater Juárez's population ranged anywhere from 1.5 to 2 million residents (7–11). The managers of the maquiladora plants strongly preferred hiring women, believing that women could be paid a lower hourly wage than men. In addition, these managers thought that women possess superior manual dexterity and therefore can effectively accomplish repetitive tasks more quickly than men. Some social critics have noted that the employment of women in much larger numbers than men provoked an acute conflict over gender roles and that perhaps this conflict fueled the feminicide (71). In addition to prompting the growth of U.S. corporate factories in Mexico, NAFTA was also seen by drug traffickers as opening new possibilities for the flow of drugs. Drug traffickers figured out that the new NAFTA procedures for foreign exchange could be used to smuggle drugs across the border from Juárez into El Paso more efficiently. Moreover, during the mid-1990s, the leader of Mexico's largest drug cartel, Amado Carrillo Fuentes, lived in Juárez, and he became "responsible for importing as much as 70 percent of the cocaine that entered the U.S. annually" (92). In 1997, Carrillo died during a seriously flawed cosmetic surgery operation designed to change his physical appearance so that he could elude law enforcement. His death triggered a blood bath in Juárez among the leaders of the remaining drug cartels, each seeking to emerge as the new "kingpin." Eventually one emerged, and throughout the late 1990s and in the 2000s, large shipments of cocaine, heroin, methamphetamines, and marijuana came into the United States through Juárez and made their way up to Washington State and New York City and all points in between. This becomes significant in the story of the Juárez feminicide because in 2002 a federal judicial police officer, Mario Héctor Varela, was gunned down in Juárez by assassins with ties to the Juárez drug cartel. He was dubbed a corrupt narco-policeman by Mexican attorney general Jorge Madrazo Cuéllar. This same police officer was part of a special police task force charged with

investigating the abductions and murders of young women in Juárez. This incident marked one of the first public links between the feminicides and the Juárez narco-traffickers (91–96).

15. Rosa Linda Fregoso, "Toward a Planetary Civil Society," in *Women and Migration: In the U.S.-Mexico Borderlands*, ed. Denise A. Segura and Patricia Zavella (Durham: Duke University Press, 2007), 52.

16. While sources agree that María Sagrario González Flores worked at a maquiladora plant, there is disagreement about the name of the plant where she worked. Journalist Diana Washington Valdez claims that she worked at General Electric. See Valdez, *Killing Fields*, 35. Journalist Teresa Rodríguez claims she worked for Capco Crane & Hoist, a New England–based crane manufacturer located outside of Boston. See Rodríguez, Montané, and Pulitzer, *Daughters of Juárez*, 76.

Maquiladoras are U.S.-owned factories located in Mexico for the purpose of taking advantage of low-wage Mexican labor and tax breaks from the U.S. government. While a number of these factories were located in Juárez before 1993, the signing of NAFTA that year created an accelerated growth in the number of factories and the size of the workforce. By 1994 maquiladoras in Juárez employed over 200,000, which was the largest maquiladora workforce on the border.

17. Valdez, *Killing Fields*, 35–42; Rodríguez, Montané, and Pulitzer, *Daughters of Juárez*, 75–90.

18. The idea of these victims leading a *doble vida* ("double life") became one of the narratives put forward by the state. See Fregoso, "Toward a Planetary Civil Society," 37–39.

19. Rodríguez, Montané, and Pulitzer, *Daughters of Juárez*, 75–90.

20. Fregoso, "Toward a Planetary Civil Society," 37.

21. Valdez, *Killing Fields*, 8, 13, 49, 54, 90, 119, 207, 232, 244; Rodríguez, Montané, and Pulitzer, *Daughters of Juárez*, 36, 38, 41.

22. Valdez, *Killing Fields*, 161, 232, 233, 238.

23. Patriarchy, according to Rosemary Radford Ruether, is "the 'rule of the father,' . . . [and] refers to systems of legal, social, economic, and political relations that validate and enforce the sovereignty of male heads of families over dependent persons in the household. In classical patriarchal systems, . . . dependent persons included wives, unmarried daughters, dependent sons, and slaves, male and female." See Rosemary Radford Ruether, *Women Healing Earth* (London: SCM, 1996), 205–6.

24. Elisabeth Schüssler Fiorenza distinguishes kyriarchy from patriarchy. Kyriarchy is "the Greek word for the domination of elite propertied men over women and other men, whereas patriarchy is generally understood in feminist discourses in terms of western sex/gender system which posits a man/woman opposition." Elisabeth Schüssler Fiorenza, *Bread Not Stone: The Challenge of Feminist Biblical Interpretation* (Boston: Beacon, 1984), 211. More specifically, Schüssler Fiorenza clarifies that the "neologism *kyriarchy-kyriocentrism* (from Greek *kyrios* meaning lord, master, father, husband) seeks to express this interstructuring of domination and to replace the commonly used term *patriarchy*, which is often understood in terms of binary gender dualism. I have introduced this neologism as an analytic category in order to be able to articulate a more comprehensive systematic analysis, to underscore the complex interstructuring of domination, and to locate sexism and misogyny in

the political matrix or, better, patrix of a broader range of oppressions." Elisabeth Schüssler Fiorenza, *Rhetoric and Ethic: The Politics of Biblical Studies* (Minneapolis: Fortress Press, 1999), 5. See also Elisabeth Schüssler Fiorenza, *But She Said: Feminist Practices of Biblical Interpretation* (Boston: Beacon, 1992), 114–18, 122–25; Elisabeth Schüssler Fiorenza, *Jesus: Miriam's Child, Sophia's Prophet: Critical Issues in Feminist Christology* (New York: Continuum, 1994), 36.

25. Fregoso, "Toward a Planetary Civil Society," 54.

26. Catherine Bell, *Ritual: Perspectives and Dimensions* (New York: Oxford University Press, 1997), 82.

27. Fregoso, "Toward a Planetary Civil Society," 50–54.

28. Ibid., 51.

29. Valdez, *Killing Fields*; Fregoso, "Toward a Planetary Civil Society," 50.

30. Fregoso, "Toward a Planetary Civil Society," 36.

31. Ibid., 36.

32. Valdez, *Killing Fields*, 286.

33. While this chapter focuses on the feminicide taking place in Juárez, Chihuahua, I want to acknowledge that this type of tragedy has an all-too-long history and is regrettably present in many other communities today. There are similar patterns of the brutal killing of women in other parts of Mexico (e.g., Chihuahua City, Tijuana, Mexicali, Chiapas, Oaxaca, Quintana Roo, among others) as well as in Guatemala, Honduras, and Canada, to name a few. See Valdez, *Killing Fields*, 255–63; Ikonen, "Feminicide." See also Amnesty International's website at http://www.amnesty.org /en/campaigns/stop-violence-against-women. Tragically, the evil of femicide bears a long history, with numerous examples. One among them is the femicide in Uzbekistan between 1927 and 1930. See Marianne Kamp, "Femicide as Terrorism: The Case of Uzbekistan's Unveiling Murders," in *Belief and Bloodshed: Religion and Violence across Time and Tradition*, ed. James K. Wellman Jr. (Lanham: Rowman & Littlefield, 2007), 131–44.

34. Natalia Gómez Quintero and Noemí Gutiérrez, "Culpan a Minifaldas y Escotes de Ataques," *El Universal*, January 16, 2009, http://www2.eluniversal.com .mx/pls/impreso/version_imprimir.html?id_nota=165128&tabla=nacion; Rodríguez, Montané, and Pulitzer, *Daughters of Juárez*, 75–90.

35. Rebecca S. Chopp, *The Praxis of Suffering: An Interpretation of Liberation and Political Theologies* (Maryknoll: Orbis, 1986), 2.

36. Paul Farmer, "On Suffering and Structural Violence: A View from Below," in *Social Suffering*, ed. Arthur Kleinman, Veena Das, and Margaret Lock (Berkeley: University of California Press, 1997), 272.

37. Robert McAfee Brown, *Liberation Theology: An Introductory Guide* (Louisville: Westminster John Knox, 1993), 44.

38. Arthur Kleinman, Veena Das, and Margaret Lock, eds., *Social Suffering* (Berkeley: University of California Press, 1997), x–xi.

39. Kleinman, Das, and Lock, *Social Suffering*, x–xi.

40. Arthur Kleinman and Joan Kleinman, "The Appeal to Experience; The Dismay of Images: Cultural Appropriations of Suffering in Our Times," in *Social Suffering*, ed. Arthur Kleinman, Veena Das, and Margaret Lock (Berkeley: University of California Press, 1997), 2.

41. Ibid., 9.

42. Ibid., 18.

43. For an extended discussion of praxis and suffering see Chopp, *Praxis of Suffering*.

44. Kleinman, Das, and Lock, *Social Suffering*, xii.

45. Ibid., xii–xiii.

46. Ibid., ix.

47. These descriptors of "social suffering" are found in a Boston College graduate course syllabus authored by Dr. M. Shawn Copeland for her fall 2006 course titled *Social Suffering*.

48. For an extended example of "effective history," see Nancy Pineda-Madrid, "'Holy Guadalupe . . . Shameful Malinche?': Excavating the Problem of 'Female Dualism,' Doing Theological Spade Work," *Listening: Journal of Religion and Culture* 44/2 (Spring 2009): 71–87.

49. Hans-Georg Gadamer, *Truth and Method*, trans. Joel Weinsheimer and Donald G. Marshall, 2nd rev. ed. (New York: Continuum, 1997), 265–379.

50. Kleinman, Das, and Lock, *Social Suffering*, ix.

51. Ibid.

52. Ibid., xi.

53. Farmer, "On Suffering and Structural Violence," 261.

54. Many of these questions are suggested in Paul Farmer, "On Suffering and Structural Violence."

55. Rodríguez, Montané, and Pulitzer, *Daughters of Juárez*, 177–95, 261–89.

56. Fregoso, "Toward a Planetary Civil Society"; Alicia Schmidt Camacho, "La Ciudadana X: Reglamentando Los Derechos de las Mujeres en la Frontera México-Estados Unidos," in *Bordeando La Violencia Contra Las Mujeres en al Frontera Norte De México*, ed. Julia Monárrez Fragoso and María Socorro Tabuenca Córdoba (Mexico: El Colegio de la Frontera Norte, 2007), 19–48.

57. Kathleen Staudt, *Violence and Activism at the Border: Gender, Fear, and Everyday Life in Ciudad Juárez* (Austin: University of Texas Press, 2008), xi.

58. Elisabeth Schüssler Fiorenza, "Breaking the Silence—Becoming Visible," in *The Power of Naming: A Concilium Reader in Feminist Liberation Theology*, ed. Elisabeth Schüssler Fiorenza (Maryknoll: Orbis, 1996), 164.

59. Schmidt Camacho, "La Ciudadana X," 36–40; Fregoso, "Toward a Planetary Civil Society," 50–54; Staudt, *Violence and Activism at the Border*, 5.

60. This argument was made by Victor Quintana, a 2006 PRD (Revolutionary Democratic Party) candidate and professor of social communication at the Autonomous University of Juárez. For a discussion of his comments, see Saul Landau and Sonia Angulo Chaidez, "J.Lo Investigates the Juárez Murders," *Transnational Institute* (http://tni.org), June 2007, http://tni.org/article/jlo-investigates-juarez-murders.

61. Steev Hise, *On the Edge*, A new documentary about the femicide in Ciudad Juárez (IA Productions, 2006), 58 minutes.

62. Fregoso, "Toward a Planetary Civil Society," 40.

63. Ibid., 40, 41.

64. Ibid., 40.

65. Ibid, 40–42.

66. Ibid, 42–43.

67. Ibid., 46.

68. Ibid., 46–47.

69. Ibid., 38.

70. Ibid., 39.

71. Ibid.

72. Ibid.

73. Ibid, 50. See also Schmidt Camacho, "La Ciudadana X."

74. Staudt, *Violence and Activism at the Border*, 5.

75. Schmidt Camacho, "La Ciudadana X," 21.

76. In reference to a human being, *illegal* is a patently erroneous and highly offensive term. The very word connotes lack of any political standing or any right to citizenship in the polis. An act is "illegal," meaning that you as a member of the polis have violated one of the agreed upon standards set by the polis. A human being cannot be "illegal."

77. Schmidt Camacho, "La Ciudadana X," 37. Translation mine.

78. Ibid.

79. Rodríguez, Montané, and Pulitzer, *Daughters of Juárez*, 178, 252.

80. Ibid., 41, 231–60.

81. Ibid., 105, 113–25.

82. Maher, "Daring to Dream," 192.

83. Gómez Quintero and Gutiérrez, "Culpan a Minifaldas y Escotes de Ataques"; Jesusa Cervantes, "Cuestiona PRD Doble Moral de la Iglesia," *Proceso*, January 16, 2009.

84. Graciela Atencio, "El Feminicidio es el Exterminio de la Mujer en el Patriarcado: Monárrez Fragoso," *La Jornada* September 1, 2003, http://www.jornada .unam.mx/2003/09/01/articulos/61_juarez_monarrez.htm. Of particular note is the work of Mercy Sister Betty Campbell and Carmelite priest Father Peter Hinde and their ministry at Tabor House as well as the work of Ruben García of Casa Peregrina, all in Juárez.

85. Conferencia del Episcopado Mexicano, "Que en Cristo Nuestra Paz México Tenga Vida Digna," March 2010, http://www.cem.org.mx/prensa/comunicados-de -prensa/2390-que-en-cristo-nuestra-paz-mexico-tenga-vida-digna.html; Conferencia del Episcopado Mexicano, "Sedientos de las Estructuras Que Garanticen la Paz en México," March 9, 2010, http://www.cem.org.mx/prensa/comunicados-de-prensa/; Conferencia del Episcopado Mexicano, "Les Anunciamos a Jesucristo 'Su Venida Nos Ha Traído la Buena Noticia de la Paz' (Ef. 2, 17)," November 19, 2009, http://www .cem.org.mx/prensa/comunicados-de-prensa/.

86. Obispos de la P. E. de Chihuahua, "Déjense Reconciliar por Dios," March 2, 2009, http://www.cem.org.mx/secciones/diocesis-y-prelaturas/135-mensaje-cuaresma -p-e-chihuahua.html.

87. See "Que en Cristo Nuestra Paz México Tenga Vida Digna," par. 70.

88. Rodríguez, Montané, and Pulitzer, *Daughters of Juárez*, 175–78.

89. Ibid., 293.

90. Ibid., 72, 250. See also Valdez, *Killing Fields*, 35–42.

Chapter 2: Suffering, Social Imaginaries, and the Making of Evil

1. Emilie M. Townes, *Womanist Ethics and the Cultural Production of Evil* (New York: Palgrave Macmillan, 2006).

2. Charles Taylor, *Modern Social Imaginaries* (Durham: Duke University Press, 2004), 8–9, 24, 26

3. Ibid., 23.

4. Ibid., 183.

5. Kwok Pui-lan argues as much when she identifies the need for a reconceptualization of the relation between theology and empire. Analysis of the "theology-empire" relation would help us get at the underside of our social imagination. She rightly claims that we need to examine "the circulation of theological symbols and cultural capital in the colonial period and its permutations in late capitalism. An important theological agenda will be to analyze the use of theological symbols for the colonization of women's minds and bodies, as well as the reappropriation of such symbols for resistance, subversion, and empowerment." Kwok Pui-lan, *Postcolonial Imagination and Feminist Theology* (Louisville: Westminster John Knox, 2005), 144.

6. Octavio Paz, *The Labyrinth of Solitude, and The Other Mexico, Return to the Labyrinth of Solitude, Mexico and the United States, The Philanthropic Ogre*, trans. Lysander Kemp, Yara Milos, and Rachel Phillips Belash (New York: Grove, 1985), 332.

7. See, for example, Norma Alarcón, "Chicana's Feminist Literature: A Re-Vision Through Malintzin/or Malintzin: Putting Flesh Back on the Object," in *This Bridge Called My Back: Writings by Radical Women of Color*, ed. Cherríe Moraga and Gloria Anzaldúa, 2nd ed. (New York: Kitchen Table: Women of Color Press, 1983), 186–87.

8. Patriarchy, according to Rosemary Radford Ruether, is "the 'rule of the father,' . . . [and] refers to systems of legal, social, economic, and political relations that validate and enforce the sovereignty of male heads of families over dependent persons in the household. In classical patriarchal systems . . . dependent persons included wives, unmarried daughters, dependent sons, and slaves, male and female." See Rosemary Radford Ruether, *Women Healing Earth* (London: SCM, 1996).

9. The term means the violated woman.

10. Paz, *Labyrinth of Solitude*, 80, 81. In 2004 then–Boston Red Sox starting pitcher Pedro Martinez, after a tension-filled American League Championship game with the New York Yankees, remarked, "They beat me. They're that good right now. They're that hot. I just tip my hat and call the Yankees my daddy." His remark represents a contemporary example of this kind of thinking.

11. Paz backhandedly acknowledges his oversight in his dubious attempt to give some account of the extraordinary contributions of the Mexican intellectual Sor Juana Inés de la Cruz Paz: *Labyrinth of Solitude*, 109–16. See Octavio Paz, *Sor Juana Inés de la Cruz o Las Trampas de la Fe* (Barcelona: Seix Barral, S.A., 1982).

12. Alicia Schmidt Camacho, "La Ciudadana X: Reglamentando Los Derechos de las Mujeres en la Frontera México-Estados Unidos," in *Bordeando La Violencia Contra Las Mujeres en al Frontera Norte De México*, ed. Julia Monárrez Fragoso and

Maria Socorro Tabuenca Córdoba (Mexico: El Colegio de la Frontera Norte, 2007), 34. Translation mine.

13. Kathleen Staudt, *Violence and Activism at the Border: Gender, Fear, and Everyday Life in Ciudad Juárez* (Austin: University of Texas Press, 2008), 36.

14. Marcella Althaus-Reid, "When God Is a Rich White Woman Who Does Not Walk: The Hermeneutical Circle of Mariology and the Construction of Femininity in Latin America," *Theology and Sexuality* 1 (September 1994): 55–72.

15. Silvana Paternostro, *In the Land of God and Man: Confronting Our Sexual Culture* (New York: Dutton, 1998).

16. Townes, *Cultural Production of Evil*, 12.

17. Ibid., 13.

18. Ibid., 7.

19. Ibid., 18.

20. Ibid., 16.

21. Hannah Arendt, *The Jew as Pariah: Jewish Identity and Politics in the Modern Age* (New York: Grove, 1978), 251.

22. Townes, *Cultural Production of Evil*, 20.

23. Norma Alarcón describes "Chicana" as follows: "Thus, the name Chicana, in the present, is the name of resistance that enables cultural and political points of departure and thinking through the multiple migrations and dislocations of women of 'Mexican' descent. The name Chicana is not a name that women (or men) are born to or with, as is often the case with 'Mexican,' but rather it is consciously and critically assumed and serves as point of redeparture for dismantling historical conjunctures of crisis, confusion, political and ideological conflict, and contradictions of the simultaneous effects of having 'no names,' having 'many names,' not 'know[ing]' her names,' and being someone else's 'dreamwork.' . . . In the Mexican-descent continuum of meanings, Chicana is still the name that brings into focus the interrelatedness of class/race/gender into play and forges the link to actual subaltern native women in the U.S./Mexican dyad." See Norma Alarcón, "Chicana Feminism: In the Tracks of the Native Woman," in *Living Chicana Theory*, ed. Carla Trujillo (Berkeley: Third Woman Press, 1998), 374, 379. In this chapter and throughout the book, I use the term "Latina" for the purpose of signifying women of Latin American ancestry who live in the United States. I use the term "Chicana" to indicate a more specific population, namely women who are of Mexican or Mexican American ancestry and who identify themselves as Chicanas. As noted above, the term "Chicana" indicates a particular consciousness.

24. Alma M. García, ed., *Chicana Feminist Thought: The Basic Historical Writings* (New York: Routledge, 1997), 116.

25. Anne E. Carr, *Transforming Grace: Christian Tradition and Women's Experience* (San Francisco: HarperSanFrancisco, 1988), 38.

26. Rosemary Radford Ruether, *Sexism and God-Talk: Toward a Feminist Theology* (Boston: Beacon, 1983), 147.

27. Berta Esperanza Hernández-Truyol, "Culture and Economic Violence," in *The Latino Condition: A Critical Reader*, ed. Richard Delgado and Jean Stefancic (New York: New York University Press, 1998), 536.

28. Anna NietoGomez, "La Chicana—Legacy of Suffering and Self-Denial," in *Chicana Feminist Thought: The Basic Historical Writings*, ed. Alma M. García (New York: Routledge, 1997), 48–49.

29. José E. Limón, "La Llorona, The Third Legend of Greater Mexico: Cultural Symbols, Women, and the Political Unconscious," in *Between Borders: Essays on Mexicana/Chicana History*, ed. Adelaida R. Del Castillo (Encino: Floricanto, 1990), 408.

30. Sandra Cisneros, "Woman Hollering Creek," in *Woman Hollering Creek and Other Stories* (New York: Vintage, 1992), 43–56.

31. Joan Baez, "La Llorona (The Weeping Woman)," in *Gracias A La Vida (Here's to Life)*, CD Audio (A & M Records, 1974).

32. Tey Diana Rebolledo, *Women Singing in the Snow: A Cultural Analysis of Chicana Literature* (Tucson: University of Arizona Press, 1995), 63.

33. Rebolledo, *Women Singing in the Snow*, 63.

34. Ibid., 77–78.

35. Paz, *Labyrinth of Solitude*, 75, 79.

36. Limón, "La Llorona." For an extended discussion of La Llorona in the context of religion and the U.S.-Mexican borderlands, see Luis D. León, *La Llorona's Children: Religion, Life, and Death in the U.S.-Mexican Borderlands* (Berkeley: University of California Press, 2004).

37. While "Aztec" is the more widely recognized term, many scholars today use the term "Nahua," which several scholars regard as more accurate. See J. Jorge Klor de Alva's introduction in Miguel León-Portilla, *The Aztec Image of Self and Society: An Introduction to Nahua Culture* (Salt Lake City: University of Utah Press, 1992), vii–xxiii.

38. Davíd Carrasco, *City of Sacrifice: The Aztec Empire and the Role of Violence in Civilization* (Boston: Beacon, 1999), 6.

39. Carrasco, *City of Sacrifice*, 6–7.

40. "The Birth of Huitzilopochtli, Patron God of the Aztecs," in *Native Mesoamerican Spirituality*, ed. Miguel Léon-Portilla (New York: Paulist, 1980), 220–25.

41. Carrasco, *City of Sacrifice*, 63. See also Cherríe Moraga, *The Last Generation: Prose and Poetry* (Boston: South End, 1993), 72–76.

42. Carrasco, *City of Sacrifice*, 62; Davíd Carrasco, *Quetzalcoatl and the Irony of Empire: Myths and Prophecies in the Aztec Tradition*, 2nd ed. (Chicago: University of Chicago Press, 1992), 167.

43. Carrasco, *City of Sacrifice*, 65, 188–210.

44. Walter Wink, *Engaging the Powers: Discernment and Resistance in a World of Domination* (Minneapolis: Fortress Press, 1992), 14. See also Paul Ricoeur, *The Symbolism of Evil*, trans. Emerson Buchanan (Boston: Beacon, 1969), 175–210. I want to thank Larry Gordon for sharing this insight with me.

45. Wink, *Engaging the Powers*, 14.

46. Ibid., 17–25.

47. Not infrequently, interpretations of the lives of both Sor Juana Inés de la Cruz and Frida Kahlo have been caricatured along this trajectory of iconic figures who represent the "women-suffering" relation explored in this chapter. No doubt, both knew a great deal of suffering in their lives. However, my point is that their suffering is often idealized and tinged with longing.

48. Cisneros, "Woman Hollering Creek," 43–56; Verónica A. Guerra, "The Silence of the Obejas: Evolution of Voice in Alma Villanueva's 'Mother, May I' and Sandra Cisneros' 'Woman Hollering Creek,'" in *Living Chicana Theory*, ed. Carla Trujillo (Berkeley: Third Woman, 1998), 320–51; Nancy Pineda-Madrid, "In Search of a Theology of Suffering, Latinamente," in *The Ties That Bind: African-American and Hispanic-American/Latino Theology in the United States*, ed. Anthony B. Pinn and Benjamin Valentin (New York: Continuum, 2001), 187–99.

49. Paz, *Labyrinth of Solitude*, 35–39.

50. Ibid., 38–39.

51. Ibid., 39.

52. Arthur Kleinman, Veena Das, and Margaret Lock, eds., *Social Suffering* (Berkeley: University of California Press, 1997), xiii.

53. Lawrence L. Langer, "The Alarmed Vision: Social Suffering and Holocaust Atrocity," in *Social Suffering*, ed. Arthur Kleinman, Veena Das, and Margaret Lock (Berkeley: University of California Press, 1997), 47.

54. Arthur Kleinman and Joan Kleinman, "The Appeal to Experience; The Dismay of Images: Cultural Appropriations of Suffering in Our Times," in *Social Suffering*, ed. Arthur Kleinman, Veena Das, and Margaret Lock (Berkeley: University of California Press, 1997), 8.

55. Schmidt Camacho, "La Ciudadana X," 25. Translation mine.

56. Hannah Arendt, *The Origins of Totalitarianism* (San Diego: Harcourt, 1976), 446.

57. Keith Doubt, *Understanding Evil: Lessons from Bosnia* (New York: Fordham University Press, 2006), 126.

58. Guillermo Gómez-Peña, *The New World Border: Prophecies, Poems, and Locuras for the End of the Century* (San Francisco: City Lights, 1996), 25.

59. David Tracy, "Saving from Evil: Salvation and Evil Today," in *The Fascination of Evil*, ed. David Tracy and Hermann Häring (London: SCM, 1998), 107.

60. Ibid., 108.

61. Ibid., 107–8.

62. Elizabeth A. Johnson, "Jesus and Salvation," in *CTSA Proceedings*, ed. Paul Crowley (Santa Clara: CTSA, 1994), 49:6.

63. J. Denny Weaver, *The Nonviolent Atonement* (Grand Rapids: Eerdmans, 2001), 90–91.

64. Ruether, *Sexism and God-Talk*, 116–38.

65. Ibid., 122.

66. Elizabeth A. Johnson, *She Who Is: The Mystery of God in Feminist Theological Discourse* (New York: Crossroad, 1992), 151.

67. Gebara, *Out of the Depths*, 90.

68. Ibid., 107.

69. Elizabeth A. Johnson, *Quest for the Living God: Mapping Frontiers in the Theology of God* (New York: Continuum, 2007), 51.

70. Gebara, *Out of the Depths*, 16.

71. Walter Brueggemann, *Hope within History* (Atlanta: John Knox, 1987), 9.

72. Brueggemann, *Hope within History*, 11–13.

73. Ibid., 16, 17.

74. Ibid., 20–22.
75. Gebara, *Out of the Depths*, 16.
76. Johnson, "Jesus and Salvation," 11.
77. Ibid., 10.
78. Catherine Mowry LaCugna, "God in Communion with Us—The Trinity," in *Freeing Theology: The Essentials of Theology in Feminist Perspective*, ed. Catherine Mowry LaCugna (San Francisco: HarperSanFrancisco, 1993), 92.
79. LaCugna, "God in Communion with Us," 93.

Chapter 3: Anselm and Salvation

1. While Dr. Francine Cardman provided me with detailed notes on my entire manuscript, I want to acknowledge in a particular way her contribution to this chapter. I am greatly in her debt.
2. David Brown, "Anselm on Atonement," in *The Cambridge Companion to Anselm*, ed. Brian Davies and Brian Leftow (Cambridge: Cambridge University Press, 2004), 280.
3. Elizabeth A. Johnson, "Jesus and Salvation," in *CTSA Proceedings*, ed. Paul Crowley (Santa Clara: CTSA, 1994), 49:5.
4. John P. Galvin, "Jesus Christ," in *Systematic Theology: Roman Catholic Perspectives*, ed. Francis Schüssler Fiorenza and John P. Galvin (Minneapolis: Fortress Press, 1991), 275.
5. Ibid., 277.
6. G. R. Evans, "Anselm's Life, Works, and Immediate Influence," in *The Cambridge Companion to Anselm*, ed. Brian Davies and Brian Leftow (Cambridge: Cambridge University Press, 2004), 5.
7. Evans, "Anselm's Life, Works, and Immediate Influence," 8–9.
8. David Knowles, *The Evolution of Medieval Thought*, ed. D. E. Luscombe and C. N. L. Brooke, 2nd ed. (London: Longman, 1988), 72–84.
9. Ibid., 165.
10. R. W. Southern, *Saint Anselm: A Portrait in a Landscape* (Cambridge: Cambridge University Press, 1990), 73.
11. Brown, "Anselm on Atonement," 288–89.
12. Flora A. Keshgegian, "The Scandal of the Cross: Revisiting Anselm and His Feminist Critics," *Anglican Theological Review* 82/3 (Summer 2000): 5.
13. Evans, "Anselm's Life, Works, and Immediate Influence," 18.
14. Brown, "Anselm on Atonement," 286.
15. I want to acknowledge Francine Cardman for this insight.
16. Brock and Parker, *Saving Paradise*, 265.
17. Anthony W. Bartlett, *Cross Purposes: The Violent Grammar of Christian Atonement* (Harrisburg: Trinity International, 2001), 95.
18. Bartlett, *Cross Purposes*, 96.
19. *Fourth Lateran Council*, constitutions 1: "On the Catholic Faith."
20. Southern, *Saint Anselm*, 198–202.
21. Brock and Parker, *Saving Paradise*, 268.

22. There is a debate among theologians, even among feminist theologians, over whether the sometimes mirroring of the extremes of atonement theology with horrific acts of violence (e.g., counseling women to stay in physically abusive marriages) is more properly attributable to Anselm or to some of his interpreters over the centuries. The outcome of this debate, while important for other reasons, is not directly relevant to the argument of this chapter, which is that the consequences of this extreme theology of atonement carries an influence in the Juárez feminicide, regardless of its source. See Keshgegian, "Scandal of the Cross."

23. Brown, "Anselm on Atonement," 290-91.

24. Jaroslav Pelikan, *The Growth of Medieval Theology (600–1300)*, The Christian Tradition: A History of the Development of Doctrine, vol. 3 (Chicago: University of Chicago Press, 1978), 106.

25. Ibid., 118–19.

26. Ibid., 126.

27. Ibid., 127.

28. Southern, *Saint Anselm*, 208.

29. Ibid.

30. *CDH* 1.7 and 2.19.

31. Pelikan, *Growth of Medieval Theology*, 144.

32. Southern, *Saint Anselm*, 209.

33. All such citations are from *Cur Deus Hom*, as translated in Brian Davies and G. R. Evans, eds., *Anselm of Canterbury: The Major Works* (Oxford: Oxford University Press, 1998).

34. Southern, *Saint Anselm*, 206; Evans, "Anselm's Life, Works, and Immediate Influence," 18–19; Pelikan, *Growth of Medieval Theology*, 139.

35. Southern, *Saint Anselm*, 206.

36. Southern, *Saint Anselm*, 206; G. R. Evans, "Anselm of Canterbury," in *The Medieval Theologians: An Introduction to Theology in the Medieval Period*, ed. G. R. Evans (Oxford: Blackwell, 2001), 99; Pelikan, *Growth of Medieval Theology*, 140.

37. Pelikan, *Growth of Medieval Theology*, 141.

38. Brown, "Anselm on Atonement," 293.

39. Southern, *Saint Anselm*, 205–7.

40. Brown, "Anselm on Atonement," 293.

41. Ibid., 293–94.

42. Eugene R. Fairweather, ed., *A Scholastic Miscellany: Anselm to Ockham*, trans. Eugene R. Fairweather, Library of Christian Classics 10 (Philadelphia: Westminster, 1956), 55.

43. My argument here is informed by the work of Charles Sanders Peirce and his understanding of the relationship between theory and practice. The most succinct account of his method is captured in his pragmatic maxim, which reads: "Consider what effects, that might conceivably have practical bearings, we conceive the object of our conception to have, then, our *conception of these effects* is the whole of our conception of the object." See Charles S. Peirce, "How to Make Our Ideas Clear," in *The Essential Peirce: Selected Philosophical Writings, Volume I (1867–1893)*, ed. Nathan Houser and Christian Kloesel (Bloomington: Indiana University Press, 1992), 132.

44. Hans-Georg Gadamer, *Truth and Method*, trans. Joel Weinsheimer and Donald G. Marshall, 2nd rev. ed. (New York: Continuum, 1997), 300.

45. Ibid., 276.

46. Ibid., 297.

47. Ibid., 302.

48. Kenneth W. Stikkers, "Royce and Gadamer on Interpretation as the Constitution of Community," *Journal of Speculative Philosophy* 15/1 (2001): 17.

49. Josiah Royce, *The Problem of Christianity* (1913; repr., Chicago: University of Chicago Press, 1968), 286–87.

50. Knowles, *Evolution of Medieval Thought*, 90–91.

51. Brock and Parker, *Saving Paradise*, 254–306.

52. M. Shawn Copeland, *Enfleshing Freedom: Body, Race, and Being* (Minneapolis: Fortress Press, 2010), 122.

53. Timothy J. Gorringe, "Atonement," in *Blackwell Companion to Political Theology*, ed. Peter Scott and William T. Cavanaugh (Malden, Mass.: Blackwell, 2007), 370.

54. J. Denny Weaver, *The Nonviolent Atonement* (Grand Rapids: Eerdmans, 2001), 2–6, 69, 79.

55. Ibid., 97.

56. María Pilar Aquino, "The Feminist Option for the Poor and Oppressed in the Context of Globalization," in *The Option for the Poor in Christian Theology*, ed. Daniel G. Groody (Notre Dame: Notre Dame University Press, 2007), 199.

57. Ivone Gebara, *Out of the Depths: Women's Experience of Evil and Salvation* (Minneapolis: Fortress Press, 2002), 107.

58. Karl Rahner, "Experience of Self and Experience of God," in *Theological Investigations*, vol. 13 (New York: Seabury, 1975), 105–21.

59. Rosemary P. Carbine, "Contextualizing the Cross for the Sake of Subjectivity," in *Cross Examinations: Readings on the Meaning of the Cross Today*, ed. Marit A. Trelstad (Minneapolis: Fortress Press, 2006), 93.

60. Delores S. Williams, *Sisters in the Wilderness: The Challenge of Womanist God-Talk* (Maryknoll: Orbis, 1993), 60–83, 161–67.

61. Gebara, *Out of the Depths*, 88–89.

62. Ibid., 88.

63. Weaver, *Nonviolent Atonement*, 69.

64. Elizabeth A. Johnson, "Redeeming the Name of Christ," in *Freeing Theology: The Essentials of Theology in Feminist Perspective*, ed. Catherine Mowry LaCugna (New York: Harper & Row, 1993), 119.

65. Ibid., 119, 120.

66. Elizabeth A. Johnson, *She Who Is: The Mystery of God in Feminist Theological Discourse* (New York: Crossroad, 1992), 72.

67. Weaver, *Nonviolent Atonement*, 90.

68. Keshgegian, "Scandal of the Cross."

69. Weaver, *Nonviolent Atonement*, 54–58.

70. Copeland, *Enfleshing Freedom*, 101–2.

71. Walter Brueggemann, *Hope within History* (Atlanta: John Knox, 1987).

72. Lisa Isherwood, *Introducing Feminist Christologies* (Cleveland: Pilgrim, 2002), 31–32.

73. Darby Kathleen Ray, "Anselm of Canterbury," in *Empire and the Christian Tradition: New Readings of Classical Theologians*, ed. Kwok Pui-lan, Don H. Compier, and Joerg Rieger (Minneapolis: Fortress Press, 2007), 136.

74. Ray, "Anselm of Canterbury," 135–37.

75. Catherine Mowry LaCugna, *God for Us: The Trinity and Christian Life* (New York: HarperCollins, 1973), 292.

76. Ibid., 274.

77. Aquino, "Feminist Option for the Poor," 201.

78. David Tracy, "Saving from Evil: Salvation and Evil Today," in *The Fascination of Evil*, ed. David Tracy and Hermann Häring (London: SCM, 1998), 114–15.

Chapter 4: Responding to Social Suffering—Practices of Resistance

1. Edward Schillebeeckx, *Church: The Human Story of God*, trans. John Bowden (New York: Crossroad, 1994), 4.

2. Ibid., 11.

3. Kathleen Staudt, *Violence and Activism at the Border: Gender, Fear, and Everyday Life in Ciudad Juárez* (Austin: University of Texas Press, 2008), 79.

4. "Day of the Dead." Also known as All Saints Day.

5. Staudt, *Violence and Activism at the Border*, 79.

6. Mark Ensalaco, "Murder in Ciudad Juárez: A Parable of Women's Struggle for Human Rights," *Violence against Women* 12/5 (May 2006): 428.

7. Melissa W. Wright, "A Manifesto against Femicide," *Antipode* 33/3 (2001): 556.

8. Ensalaco, "Murder in Ciudad Juárez," 428; Canadian Press, "Controversy Greets New Mexican Ambassador: Former State Governor Refused Inquiry Into Rapes, Murders of Hundreds of Women," *TheStar.Com*, February 26, 2009, http://www.thestar.com/news/canada/article/593476; Staudt, *Violence and Activism at the Border*, 82.

9. Ensalaco, "Murder in Cuidad Juárez," 428.

10. Diana Washington Valdez, *The Killing Fields: Harvest of Women* (Burbank: Peace at the Border, 2006), 38.

11. Valdez, *Killing Fields*, 38.

12. Ensalaco, "Murder in Cuidad Juárez," 430.

13. Joanna Swanger, "Feminist Community Building in Ciudad Juárez: A Local Cultural Alternative to the Structural Violence of Globalization," *Latin American Perspectives* 34/2 (March 2007): 118.

14. Swanger, "Feminist Community Building in Ciudad Juárez," 115. See also Wright, "A Manifesto Against Femicide," 551. In her work, Joanna Swanger has argued for the effectiveness of subtle practices of resistance like Casa Amiga. "First, only the quiet and quotidian resistance can be sustained day-to-day for years, and given that constructing viable alternatives to neoliberal globalization is to be a process measured in decades and even centuries, this patient form of struggle, which does not lose energy in the absence of cameras or other forms of public documentation, is vital. Second, this kind of resistance tends to be far less alienating of wider segments of society. Strikes, roadblocks, and other forms of spectacular resistance that are aimed either directly or

indirectly at shutting down systems of production and/or distribution often have indirect and unintended consequences. . . . These kinds of actions can therefore antagonize segments of society that might otherwise be allied with the initiators of resistance. . . . Quieter forms of constructive resistance have a greater potential for inviting the alliances across lines of race, nationality, and class that will be necessary if the alternatives to globalization are to be viable. Third, because they are usually less overtly antagonistic and generally are not acts that can be captured in the visual media and used to stoke the fires of public imagination for good or for ill, these forms of subtle, constructive resistance tend not to occasion the brutal state-sponsored repression that is the stock in trade of neoliberalism when the public fails to be convinced of its supposed benefits." Swanger, "Feminist Community Building in Ciudad Juárez," 120.

15. John Burnett, "Who's Killing the Women of Juárez? Mexican City Haunted by Decade of Vicious Sex Crimes," *National Public Radio*, February 22, 2003, http://www.npr.org/templates/story/story.php?storyId=1171962.

16. Valdez, *Killing Fields*, 206.

17. Fregoso, "Toward a Planetary Civil Society," 55; Staudt, *Violence and Activism at the Border*, 85; Rodríguez, Montané, and Pulitzer, *Daughters of Juárez*, 166.

18. Rodríguez, Montané, and Pulitzer, *Daughters of Juárez*, 178, 179.

19. Valdez, *Killing Fields*, 69.

20. Ensalaco, "Murder in Cuidad Juárez," 428–29.

21. Fregoso, "Toward a Planetary Civil Society," 55–56; Valdez, *Killing Fields*, 75.

22. Melissa W. Wright, "The Paradox of Politics: Femicide and the Mujeres de Negro of Northern Mexico" (paper presented at the El Primer Encuentro Sobre Estudios de la Mujer en la Región Paso del Norte: Retos Frente al Siglo XXI, Ciudad Juárez, Chihuahua: El Colegio de la Frontera Norte, November 14, 2003).

23. Fregoso, "Toward a Planetary Civil Society," 55–56.

24. Valdez, *Killing Fields*, 74–75.

25. Ibid., 75.

26. Melissa W. Wright, "El Lucro, La Democracia y La Mujer Publica," in *Bordeando La Violencia Contra Las Mujeres en al Frontera Norte De México*, ed. Julia Monárrez Fragoso and María Socorro Tabuenca Córdoba (Mexico: El Colegio de la Frontera Norte, 2007), 51, 53–54.

27. Valdez, *Killing Fields*, 205.

28. Alicia Schmidt Camacho, "La Ciudadana X: Reglamentando Los Derechos de las Mujeres en la Frontera México-Estados Unidos," in *Bordeando La Violencia Contra Las Mujeres en al Frontera Norte De México*, ed. Julia Monárrez Fragoso and Maria Socorro Tabuenca Córdoba (Mexico: El Colegio de la Frontera Norte, 2007), 33–34.

29. Valdez, *Killing Fields*, 15.

30. Ensalaco, "Murder in Cuidad Juárez," 428.

31. Elizabeth A. Johnson, "Jesus and Salvation," in *CTSA Proceedings*, ed. Paul Crowley (Santa Clara: CTSA, 1994), 49:11.

32. This claim is shared by many contributors to one of the first scholarly edited collections exploring the feminicide: Julia Estela Monárrez Fragoso and María Socorro Tabuenca Córdoba, eds., *Bordeando la Violencia Contra Las Mujeres en la Frontera Norte De México* (Mexico: El Colegio de la Frontera Norte, 2007).

33. Orlando O. Espín and Sixto J. García, "Hispanic-American Theology," in *Proceedings of the Catholic Theological Society of America* 42 (1987): 115. Within the discourse of theology, one can find various definitions of Christian practices in general as well as of popular religious practices in particular. For example, Dorothy Bass offers a helpful description of Christian practices that is consonant with what I am calling popular religious practices. Along with Craig Dykstra, Bass identifies Christian practices as "things Christian people do together over time to address fundamental human needs in response to and in the light of God's active presence for the life of the world." Craig Dykstra and Dorothy C. Bass, "A Theological Understanding of Christian Practices," in *Practicing Theology: Beliefs and Practices in Christian Life*, ed. Miroslav Volf and Dorothy C. Bass (Grand Rapids: Eerdmans, 2002), 18; Craig Dykstra and Dorothy C. Bass, "Time of Yearning, Practices of Faith," in *Practicing Our Faith*, ed. Dorothy C. Bass (San Francisco: Jossey-Bass, 1997), 5. Further, practices and reflection on practices can "contribute to building up ways of life that are abundant . . . in love, justice and mercy." Dykstra and Bass, "A Theological Understanding of Christian Practices," 16. Practices may be distinguished by the following characteristics: "First, as meaningful clusters of human activity (including the activity of thinking) that require and engender knowledge on the part of practitioners, *practices resist the separation of thinking from acting*, and thus of Christian doctrine from Christian life. Second, *practices are social, belonging to groups of people across generations*—a feature that undergirds the communal quality of the Christian life. Third, *practices are rooted in the past but are also constantly adapting to changing circumstances*, including new cultural settings. Fourth, *practices articulate wisdom that is in the keeping of practitioners who do not think of themselves as theologians.*" Dorothy C. Bass, "Introduction," in *Practicing Theology: Beliefs and Practices in Christian Life*, ed. Miroslav Volf and Dorothy C. Bass (Grand Rapids: Eerdmans, 2002), 6.

34. Roberto S. Goizueta, *Caminemos Con Jesús: Toward a Hispanic/Latino Theology of Accompaniment* (Maryknoll: Orbis, 1995), 21.

35. Orlando O. Espín, *The Faith of Our People: Theological Reflections on Popular Catholicism* (Maryknoll: Orbis, 1997), 162.

36. Michelle A. González, *Afro-Cuban Theology: Religion, Race, Culture, and Identity* (Gainesville: University Press of Florida, 2006), 103–4.

37. Benjamín Valentín, *Mapping Public Theology: Beyond Culture, Identity, and Difference* (Harrisburg: Trinity International, 2002), 59; González, *Afro-Cuban Theology*, 105.

38. Goizueta, *Caminemos Con Jesús*, 23.

39. Raúl Gómez-Ruiz, *Mozarabs, Hispanics and the Cross* (Maryknoll: Orbis, 2007), 167–68; González, *Afro-Cuban Theology*, 108.

40. Alejandro García-Rivera, *St. Martin de Porres: The "Little Stories" and the Semiotics of Culture* (Maryknoll: Orbis, 1995), 20–21.

41. There are exceptions of course, one being Orlando O. Espín, "An Exploration Into the Theology of Grace and Sin," in *From the Heart of Our People: Latino/a Explorations In Catholic Systematic Theology*, ed. Orlando O. Espín and Miguel H. Díaz (Maryknoll: Orbis, 1999), 121–52.

42. María Pilar Aquino, *Our Cry for Life: Feminist Theology from Latin America* (Maryknoll: Orbis, 1993), 179.

43. Rosemary Houghton, *The Re-Creation of Eve* (Springfield: Templegate, 1985), 119.

44. Nancy Pineda-Madrid, " 'Holy Guadalupe . . . Shameful Malinche?': Excavating the Problem of 'Female Dualism,' Doing Theological Spade Work," *Listening: Journal of Religion and Culture* 44/2 (Spring 2009): 71–87; Nancy Pineda-Madrid, "Through the Leaven of Popular Catholic Practices: Women Transforming Church," in *Prophetic Witness: Catholic Women's Strategies for the Church*, ed. Colleen Griffith (New York: Herder & Herder, 2009), 188–96.

45. González, *Afro-Cuban Theology*, 105.

46. Goizueta, *Caminemos Con Jesús*, 129.

47. Fregoso, "Toward a Planetary Civil Society," 55.

48. María Pilar Aquino, "The Feminist Option for the Poor and Oppressed in the Context of Globalization," in *The Option for the Poor in Christian Theology*, ed. Daniel G. Groody (Notre Dame: Notre Dame University Press, 2007), 202. For a definition of *kyriarchy* see endnote 29 in chapter 1.

49. Espín, *Grace and Humanness*, 104–19; Espín, *Faith of Our People*, 111–55; González, *Afro-Cuban Theology*, 102–20; Isasi-Díaz, *Mujerista Theology*, 74–75.

50. Goizueta, *Caminemos Con Jesús*, 111.

51. Valdez, *Killing Fields*, 241–42.

52. Ibid.

53. Walter Brueggemann, *Hope within History* (Atlanta: John Knox, 1987), 11.

54. Michel de Certeau, *The Practice of Everyday Life*, trans. Steven Rendall (Berkeley: University of California Press, 1984), 16–17.

55. Dominican American Julia Álvarez published a fictionalized account of their lives. See Julia Álvarez, *In the Time of the Butterflies* (New York: Plume, 1994).

56. Ignacio Ellacuría, "The Crucified People," in *Systematic Theology: Perspectives from Liberation Theology*, ed. Jon Sobrino and Ignacio Ellacuría (Maryknoll: Orbis, 1993), 257.

57. Staudt, *Violence and Activism at the Border*, 19.

58. Wright, "El Lucro," 76–77.

59. Swanger, "Feminist Community Building in Ciudad Juárez," 111.

60. Staudt, *Violence and Activism at the Border*, 19.

61. Ibid., 104–5.

62. Ignacio Ellacuría, "The Crucified People," in *Mysterium Liberationis: Fundamental Concepts in Liberation Theology*, ed. Ignacio Ellacuría S.J. and Jon Sobrino S.J. (Maryknoll: Orbis, 1993), 580–603.

63. Brueggemann, *Hope within History*, 19.

64. Wright, "El Lucro," 77. Translation mine.

65. Carolyn G. Heilbrun, *Writing a Woman's Life* (New York: Norton, 1988), 18.

66. Brueggemann, *Hope within History*, 20.

67. Elisabeth Schüssler Fiorenza, *Bread Not Stone: The Challenge of Feminist Biblical Interpretation* (Boston: Beacon, 1984), 21.

68. Goizueta, *Caminemos Con Jesús*, 148.

69. Amy Hollywood, "Practice, Belief, and Feminist Philosophy of Religion," in *Feminist Philosophy of Religion*, ed. Pamela Sue Anderson and Beverley Clack (New York: Routledge, 2004), 225–37.

70. Roger Haight, *Jesus: Symbol of God* (Maryknoll: Orbis, 1999), 355.

Chapter 5: On the Possibility of Salvation

1. Ignacio Ellacuría, "The Historicity of Christian Salvation," in *Mysterium Liberationis: Fundamental Concepts in Liberation Theology*, ed. Ignacio Ellacuría S.J. and Jon Sobrino S.J. (Maryknoll: Orbis, 1993), 251, 2.

2. Ibid, 2.

3. Elizabeth A. Johnson, "The Word Was Made Flesh and Dwelt Among Us: Jesus Research and Christian Faith," in *Jesus: A Colloquium in the Holy Land*, ed. Doris Donnelly (New York: Continuum, 2001), 159.

4. Walter Wink, *Engaging the Powers: Discernment and Resistance in a World of Domination* (Minneapolis: Fortress Press, 1992).

5. J. Denny Weaver, *The Nonviolent Atonement* (Grand Rapids: Eerdmans, 2001), 90.

6. Ibid., 90–91.

7. Ibid., 13.

8. Josiah Royce, *The Sources of Religious Insight* (1912; repr., Washington, D.C.: Catholic University of America Press, 2001), 226.

9. Ibid., 213–54; Josiah Royce, *Metaphysics (His Philosophy 9 Course of 1915–1916)*, ed. William Ernest Hocking, Richard Hocking, and Frank Oppenheim (Albany: SUNY, 1998), 276. In some ways the idea of the "irrevocable past" is consonant with Johann Baptist Metz's notion of "dangerous memories." See Johann Baptist Metz, *Faith in History and Society: Toward a Practical Fundamental Theology*, ed. and trans. J. Matthew Ashley (1977; repr., New York: Crossroad, 2007), 97–113.

10. Royce, *Sources of Religious Insight*, 153–54.

11. Ibid., 202–3, 232–35; Josiah Royce, *The Philosophy of Loyalty*, ed. John J. McDermott (1908; repr., Nashville: Vanderbilt University Press, 1995), 58–61.

12. This is not to affirm a modern totalizing notion of human progress. History is radically contingent and "human progress" invariably ambiguous. The chaotic, tragic, out-of-control evils of the twentieth century no doubt teach us that the vagaries of history place notions of human progress in doubt.

13. Edward Schillebeeckx, *Church: The Human Story of God*, trans. John Bowden (New York: Crossroad, 1994), 11–13.

14. Ignacio Ellacuría, *Freedom Made Flesh: The Mission of Christ and His Church*, trans. John Drury (Maryknoll: Orbis, 1976), 3.

15. For a more extended discussion, see Ellacuría, *Freedom Made Flesh*, 3–19.

16. Ellacuría, "Historicity of Christian Salvation," 255.

17. Ellacuría, *Freedom Made Flesh*, 16, 18. Emphasis mine.

18. Frank M. Oppenheim, *Royce's Mature Ethics* (Notre Dame: University of Notre Dame Press, 1993), 173.

19. Ellacuría, *Freedom Made Flesh*, 18.

20. Josiah Royce, *The Problem of Christianity* (1913; repr., Chicago: University of Chicago Press, 1968), 343–62; Oppenheim, *Royce's Mature Ethics*, 172–75.

21. Josiah Royce, *Studies of Good and Evil: A Series of Essays upon Problems of Philosophy and of Life* (New York: D. Appleton, 1898), 23.

22. Ibid., 24.

23. Jon Sobrino, *Christ the Liberator: A View from the Victims*, trans. Paul Burns (Maryknoll: Orbis, 2001), 48.

24. Denis Edwards, *Breath of Life: A Theology of the Creator Spirit* (Maryknoll: Orbis, 2004).

25. Miguel H. Díaz, "Outside the Survival of Community There Is No Salvation: A U.S. Hispanic Catholic Contribution to Soteriology," in *Building Bridges, Doing Justice: Constructing a Latino/a Ecumenical Theology*, ed. Orlando O. Espín (Maryknoll: Orbis, 2009), 101.

26. Royce, *Problem of Christianity*, 41, 344.

27. Royce, *Problem of Christianity*, 41. Josiah Royce and William James were friendly adversaries who argued about whether or not experience was not only individual but also social. Royce argued that experience was both personal and social. James disagreed with Royce. Their markedly different approach can be found in comparing two of their classic works, Royce's *Sources of Religious Insight* with James's *The Varieties of Religious Experience*. Royce wrote *Sources* after James had passed away, and in it Royce critiqued James's understanding of experience as primarily individual. See Royce, *Sources of Religious Insight*; William James, *The Varieties of Religious Experience* (1902; repr., New York: Penguin, 1982).

28. Royce, *Problem of Christianity*, 229–342.

29. Royce, *Problem of Christianity*, 229–49, 273–95. See also Nancy Pineda-Madrid, "Traditioning: The Formation of Community, The Transmission of Faith," in *Futuring the Past: Explorations in the Theology of Tradition*, ed. Orlando Espín and Gary Macy (Maryknoll: Orbis, 2006), 210–14.

30. Royce, *Problem of Christianity*, 75–98, 229–72. In addition to the three dynamic processes that I examine, Royce identifies three more. These additional three are: (1) communities must be capable of real communication, (2) communities need the voluntary cooperation of their members, and (3) communities must be loved first by their members. For a straightforward, succinct summary of Royce's theory of community, see John J. Markey O.P., *Creating Communion: The Theology of the Constitutions of the Church* (New York: New City, 2003), 127–40. Because community is the cornerstone for all of his work, Royce explains some dimension of his theory of community in almost all of his writings. See for example Royce, *Sources of Religious Insight*, 37–75, 166–210, 257–97; Royce, *Metaphysics*, 24–32.

31. Royce, *Problem of Christianity*, 256–58. See also Mary McClintock Fulkerson, *Places of Redemption: Theology for a Worldly Church* (New York: Oxford University Press, 2007), 38–39.

32. Mary Catherine Hilkert, "Cry Beloved Image: Rethinking the Image of God," in *In the Embrace of God: Feminist Approaches to Theological Anthropology*, ed. Ann O'Hara Graff (Maryknoll: Orbis, 1995), 196.

33. The Mirabal sisters' opposition to the brutal dictator Rafael Trujillo initially meant repeated incarceration and torture for Minerva and María Teresa Mirabal. However, on November 25, 1960, Trujillo's men beat three of the Mirabal sisters and their driver to death. In December of 1999 the United Nations General Assembly declared November 25, the day that three of the Mirabal sisters were murdered, a day to be observed as International Day for the Elimination of Violence against Women. For a fictionalized account of their story, see Julia Álvarez, *In the Time of the Butterflies* (New York: Plume, 1994).

34. Royce, *Problem of Christianity*, 253–65.

35. Ibid., 253–56.

36. Ibid., 243.

37. Ibid., 243, 242–45.

38. Ibid., 245.

39. Ibid., 248.

40. Ada María Isasi-Díaz, "Mujerista Narratives: Creating a New Heaven and a New Earth," in *Essays in Honor of Letty M. Russell*, ed. Margaret A. Farley and Serene Jones (Louisville: Westminster John Knox, 1999), 231.

41. Ibid.," 231.

42. Royce, *Problem of Christianity*, 229–405.

43. Theologians writing from a U.S. Latino/a perspective have consistently insisted upon relationality and community as fundamental to a Latino/a understanding of reality. While U.S. Latino/a theologians define and describe relationality differently from one another, it nonetheless holds a place of prominence in this body of work. The following are but a few examples. Miguel H. Díaz exemplifies this understanding when he writes: "The emphasis on community predisposes U.S. Hispanic anthropology to consider more so than Rahner can with his individual starting point, those commonly shared experiences out of which the self is born. The U.S. Hispanic theological focus on *pueblo*, family, *mestizaje*, and the socio-political implications of these experiences exemplify my point. In all of these experiences the self is understood as a socially constituted self who exists and exercises his or her freedom not prior to or separate from, but within a given set of pre-existent relationships to other," Díaz, *On Being Human*, 133. Many feminist theologians have likewise read salvation as inherently and unavoidably social. Theologians in the discourse of science and religion are advancing a similar view. My contribution is to suggest how a new context, that of the Juárez feminicide, affirms and extends this insight and might break new ground in our understanding.

44. Royce, *Problem of Christianity*, 42, 206, 329.

45. Ellacuría, "Crucified People," 263.

46. Jon Sobrino, *The Principle of Mercy: Taking the Crucified People from the Cross*, trans. Various (Maryknoll: Orbis, 1994), 55.

47. Ellacuría, "Crucified People," 260.

48. If we hold that the world is essentially interrelated—as most liberationist theologies have claimed—nowhere is the strength of this argument more poignant than in how the human search for salvation is related to our conception of reality in general. With a conception of the universe as suffused "through and through" by social categories, a philosophical understanding of reality well developed by Josiah Royce, we can lay a substantive foundation for the assertion that community is the condition for the possibility of salvation. See Royce, *Problem of Christianity*; Royce, *Metaphysics*.

49. Royce, *Problem of Christianity*, 306.

50. María Pilar Aquino, "The Feminist Option for the Poor and Oppressed in the Context of Globalization," in *The Option for the Poor in Christian Theology*, ed. Daniel G. Groody (Notre Dame: Notre Dame University Press, 2007), 199.

51. Elizabeth A. Johnson, "Redeeming the Name of Christ," in *Freeing Theology: The Essentials of Theology in Feminist Perspective*, ed. Catherine Mowry LaCugna (New York: Harper & Row, 1993), 120.

52. "Sex" and "gender" are distinct from one another. According to Elizabeth A. Johnson: *"Sex* refers to the biologically distinct designs of the male and female body that function in reproduction, a physiological constant normally needing surgical intervention to be changed. *Gender* is not a given in the same sense. It is the socially constructed expectation of how sexually embodied male and female persons should act, what characteristics each should develop, and what social roles they will be allowed to play. As Gerda Lerner writes, gender is "the cultural definition of behavior as appropriate to the sexes in a given society at a given time." Complete with linguistic and symbolic expressions, gender organizes the relation between the sexes in a given time and place. Because they are historical constructions, gender definitions can and do change from age to age—including in spectacular ways in our own—while sex remains a constant." See Elizabeth A. Johnson, *Truly Our Sister: A Theology of Mary in the Communion of Saints* (New York: Continuum, 2003), 20–21.

53. Ellacuría, "Crucified People," 257.

54. Ignacio Ellacuría, "Discernir el Signo de los Tiempos," *Diakonia* 17 (1981): 59.

55. Sobrino, *Principle of Mercy*, 52.

56. Johnson, "Jesus and Salvation," 10.

57. Royce, *Problem of Christianity*, 318–19.

58. Most normative presentations of systematic theology locate soteriology or the problem of salvation (also termed redemption) as a subset of Christology. In the simplest of terms, salvation is understood as the work of Jesus the Christ. By focusing on the primacy of the Spirit, Royce suggests a radical, though consonant, departure from the norm. Royce also claimed that Christianity could be understood as essentially concerned with two overriding concerns: (1) who the historical person Jesus was and what kind of life he counseled, and (2) what the interpretations were of later generations of believers who not only professed belief in Jesus as the Christ but also developed teachings that go beyond what Jesus himself taught. See ibid., 63–66, 68.

59. Royce, *Problem of Christianity*, 119.

60. Royce, *Problem of Christianity*, 404. The "Beloved Community" is a Roycean term of art that can be equated to the reign of God. Martin Luther King, who often wrote of the Beloved Community, adopted this term from Josiah Royce.

61. Catherine Mowry LaCugna, *God for Us: The Trinity and Christian Life* (New York: HarperCollins, 1973), 292.

62. Ellacuría, "Historicity of Christian Salvation," 263–64.

63. Ellacuría, "Crucified People," 277.

64. Johnson, "Jesus and Salvation," 10.

65. Roberto S. Goizueta, *Christ Our Companion: Toward a Theological Aesthetics of Liberation* (Maryknoll: Orbis, 2009), 23.

66. Elisabeth Schüssler Fiorenza, *Jesus: Miriam's Child, Sophia's Prophet: Critical Issues in Feminist Christology* (New York: Continuum, 1994), 123–26.

67. Ibid., 125.

68. Ibid., 125.

69. Ellacuría, "Crucified People," 258.

70. Schüssler Fiorenza, *Jesus*, 125.

For Further Reading

Acuña, Rodolfo. *Occupied America: A History of Chicanos*. New York: Harper and Row, 1988.

Aquino, María Pilar. *Our Cry for Life: Feminist Theology from Latin America*. Maryknoll: Orbis, 1993.

Aquino, María Pilar, Daisy L. Machado, and Jeanette Rodríguez, eds. *Religion, Feminism and Justice: A Reader in Latina Feminist Theology*. Austin: University of Texas Press, 2002.

Aquino, María Pilar, and María José Rosado-Nunes, eds. *Feminist Intercultural Theology: Latina Explorations for a Just World*. Maryknoll: Orbis, 2007.

Brading, D. A. *Mexican Phoenix: Our Lady of Guadalupe: Image and Tradition across Five Centuries*. Cambridge: Cambridge University Press, 2001.

Brock, Rita Nakashima, and Rebecca Ann Parker. *Saving Paradise: How Christianity Traded Love of This World for Crucifixion and Empire*. Boston: Beacon, 2008.

Brock, Rita Nakashima et al., eds. *Off the Menu: Asian and Asian North American Women's Religion and Theology*. Louisville: Westminster John Knox, 2007.

Carrasco, Davíd. *City of Sacrifice: The Aztec Empire and the Role of Violence in Civilization*. Boston: Beacon, 1999.

Chopp, Rebecca S. *The Praxis of Suffering: An Interpretation of Liberation and Political Theologies*. Maryknoll: Orbis, 1986.

Clifford, Anne M., and Anthony J. Godzieba, eds. *Christology: Memory, Inquiry, Practice*. Maryknoll: Orbis, 2003.

Cone, James. *A Black Theology of Liberation*. Philadelphia: Lippincott, 1970.

Copeland, M. Shawn. *Enfleshing Freedom: Body, Race, and Being*. Minneapolis: Fortress Press, 2010.

Das, Veena et al., eds. *Remaking a World: Violence, Social Suffering, and Recovery*. Berkeley: University of California Press, 2001.

Daly, Mary. *Beyond God the Father: Towards a Philosophy of Women's Liberation*. London: Women's, 1986.

De Luna, Anita. *Faith Formation and Popular Religion: Lessons from the Tejano Experience*. Lanham: Rowman and Littlefield, 2002.

Del Castillo, Adelaida R., ed. *Between Borders: Essays on Mexicana/Chicana History*. Encino: Floricanto, 1990.

Díaz, Miguel H. "Outside the Survival of Community There Is No Salvation: A U.S. Hispanic Catholic Contribution to Soteriology." In *Building Bridges, Doing Justice: Constructing a Latino/a Ecumenical Theology*, edited by Orlando O. Espín, 91–111. Maryknoll: Orbis, 2009.

———. *On Being Human: U.S. Hispanic and Rahnerian Perspectives*. Maryknoll: Orbis, 2001.

Elizondo, Virgilio. *Galilean Journey: The Mexican-American Promise*. Maryknoll: Orbis, 1983.

———. *Guadalupe: Mother of the New Creation*. Maryknoll: Orbis, 1997.

Ellacuría, Ignacio. "The Crucified People." In *Mysterium Liberationis: Fundamental Concepts in Liberation Theology*, edited by Ignacio Ellacuría and Jon Sobrino, 580–603. Maryknoll: Orbis, 1993.

———. "The Historicity of Christian Salvation." In *Mysterium Liberationis: Fundamental Concepts in Liberation Theology*, edited by Ignacio Ellacuría and Jon Sobrino, 251–89. Maryknoll: Orbis, 1993.

———. *Freedom Made Flesh: The Mission of Christ and His Church*. 1973. Translated by John Drury. Maryknoll: Orbis, 1976.

Espín, Orlando O. *The Faith of Our People: Theological Reflections on Popular Catholicism*. Maryknoll: Orbis, 1997.

Espín, Orlando O., and Gary Macy, eds. *Futuring the Past: Explorations in the Theology of Tradition*. Maryknoll: Orbis, 2006.

Farmer, Paul. *Pathologies of Power: Health, Human Rights, and the New War on the Poor*. Berkeley: University of California Press, 2005.

Fortune, Marie M. *Sexual Violence: The Sin Revisited*. Cleveland: Pilgrim, 2005.

Fregoso, Rosa Linda, and Cynthia Bejarano, eds. *Terrorizing Women: Feminicide in the Americas*. Durham: Duke University Press, 2010.

García-Rivera, Alejandro. *The Community of the Beautiful: A Theological Aesthetics*. Collegeville: Liturgical, 1999.

———. *A Wounded Innocence: Sketches for a Theology of Art*. Collegeville: Liturgical, 2003.

Gaspar de Alba, Alicia, and Georgina Guzmán, eds. *Making a Killing: Femicide, Free Trade, and La Frontera*. Austin: University of Texas Press, 2010.

Gebara, Ivone. *Out of the Depths: Women's Experience of Evil and Salvation*. Minneapolis: Fortress Press, 2002.

Goizueta, Roberto S. *Caminemos Con Jesús: Toward a Hispanic/Latino Theology of Accompaniment*. Maryknoll: Orbis, 1995.

———. *Christ Our Companion: Toward a Theological Aesthetics of Liberation*. Maryknoll: Orbis, 2009.

González, Michelle A. *Afro-Cuban Theology: Religion, Race, Culture, and Identity*. Gainesville: University Press of Florida, 2006.

———. *Sor Juana: Beauty and Justice in the Americas*. Maryknoll: Orbis, 2003.

González, Justo L. *Mañana: Christian Theology from a Hispanic Perspective*. Nashville: Abingdon, 1990.

González Rodríguez, Sergio. *Huesos en el Desierto*. Barcelona: Anagrama, 2002.

Grey, Mary. *Redeeming the Dream: Feminism, Redemption, and Christian Tradition*. London: SPCP, 1989.

Griffith, Colleen M., ed. *Prophetic Witness: Catholic Women's Strategies for Reform*. New York: Crossroad, 2009.

Gutiérrez, Gustavo. *On Job: God-Talk and the Suffering of the Innocent*. Translated by Matthew J. O'Connell. Maryknoll: Orbis, 1987.

———. *A Theology of Liberation: History, Politics, and Salvation*. Translated by Sister Caridad Inda and John Eagleson. 15th Anniversary Edition. Maryknoll: Orbis, 1988.

Isasi-Díaz, Ada María. *Mujerista Theology: A Theology for the Twenty-First Century*. Maryknoll: Orbis, 1996.

Isasi-Díaz, Ada María, and Fernando Segovia, eds. *Hispanic/Latino Theology: Challenge and Promise*. Minneapolis: Fortress Press, 1996.

Isherwood, Lisa, and Rosemary Radford Ruether, eds. *Weep Not For Your Children: Essays on Religion and Violence*. Oakville: Equinox, 2008.

Johnson, Elizabeth A. *She Who Is: The Mystery of God in Feminist Theological Discourse*. New York: Crossroad, 1992.

———. *Friends of God and Prophets: A Feminist Theological Reading of The Communion of Saints*. New York: Continuum, 1998.

Keller, Catherine. *From a Broken Web: Separation, Sexism, and Self*. Boston: Beacon, 1986.

Kleinman, Arthur, Veena Das, and Margaret Lock, eds. *Social Suffering*. Berkeley: University of California Press, 1997.

Kwok Pui-lan. *Postcolonial Imagination and Feminist Theology*. Louisville: Westminster John Knox Press, 2005.

———, ed. *Hope Abundant: Third World and Indigenous Women's Theology*. Maryknoll: Orbis, 2010.

LaCugna, Catherine Mowry. *God for Us: The Trinity and Christian Life*. New York: HarperCollins, 1973.

Machado, Daisy L. *Of Borders and Margins: Hispanic Disciples in Texas, 1888–1945*. New York: Oxford University Press, 2003.

Maher, Monica A. "The Truth Will Set Us Free: Religion, Violence, and Women's Empowerment in Latin America." In *Global Empowerment of Women: Responses to Globalization and Politicized Religions*, edited by Carolyn Elliott. New York: Routledge, 2008.

Maldonado, David, Jr., ed. *Protestantes/Protestants: Hispanic Christianity within Mainline Traditions*. Nashville: Abingdon, 1999.

Matovina, Timothy, and Gerald E. Poyo, eds. *¡Presente! U.S. Latino Catholics from Colonial Origins to the Present*. Maryknoll: Orbis, 2000.

Matovina, Timothy. "Theologies of Guadalupe: From the Spanish Colonial Era to Pope John Paul II." *Theological Studies* 70 (2009): 61–91.

———. *Guadalupe and Her Faithful: Latino Catholics in San Antonio, from Colonial Origins to the Present*. Baltimore: John Hopkins University Press, 2005.

Metz, Johann Baptist. *A Passion for God: The Mystical-Political Dimension of Christianity*. Translated by J. Matthew Ashley. New York: Paulist, 1998.

Monárrez Fragoso, Julia Estela. *Trama de Una Injusticia: Feminicidio Sexual Sistémico en Ciudad Juárez*. Tijuana: El Colegio de la Frontera Norte, 2009.

Monárrez Fragoso, Julia Estela, and María Socorro Tabuenca Córdoba, Coordinadoras. *Bordeando la Violencia Contra Las Mujeres en la Frontera Norte De México*. Tijuana: El Colegio de la Frontera Norte, 2007.

Paz, Octavio. *The Labyrinth of Solitude: The Other Mexico, Return to the Labyrinth of Solitude, Mexico and the United States, the Philanthropic Ogre*. Translated by Lysander Kemp, Yara Milos, and Rachel Phillips Belash. New York: Grove, 1985.

Peters, Ted. *God—The World's Future: A Systematic Theology for a New Era*. 2nd ed. Minneapolis: Fortress Press, 2000.

Pineda-Madrid, Nancy. "Notes toward a ChicanaFeminist Epistemology (And Why It Is Important for Latina Feminist Theologies)." In *A Reader in Latina Feminist Theology: Religion and Justice*, edited by María Pilar Aquino, Daisy L. Machado, and Jeanette Rodríguez, 241–66. Austin: University of Austin Press, 2002.

———. "Holy Guadalupe . . . Shameful Malinche?": Excavating the Problem of 'Female Dualism,' Doing Theological Spade Work." *Listening: Journal of Religion and Culture* 44/2 (Spring 2009): 71–87.

Pope, Stephen J., ed. *Hope and Solidarity: Jon Sobrino's Challenge to Christian Theology*. Maryknoll: Orbis, 2008.

Rahner, Karl. "The One Christ and the Universality of Salvation." In *Theological Investigations*, vol. 16, translated by David Morland. New York: Seabury, 1979.

Rieger, Joerg. *Christ and Empire: From Paul to Postcolonial Times*. Minneapolis: Fortress Press, 2007.

Rodríguez, Jeanette. *Our Lady of Guadalupe: Faith and Empowerment among Mexican-American Women*. Austin: University of Texas Press, 1994.

Rodríguez, Ruben Rosario. *Racism and God-Talk: A Latino/a Perspective*. New York: New York University Press, 2008.

Rodríguez, Teresa, Diana Montané, and Lisa Pulitzer. *The Daughters of Juárez: A True Story of Serial Murder South of the Border*. New York: Atria, 2007.

Royce, Josiah. *The Problem of Christianity*. Washington, D.C.: Catholic University of America Press, 2001.

————. *The Sources of Religious Insight.* 1912. Washington, D.C.: Catholic University of America Press, 2001.

Ruether, Rosemary Radford. *Sexism and God-Talk: Toward a Feminist Theology.* Boston: Beacon, 1983.

————. *Women-Church: Theology and Practice of Feminist Liturgical Communities.* San Francisco: Harper and Row, 1986.

————. *America, Amerikkka: Elect Nation and Imperial Violence.* Oakville: Equinox, 2007.

————. *Women and Redemption: A Theological History.* Minneapolis: Fortress Press, 1998.

Schillebeeckx, Edward. *Christ: The Experience of Jesus as Lord.* New York: Seabury, 1980.

————. *Church: The Human Story of God.* Translated by John Bowden. New York: Crossroad, 1994.

Schüssler Fiorenza, Elisabeth. *Bread Not Stone: The Challenge of Feminist Biblical Interpretation.* Boston: Beacon, 1984.

————. *Jesus: Miriam's Child, Sophia's Prophet: Critical Issues in Feminist Christology.* New York: Continuum, 1994.

Schwager, Raymund. *Jesus in the Drama of Salvation: Toward a Biblical Doctrine of Redemption.* New York: Herder and Herder, 1999.

Segura, Denise A., and Patricia Zavella, eds. *Women and Migration in the U.S.-Mexican Borderlands.* Durham: Duke University Press, 2007.

Sobrino, Jon. *Christ the Liberator: A View from the Victims.* Translated by Paul Burns. Maryknoll: Orbis, 2001.

————. *Jesus the Liberator: A Historical-Theological Reading of Jesus of Nazareth.* Translated by Paul Burns and Francis McDonagh. Maryknoll, New York: Orbis, 1993.

————. *The Principle of Mercy: Taking the Crucified People from the Cross.* Maryknoll: Orbis, 1994.

Sontag, Susan. *Regarding the Pain of Others.* New York: Picador, 2003.

Staudt, Kathleen. *Violence and Activism at the Border: Gender, Fear, and Everyday Life in Ciudad Juárez.* Austin: University of Texas Press, 2008.

Terrell, JoAnne Marie. *Power in the Blood: The Cross in the African American Experience.* Maryknoll: Orbis, 1998.

Tilley, Terrence W. *The Disciples' Jesus: Christology as Reconciling Practice.* Maryknoll: Orbis, 2008.

Townes, Emilie M., ed. *Embracing the Spirit: Womanist Perspectives on Hope, Salvation, and Transformation.* Maryknoll: Orbis, 1997.

————. *Womanist Ethics and the Cultural Production of Evil.* New York: Palgrave Macmillan, 2006.

————, ed. *A Troubling in My Soul: Womanist Perspectives on Evil and Suffering.* Maryknoll: Orbis, 1993.

Trelstad, Marit, ed. *Cross Examinations: Readings on the Meaning of the Cross Today.* Minneapolis: Fortress Press, 2006.

Valdez, Diana Washington. *The Killing Fields: Harvest of Women.* Burbank: Peace at the Border, 2006.

Valentín, Benjamín, ed. *New Horizons in Hispanic/Latino(a) Theology.* Cleveland: Pilgrim, 2003.

Weaver, J. Denny. *The Nonviolent Atonement.* Grand Rapids: Eerdmans, 2001.

Welch, Sharon D. *Communities of Resistance and Solidarity: A Feminist Theology of Liberation.* Maryknoll: Orbis, 1985.

Williams, Delores S. *Sisters in the Wilderness: The Challenge of Womanist God-Talk.* Maryknoll: Orbis, 1993.

Wink, Walter. *Engaging the Powers: Discernment and Resistance in a World of Domination.* Minneapolis: Fortress Press, 1992.

Index